D0204000

CROWN OF THORNS

CROWN OF THORNS

Political Martyrdom in America from Abraham Lincoln to Martin Luther King, Jr.

Eyal J. Naveh

New York University Press

NEW YORK AND LONDON

Library of Congress Cataloging-in-Publication Data
Naveh, Eyal J., 1952–
   Crown of thorns : political martyrdom in America from Abraham
Lincoln to Martin Luther King, Jr. / Eyal J. Naveh.
      p. cm.
   Based on the author's dissertation.
   Includes bibliographical references.
   ISBN 0-8147-5765-0
      1. United States—Politics and government—1865–1933.   2. United
States—Politics and government—1933–1945.   3. United States—
Politics and government—1945–   4. Political culture—United
States—History.   5. Religion and politics—United States—History.
6. Martyrs—United States—History.   7. United States—
Religion—19th century.   8. United States—Religion—1901–1945.
9. United States—Religion—1945–   I. Title.
E661.N38   1990
306.2'0973—dc20   89-12951
                                                               CIP

New York University Press books are printed on acid-free paper,
and their binding materials are chosen for strength and durability.

Book design by Ken Venezio

Contents

Acknowledgments

I am indebted to several people for their advice and assistance in writing this book. First and foremost, I am grateful to my dissertation adviser, Paula S. Fass, who supervised every stage of the writing with immense care and helped me to clarify my ideas and improve my writing. Her suggestions and criticism, advice and encouragement, were extremely valuable and beneficial to me during the various stages of the research and writing. I am also grateful to Robert N. Bellah who provided me with a better understanding of the concept of martyrdom, and to Samuel Haber who suggested some ways of applying this concept to the American cultural context. Graduate students from the University of California, Berkeley, history department showed interest in the topic and helped with ideas and opinions. Among them Ann Hyde was of a great help.

In turning a dissertation into a book I benefited from the comments and advice of Haggai Hurvitz and Arnon Gutfeld, friends and colleagues of the department of history at Tel Aviv University. Norman Cantor read the whole manuscript and added extremely valuable remarks and suggestions. Philipa Shimrat carefully edited my work in order to clarify language and style. The Kenneth Keating Memorial Fund provided most of the financial basis for the whole project.

Lastly, my greatest debts are to Chava who joined me in this endeavor, bore the major responsibilities of raising a family, and always provided steadfast support and encouragement.

Introduction

The martyr as hero appeared in Western culture centuries before the discovery of the New World. Socrates, Leonidas, Judah the Maccabee, Julius Caesar, Joan of Arc, Galileo, Jordano Bruno, William of Orange, and many others suffered and, in most cases, sacrificed their lives, for a sublime purpose. Later generations glorified these individuals and perceived them as martyrs. Obviously, martyrdom took many forms in different civilizations and sacrifice had disparate meanings in various societies. Yet, while sacrifice dominated many pagan rituals, the martyred figure became a well-known symbolic archetype only under the monotheistic tradition and particularly in Christianity. With the triumph of Christianity in the West, the martyr became part of the collective imagination of Western civilization, embodied above all in the real as well as the symbolic figure of Jesus Christ.

The martyr suffers enormously and often dies a terrible death because of his absolute faith and total devotion to the transcendental world, which he has witnessed. The very term *martyr* means *witness*—an individual who has the ability to penetrate the divine world and to bear testimony to a divine revelation. Supernatural power determines the course of his life and decides when he should be removed from the human world. In his life he delivers a divine message to all human beings and through his suffering and tragic death this message perpetuates itself for the coming generations. Moreover, the martyr overcomes his physical existence and turns into pure spirit through the process of suffering. In most cases the martyr sacrifices himself for the sake of his community, thus atoning for the sins of all members of human society. As part of a biblical cosmic order, he appears as a messiah, analogous to the Son of God who is to return at the end of history to redeem mankind and proclaim the coming of the millennium. As hero-redeemer, the martyr transcends his particular time—often described as the premillennial reign of Evil, which explains the martyr's tragic fate—to become a herald of universal human salvation.

Christ became the most famous Christian martyr, even though his strict followers endured similar fates. St. Stephen's blood stained Jerusalem's streets before he was stoned to death. St. Peter, exhausted from the lash and the dungeon, died in torment on another cross, St. Lawrence was roasted over a slow fire, and many other followers of Christ suffered martyrdom. But the blood of martyrs became the seed of the church and explained to many Christians the triumph of their religion over the pagan world. In the period of the Reformation Jan Huss together with two hundred other Protestant martyrs suffered terrible deaths at the hands of their Catholic enemies, thus pushing mankind another step toward the desired millennium. John Foxe, who fought for the Reformation in England, provided Protestants all over the world with a monumental list of martyrs, which acquired the popular name *The Book of Martyrs*. Published first in England in March 1563, this volume reappeared with the names of additional martyred figures in 1570, 1576, and, finally, 1583. Christians in general and Protestants in particular became familiar with the image of their martyred heroes.

When the English emigrated to the New World they took Foxe's *Book of Martyrs* with them. In many Protestant homes in the American colonies the *Book of Martyrs* stood next to the family Bible, often as the only other book.[1] In the early days of the Republic most Americans were familiar with biblical, Christian, and Protestant martyrs who suffered and died to pave the way for a better mankind and world redemption. They also held the view that the Old World had strayed from its redemptive mission and therefore God had ordered Columbus to discover a new and empty continent for a liberty-loving people. On this new continent, according to the early Pilgrims and Puritans, they would build a "City upon the Hill," an example for the unregenerated world to follow. Indeed, many Americans applied religious terminology to their political experience. They interpreted the departure from Europe as an Exodus and perceived their nation as a new Israel, abiding by a divine covenant and with a holy mission, to reconstruct the perfect world, thus redeeming mankind from the Adamic fall.[2]

But, according to many Protestant leaders, America as a redeemer nation faced an enormous danger: that of deviating from its mission. History showed that after the Fall of Man God had chosen a redeemer nation but that nation had also sinned. Like the ancient Hebrews before Christ and the European Christian civilization after Christ, sinful behavior prevented a redeemer nation from fulfilling its mission. The temptation of sin would menace the American people's mission as well. Yet, before God would decide to break His covenant with a redeemer nation He would try to reform its behavior and rededicate the nation to its original mission.

Both in biblical times and throughout European history, unique individuals like the Hebrew prophets or Christian martyrs had suffered for the sins of others and had sacrificed their lives in order to change the sinful behavior of a redeemer nation. These individuals fought the powerful forces of the existing political order and suffered to promote the desired change and repentance. Their sacrifice was either atonement for other sinners, or a quest for the purification of a redeemer nation, to improve its behavior, abolish its crimes, and renew its commitment to redemption. These martyr-reformers were likely to appear in the collective mentality of many Americans as divine instruments with a mission to rededicate the American people, the new Israel, to their mission.

During the course of their history Americans had ample opportunity to develop a whole tradition of sacrifice and suffering and even to praise certain individuals as national martyrs. Puritans stressed the persecution in Europe, which had motivated them to make a new beginning in New England. Quakers and other antinomian groups glorified individuals who fought the Puritan clergy in Massachusetts. The prerevolutionary conflict with Great Britain turned some Americans into martyrs for liberty, who sacrifed their lives while fighting the tyrannical power of the empire. The signers of the Declaration of Independence acknowledged their readiness for martyrdom when they pledged their lives, their fortunes, and their sacred honor to the cause of freedom. Many Americans believed that George Washington himself made immeasurable sacrifices for the cause of liberty when he suffered with the half-clothed, half-frozen heroes at Valley Forge. Familiar with the general heritage of sacrifice and martyrdom, American authors, poets, preachers, and popular historians applied the title *martyr* to specific individuals. They thus strove to invest the American national experience with transcendent meaning and to strengthen the American national consciousness through solidarity with the sacrifice of a dead hero.

Fallen soldiers, persecuted leaders, and later, assassinated presidents, were therefore depicted by their contemporaries as martyrs who cemented the nation with their blood.

The theme of martyrdom belongs to the realms of both popular and intellectual history. It appeared in popular songs as well as in theological, philosophical, and literary expressions. In reaction to the Civil War, which produced many new martyrs, Walt Whitman acknowledged the significance of sacrifice and martyrdom to the whole national experience:

There is a cement to the whole people, subtler more understanding than anything in written constitution of courts or armies—namely the cement of a death identified thoroughly with the people at its head and for its sake. Strange (is it not) that battles, martyrs, agonies, blood, even assassination should so condense—perhaps only really lastingly condense—a nationality.[3]

During the same era Julia Ward Howe wrote what became the most popular song in the country, "The Battle Hymn of the Republic," which ends in the following verse:

In the beauty of the lilies Christ was born across the sea
With the glory in his bosom that transfigures you and me
As he died to make man holy let us die to make man free
While God is marching on.[4]

Literary uses of the themes of sacrifice and martyrdom were not confined only to a traumatic period like the Civil War. Writing almost a century later and in the relatively prosperous and peaceful time of the 1950s, W. H. Auden viewed martyrdom and human sacrifice as a necessary and sublime part of human and national existence. In "Vespers," one of the poems from Auden's "Horae Canonicae," he portrayed two contradictory figures: Arcadian and Utopian. Each of them is the antithesis of the other and obviously they have nothing in common but mutual contempt. After describing their random meetings, which merely resulted in hostile silence, Auden, nonetheless, tried to give meaning to the crossing of their paths:

Was it (as it must look to any god of cross-roads) simply a fortuitous intersection of life-paths, loyal to different fibs?

Or also a rendezvous between two accomplices who, in spite of themselves, cannot resist meeting

to remind the other (do both at bottom, desire truth?) of that half of their secret which he would most like to forget,

forcing us both, for a fraction of a second, to remember our victim (but for him
I could forget the blood, but for me he could forget the innocence),

on whose immolation (call him Abel, Remus, Whom you will, it is one Sin
offering) arcadians, utopians, our dear old bag of a democracy are alike
founded:

For without a cement of blood (it must be human, it must be innocent) no
secular wall will safely stand.[5]

While poets, philosophers and authors dealt with the abstract idea of
martyrdom and its significance for human existence, most Americans, like
many other peoples, used the familiar image of the martyr to give meaning
to specific tragedies. However, different tragic situations engendered various martyred figures who appealed to their contemporaries but whose
significance faded as their stories no longer seemed relevant to the experience of later generations. Any calamity such as a war, execution, massacre,
or assassination could turn certain individuals into short-lived martyrs.
Their martyrdom provided contemporaries with solemn ceremonies that
might "cement" them together. But most of these martyrs were limited to a
specific group and a particular time and did not become enduring national
heroes.

This study argues that only when a martyred figure is perceived by many
Americans as a prominent reformer, working and suffering in order to
regenerate the nation, can he become an enduring national martyred hero.
The more the sympathizers and followers of a persecuted or assassinated
figure can portray him as one who suffered to reform American society, as
having been sent by God or destined by history to restore Americans to their
original mission as a redeemer nation, the better are his chances of transcending his particular historical context and of becoming a legendary
martyred hero for American democracy. Neither an individual who dies
while defending and preserving the existing order, nor a person who suffered persecution while trying to overthrow this order could become such a
figure in American historical consciousness. Only a reformer who fought
for a better future—which paradoxically was perceived in terms of the
normative past—could become a revered martyr. However, his vision of a
glorious future must not negate the present; total negation of the present
characterizes the radical and revolutionary, not the reformer. Conversely,
complete affirmation of the present is the ideology of the conservative, or
bohemian, and not of the reformer. Therefore, although conservative and

radical individuals who suffered or met a tragic death could be portrayed as martyred heroes, this study will show that, unlike the martyr-reformer, these figures never became enduring martyr-legends in America.

As a study of cultural history, this book will analyze the abstract and theological concept of martyrdom in the context of a dynamic political culture that changes over time. Such an application of the concept of martyrdom to a specific culture raises two basic questions regarding the relationship between an abstract idea and a concrete culture: first, which elements in the concept of martyrdom were absorbed by the American political culture, and which were ignored or rejected; second, what period of time was most susceptible to the cultural tradition of martyrdom and whether the image of the American martyr was modified over time.

More specific questions concern the relationship between the religious and mythical aspects of the concept of martyrdom on the one hand, and the apparently nonreligious nature of American democracy on the other. Does a political system like democracy incorporate religious imagery into its ideology for legitimation? How can a system committed to life, liberty, and the pursuit of happiness explain and justify the death and suffering of its prominent leaders? Is a sacrifice on behalf of some future generation or distant cause a positive and accepted action in a culture that regards worldly well-being as the final purpose of life? How does the cult of heroism and deification combine with the American commitment to equality and the belief in the practical wisdom of the common people? This study attempts to deal with these particular problems.

In order to approach these questions historically rather than theoretically, the chapters will focus primarily upon famous American political leaders who suffered persecution or a tragic death and thus possessed the potential for becoming martyred figures. The primary sources upon which the research is based are public addresses that refer to the death and suffering of these individuals. The material examined includes diverse documents such as obituaries and editorials in newspapers and magazines, religious sermons and public eulogies, centennial celebrations and "in memoriam" orations, iconography and artistic portraits, history text books, biographies, poetry, and other literature. Such vast amounts of material require careful selection, and therefore I used only well-known public addresses and tributes that included, aside from references to the individual's character, a meaningful lesson for potential listeners and readers. These tributes aimed at depicting an image of a martyr relevant to the

American democratic culture. By tracing this martyr image over a long period of time, the study intends to demonstrate the relevance of the theme in various contexts of American history. Specifically, when the tributes and memorial addresses outlived the generation of the particular persecuted leader, they proved his ability to become an enduring national martyr.

A chronological approach has been used in the structure of the book. The first chapter focuses on the first political movement that utilized martyrdom as an ideological device—the radical abolitionists. It is followed by the image of the first famous martyr who died for the cause, John Brown. The third chapter analyzes the image of Abraham Lincoln as an enduring national martyr. The fourth counterposes the martyr image of two other assassinated presidents in a later period and explains why Lincoln "belongs to the age" whereas James A. Garfield and William McKinley sank into oblivion shortly after their deaths. The fifth chapter deals with the general attitude toward the tradition of martyrdom around the turn of the century and in particular among progressive reformers. It is followed by a chapter on the radical martyrs who suffered because they opposed basic elements of the American political and economic establishment. The last chapter attempts to analyze the culture of sacrifice and martyrdom in contemporary America, focusing in particular upon the image of Martin Luther King, Jr., as a new enduring martyr hero.

There has been little historical analysis of the concept of martyrdom in the context of American political culture. Unlike the figure of the yeoman farmer, the self-made man, or the frontier cowboy, the martyred leader has received little attention from American historians, despite the domestic violence in America that has frequently been directed against American leaders.[6] Four presidents have been shot to death in the United States, four more died in office, and some presidents suffered personal tragedies under the enormous burden of responsibility. All these leaders were depicted by their contemporaries as martyrs and suffering servants. Yet political violence in the United States struck not only at the head of the nation but also at other politicians and various leaders of specific groups, such as abolitionists, Mormons, trade unionists, anarchists, blacks, and Civil Rights activists. Thus it seems that the American political experience is an appropriate arena for a historical discussion and analysis of the concept of martyrdom.

A range of secondary literature has examined the concept of martyrdom from theological, philosophical, literary, and psychological perspectives. These have supplied me with the necessary analytical framework as well as valuable examples of martyred figures. Mircea Eliade, in *The Sacred and The Profane,* and René Girard, in *Violence and the Sacred,* discuss the significance of sacrifice in premonotheistic cultures. A collection of essays, *Suffering and Martyrdom in the New Testament,* edited by William Horbury and Brian McNeil, explore the various Christian aspects of martyrdom. Together with Flavian Dougherty, *The Meaning of Human Suffering,* these essays explained the relation between martyrdom, sacrifice, and the monotheistic tradition. Martin Foss in *Death, Sacrifice and Tragedy* approached the subject from an existentialist philosophical perspective, and Eric Hoffer, in *The True Believer,* analyzed the psychology of a potential martyr who decides to sacrifice his life for an ultimate purpose. Bruce A. Rosenberg, in *Custer and the Epic of Defeat,* compared the image of General Custer, the famous American military martyr, to other martyred figures in Western culture. Using the epic as a distinct literary form, this book made an interesting analogy between different discourses that depict the martyr as an inspirational, mythical, and legendary hero.

Many biographies have dealt with assassinated leaders in the United States and usually refer to their martyr image in the last chapter. They do not, however, analyze the meaning of this image and its persistence over time. Between the biographies that focus on a particular martyr-hero, or on specific movements that used the concept of martyrdom on the one hand, and the abstract and theoretical discussions of the idea of martyrdom on the other hand, there is a substantial gap. In analyzing the theme of martyrdom and the image of the political martyr within the context of American historical experience, the coming chapters attempt to bridge this gap.

1

Suffering for the Sin of Slavery

Although the symbolic figure of the martyr in its religious setting was familiar to most Americans, the concept of sacrifice, suffering, and martyrdom, became an important ideological component of American political discourse only in the midnineteenth century. The first group to use these concepts politically were the radical members of the anti-slavery reform movement, known as the abolitionists. A famous English author, Harriet Martineau, who visited America in the 1830s, wrote about the abolitionists in her book *The Martyr Age of the United States*. She urged her English readers to view the abolitionists as

the true republicans . . . the sufferers, the moral soldiers who have gone out armed only with faith, hope, and charity. . . . Let us not wait . . . for another century to greet the confessors and martyrs who stretch out their strong arm to bring down Heaven upon our earth; but even now . . . let us make our reverent congratulations heard over the ocean which divides us from the spiritual potentates of our age.[1]

Indeed this radical reform movement, which rejected any compromise on the issue of slavery and refused to use conventional political channels to promote its goal, resorted to the martyr tradition as an ideological device and made martyrdom a leitmotif of its rhetoric. Operating as a small but very influential reform movement from the third decade of the nineteenth century until the Civil War, the radical abolitionists were the first group to demonstrate the significance that martyrdom had for dedicated reformers. Faced with overwhelming opposition both in the South and the North, the abolitionists cultivated in certain important aspects a sense of self-sacrifice

9

and martyrdom. They asserted that martyr figures were instruments of redemption, whose struggle for reform would help America purge itself of the sin of slavery.

The abolitionists operated in a period when numerous evangelical reform groups were active. Many Americans at this time were receptive to the political implications of religious concepts and generally interpreted their historical experience in moral, pietistic, and even theological terms. They took biblical symbols seriously and incorporated them into what can be defined as a distinct civil religion.[2] Thus the concepts of sin, sacrifice, martyrdom, and redemption, which abolitionists emphasized in their political struggle, were in accordance with the general pietistic climate of opinions. Many Americans believed that their society had the mission to re-create the perfect Garden of Eden through a cycle of sin, suffering, and sacrifice. Such convictions enhanced the potential of a particular reformer who suffered for his cause for becoming a revered martyr figure.

Certainly, not every reform movement celebrated the idea of martyrdom for the cause, and many reformers did not value such sacrifice as a worthy act that would promote the goal of their reform. Even those reformers who might have perceived themselves as potential martyrs did not necessarily succeed in conveying such an image to their friends and followers and thus the image did not become a common ideology of their reform movement. Moreover, even when a reform movement used martyrdom as an ideological device and had a celebrated figure who had been martyred for the cause, this figure was unlikely to have an impact on the indifferent masses of the population and become a recognized national martyr.

By contrast, when the leaders of radical abolitionism stressed the martyr tradition, they seemed to have a certain impact on the American people as a whole. The social profile of the movement, their self-image as reformers, the tactics of the struggle, their very cause, and their perception of their enemy—all these factors reinforced the ideology of martyrdom and spread it among the Northern public in general. Historian Hazel Catherine Wolf noted in her book *On Freedom's Altar* that personal agony and the ability to interpret suffering as God's favor provided the abolitionists with fire and momentum.[3] This book certainly minimized the real opposition that radical abolitionists faced throughout the country, by suggesting that they were motivated as much by personal psychological needs as by the moral evil of slavery. By contrast, it seems to me that the antiabolitionist climate of opinion of *ante bellum* America, together with a profound moral preoccupation on the part of the abolitionists with the American destiny and fate, accounted for their tendency to rely heavily upon the rhetoric of self-sacrifice and martyrdom.

Comprised mostly of Northern whites, the radical abolitionists fought to redeem the whole country from the sin of slavery. Many of them were Quakers who had a long tradition of martyrdom, and many would have enjoyed prestigious careers had they not chosen to engage in the struggle to free slaves. This social profile helped abolitionists to develop a martyr image: they could be depicted as ultimate altruists fighting and suffering not for their own self-interest but rather for the salvation of others, for "creatures" that were below them. In that sense they fitted into the whole tradition that viewed the martyr as free of self-interest, as one who suffered persecution because his destiny determined for him a life of service to others. "I have opened my mouth for the dumb, I have pleaded the cause of the poor and oppressed," wrote the Reverend Elijah P. Lovejoy, the abolitionist who sacrificed his life for his ideas. "For these things I have seen my family scattered, my office broken, my furnitures . . . destroyed . . . my life threatened. . . . Yet none of these things have moved me from my purpose."[4] Another member of the movement, George Thompson, wrote from jail, "We long to be instrumental in doing something for our brethren in bonds. . . . To die for the slave I felt willing."[5]

Resistance to unjust laws together with a devotion to nonviolence characterized the tactics of the radical abolitionists. These tactics recalled the example of biblical and Christian martyrs who refused to obey immoral laws, but preached nonviolence and preferred self-sacrifice to violent struggle. These tactics helped the abolitionists not only to develop an ideology of martyrdom but also to present themselves to their supporters and followers in the North as real or potential martyrs. Committed to nonviolence, they portrayed themselves merely as victims of violence and thus increased their potential for becoming martyrs. Abolitionists asserted that the more a persecuted member was committed to the ideal of nonviolence, the more deserving he was to the title of *martyr*. His martyrdom in turn served to convince indifferent members of the society to support the cause of reform and even converted new members to the movement.

Abolitionists had a single cause of reform—to eradicate slavery from the land and thereby to redeem the people from this terrible sin. A single cause enhanced the ideology of martyrdom far more than support for many reform ideals. A single outstanding cause could command the attention of large segments of the society and could arouse total, passionate commitment. The clearer the ideal, the easier it became for a reformer to be completely identified with it. Likewise, one universal evil that could be portrayed as a sin was better than many abuses that could be depicted as social shortcomings. The focus of attention upon one great evil that inhibited the one central reform cause placed the specific demand for reform in a universal and even cosmic context and enabled radical abolitionists to interpret their struggle for reform as a fight between the universal forces of Good and Evil. Consequently they perceived themselves as the avant-garde in this war, willing to sacrifice their lives for the sake of redeeming the country from the sin of slavery.

Abolitionists assumed that the cosmic nature of the antislavery struggle necessitated martyrdom. They viewed slavery as a sin that prevented human redemption and required human sacrifice. As Adam had rebelled against God, so a slaveholder was a rebel against divine authority. According to William Lloyd Garrison, the founder and leader of the American Anti-Slavery Society, when a man presumed that he owned another man he competed with God for control and government over mankind and therefore he defied the divine principle that all human beings were accountable only to God.[6] Henry Wright, another radical abolitionist, defined abolitionism as a fight to redeem man from the dominion of man.[7] Hence, by fighting a profound sin abolitionists rose to the cosmic plane as God's messengers aimed at redeeming humanity from the sin of slavery.

"I determined at every hazard to lift up the standard of emancipation," wrote Garrison in the first editorial of the *Liberator,* the official organ of the abolitionists.[8] In another editorial he declared that he would not hold his peace on the subject of slavery and oppression. "If need be who would not die a martyr to such a cause?"[9] Early in his career Garrison expressed his quest for self-sacrifice: "My trust is in God, my aim is to walk in the footsteps of his son, my rejoicing to be crucified to the world, and the world to me."[10] Among his favorite subjects were himself, his persecution, and his probable martyrdom. These themes appeared again and again in his editorials, speeches, personal letters, and poems. Garrison felt that the closer he approached martyrdom, the greater would be the success of his agitation on behalf of the slave.[11]

This quest for martyrdom was not simply a personal obsession of the leader of the American Anti-Slavery Society. Many other members shared the belief that personal sacrifice was necessary to promote the abolition of slavery. When a mob disrupted a Boston women's antislavery meeting demanding the life of Garrison, the mayor of Boston put him in a protective jail. When the mayor asked the ladies to go home for their own safety, Mrs. Maria W. Chapman, an organizer of the meeting, responded: "If it is the last bulwark of freedom we may as well die here as anywhere."[12] Wendell Phillips, second only to Garrison among the ranks of abolitionists, stressed the value of martyrdom in his speeches throughout the struggle and even after the emancipation. He proudly stated at Helen Eliza Garrison's funeral on January 27, 1876, that "trained among Friends [Quakers] with the blood of martyrdom and self sacrifice in her veins, she came so naturally to the altar."[13]

But Garrison, along with Phillips, Theodore Weld, Frederick Douglass, and many other prominent leaders of the Anti-Slavery Society never really experienced "the altar." Despite their willingness to be sacrificed to the cause, most of the well-known leaders of the movement did not meet a tragic death. They continued to live valuable and meaningful lives long after slavery had been abolished and they died from natural causes in their seventies and eighties. Other abolitionists, less familiar to the general public, suffered attacks, injuries, and even persecution in their struggle against slavery. These persecuted members were necessary to the antislavery movement, since they provided the connection of blood that bound all committed abolitionists in sacrificial ties. Yet most of these persecuted abolitionists did not reach national prominence.

The first and only effective martyr to the abolition movement was Elijah P. Lovejoy. He was killed by a mob in Dalton, Illinois, on November 17, 1837, and his personal destruction came to be regarded as a forecast of the fate that all human liberty must suffer if slavery were perpetuated. He won the martyr's crown because he died and lost, not because he triumphed. His death also affected for a short time members outside of the abolitionists' ranks. For a decade after Lovejoy's death, lust for martyrdom permeated abolitionism, and many individuals demonstrated in life what he had demonstrated in death. But without the death ritual their suffering had only a slight impact on the public in general.

Abolitionists offered plentiful examples of such "living" martyrs. Prudence Crandel, a Quaker woman, was arrested after admitting a black girl to her school. She proved that Northerners as well as Southerners would not tolerate the education of black children. Theodore Weld suffered mockery and violence while preaching black freedom and temporarily lost his voice. James G. Birney, a Southerner ex-slaveholder, lost his wealth, prestige, and status when he joined the abolitionists' ranks. Thus he was perceived as a martyr to his conscience. Alanson Work, James E. Burr, and George Thompson were jailed and sentenced when caught by Southern and Northern authorities while assisting slaves across the Mississippi River. Amos Dresser was beaten, and Jonathan Walker was humiliated and tortured by proslavery foes, who branded his hand. This branded hand— reminiscent of Jesus' bleeding hands—became a symbol of the abolition crusader's love and charity for the black man. Stephen S. Foster, who preached abolitionism from the pulpit in defiance of church authorities, supplied the movement with a profound example of suffering and tribulations. He declared that in one year church members had dragged him from places of worship twenty-four times, that they had twice thrown him from second-story windows and seriously injured him, that he had paid fines for preaching the Gospel, that he had been forced to escape assassins, and that he had been jailed more times than he could count. Such concrete examples reinforced the ideology of martyrdom, expanded the martyr tradition, and constantly stressed the abolitionist's willingness to suffer for his goal of freeing the Negro.[14] These examples supplied the raw material to the rhetoric of martyrdom.

In a eulogy to Lovejoy, Pastor Thomas T. Stone noted that he had consecrated himself to God by working and dying for others. Stone defined slavery as a curse not only to the slave but to the master, the country, the nation, and all humankind. He also emphasized that slavery was a blasphemy against God and violence to man. Therefore God had called upon Lovejoy to plead for the oppressed and had caused his death in order to promote the destruction of slavery.

The lovers of truth . . . will remember him and his blood they will feel to be the seed of glorious harvest, which trust shall gather in when the time of harvest comes. . . . Yes they are, who will feel themselves anew baptized into the name of God's holy truth . . . who will live for it so long as it lets them live, and who will die for it when it needs their death, to seal it afresh.[15]

Other obituaries explained Lovejoy's murder in similar terms and interpreted his martyrdom as part of a divine plan.[16]

In an attempt to elucidate the divine context of their suffering many abolitionists resorted to an analogy with Jesus Christ. "I do not forget that Christ and his apostles . . . were buffeted, calumniated and crucified," wrote Garrison, "and therefore my soul is as steady to its pursuit as the needle to the pole."[17] In his last public appearance, the Reverend Mr. Lovejoy himself defended his writing of antislavery articles in a Christ-like mode: "I can die at my post but I can not desert it," he told his audience at a public meeting in Alton. "I forgive my enemies and with the best assurance . . . in life or death, nothing can separate me from my Redeemer."[18] Likewise, George Thompson wrote to a friend from jail, "If I am thus to be sacrificed I submit cheerfully, rejoicing that I am counted worthy to suffer . . . for the name of Jesus."[19]

Such identification with Christ affirmed the doctrine of nonresistance as the only way to achieve victory over the sin of slavery. Sacrifice, total submission to suffering and torture was the way of the martyr who never offended his foes and never resorted even to methods of self-defence. For a devoted abolitionist, Christ was the supreme example, and the message of the Sermon on the Mount was a categorical imperative. "We find nothing but self sacrifice, willing martyrdom . . . peace and good will and the prohibition of all retaliatory feelings," commented William Lloyd Garrison on Henry Ward Beecher's statement that some abolitionists would scoff at the idea of holding a sword or rifle in a Christian state of mind. "He [Jesus] plainly prohibited war in self defence, and substituted martyrdom therefore. . . . When he said 'father forgive them they know not what they do' he did not treat them as a herd of buffaloes, but poor misguided and lost men. We believe in his philosophy, we accept his instruction."[20]

While not all abolitionists were so committed to the doctrine of nonresistance, Garrison himself and his close followers did emphasize this element as essential to a perfect martyrdom. Along with his praise of the Reverend Elijah P. Lovejoy, Garrison wrote in the *Liberator* that he regretted the martyred minister's use of self-defence.[21] In a sermon for Thanksgiving Day of 1837 the Reverend Hubbard Winslow declared in Boston that

the moral . . . glory of the event considered as martyrdom in the cause of Christ is greatly obscured by the fact that the persecuted party forsook the wisdom of Christ for their own wisdom. Christ said that "All they that take the sword, shall perish by the sword. . . . If they persecute you in the city, flee to another." That is, do not arm yourself with weapons.[22]

Lovejoy's death was almost perfect according to the doctrine of self-sacrifice. However, the fact that some of his friends used "carnal weapons" in self-defence belittled his martyrdom.

The analogy with Christ helped to explain that the fate of the antislavery reform movement was part of the Christian eschatology. It provided a better understanding of the redeemer's destiny and required abolitionists to submit themselves to similar martyrdom in order to advance the Second Coming. "He who is for us is more than they who are against us—that the battle is the Lord's and victory sure," stated the *Liberator*. "Our grand object is to hasten that glorious day when the songs of the heavenly host at the birth of Jesus shall rise in the chorus to heaven . . . from the lips of the people of every tribe and tongue, and nation, at the universal conquest and reign of that same Jesus the Crucified."[23]

When Garrison wrote about the Boston mobbing event in the *Liberator* he drew from his personal experience a universal and even cosmic lesson. "The struggle is between Right and Wrong, Liberty and Slavery, Christianity and Atheism, Northern Freedom and Southern Taskmaster."[24] Later, after the Civil War, Garrison wrote that the battle between the forces of Light and the forces of Darkness was not over yet, and "those who shall hereafter go forth to defend the righteous cause, no matter at what cost . . . cannot fail to derive strength and inspiration from the anti-slavery movement."[25]

Abolitionists used martyrdom not only within a cosmic context but also with regard to the specific American political culture. Liberty constituted perhaps the main ideological concept of this culture and indeed, abolitionists reiterated the importance of martyrdom for liberty. The freedom that most Americans celebrated as a precondition for their democracy seemed a mockery to radical abolitionists. Hence, they viewed themselves as freedom fighters confronted by the tyranny of the slave power, which, in their opinion, had ruled America. The violent attempts to silence them reinforced this perception of themselves as freedom fighters. Abolitionists fought not only for freedom from bondage for blacks, but also for freedom of speech, freedom of the press, freedom of assembly, freedom of expression, and so on. In this struggle slaveholders were not their only enemy, but also the violent mob that broke up their meetings and the distinguished politicians and clergymen who stood behind such violent action. "The great question to be settled," wrote Garrison "is . . . whether freedom is with us —THE PEOPLE OF THE UNITED STATES—a reality or a mockery, whether the liberty of speech and of press . . . is still to be enjoyed . . . or whether padlocks are to be put upon our lips, gags in our mouths and shackles upon the great palladium of human rights, the press."[26] He deliberately used images of human bondage to describe the dangers liberty faced in America.

Liberty was an ideal shared by all Americans. Therefore, when Lovejoy was killed while defending his right to express his ideas, most prominent citizens outside the abolitionists' ranks described him as a martyr for freedom of the press, rather than for the cause of abolitionism. William Ellery Channing, the founder of Unitarianism, told his Boston congregation that a martyr of freedom of the press had fallen. "A citizen has been murdered . . . in exercising what I hold to be the dearest right of a citizen. . . . It is the consumation of a long series of assaults on public order, on freedom, on the majesty of the law."[27] The general press reacted in a similar way. Northern papers, such as the *New York Evening Post,* the *Daily Advocate,* the *Pittsburgh Times,* the *Philadelphia Observer,* or the *Painesville* [Ohio] *Republican,* saw Lovejoy as a victim of an outrageous attack upon the freedom of speech and the press.[28] "If this American blood—shed in the defense of the freedom of the press and the right of every American citizen to think, speak, and print his own honest opinions—be not signally vindicated our representative institutions, our boasted freedom, our vaunted safety of property and life will become, and deserve to become, the scoff and derision of the world," wrote the *New York American.*[29] Even the Southern press joined the general condemnation of the murder, complaining that it turned an agitator and foe into a martyr for law and order.[30]

Yet, according to abolitionists, the liberty for which Lovejoy had died was neither an already-achieved law and order nor the Constitutional freedom of speech. Thus, they interpreted their own tribulations not as an assault upon their right to free speech but rather as a necessary price to pay in the struggle that aimed to bring liberty to America by destroying the tyranny of slavery.[31] From an abolitionist perspective liberty did not exist in America as long as slavery was a legal institution. As a tactical device the abolitionists challenged the tolerance of the public and showed that many Americans refused to grant them the liberties to which they were entitled by the Constitution. But in substance all such "liberties" were a mockery for them, and Constitutional rights were nothing but deceit and fraud since these liberties and rights accepted human bondage.

Wendell Phillips demonstrated this contempt for the legal rights of the Constitution in an extreme way. When Congress legislated the Fugitive Slave Act, Phillips declared that the Constitution of the United States was a covenant with death. "We presume to believe the Bible outweighs the statute-book," he stated, "My curse be on the Constitution of the United States."[32] In another reaction to this law he proclaimed: "I am not to be bullied by institutions. I am not to be frightened by parchment. Forms and theories are nothing to me. Majorities are nothing."[33] For a true reformer like Phillips the whole legal cornerstone of democracy was a wicked attempt to camouflage an evil tyranny with a legal cover.

Indeed, abolitionists sometimes defied legal authorities. Lovejoy preached antislavery in St. Louis knowing that he challenged state laws. He declared his willingness to bear the consequences.[34] In Alton he insisted on opening a printing house for his paper despite public objection. "While I value the good opinion of my fellow-citizens as highly as anyone, I may be permitted to say that I am governed by higher considerations than either the favor or the fear of man."[35] Garrison refused to be engaged in any legal battle or to agree to any compromise. He rejected the political abolitionists who formed the Liberty party. Even running for office on an abolitionist platform was a sin according to Garrison, since by forming a party people acquiesced to the system of evil laws.[36] In a book, *The Fugitive Slave Law of the United States,* Charles B. Stearns wrote that obedience to God required resistance to tyrants and the breaking of their regimes. "Law is not binding to man. Only when it is right. . . . The moment a man yields his points and obeys the laws of man in preference to the law of God, that moment he is a fallen being and a rebel against Jehovah."[37]

Many leaders of radical abolitionism saw some "high law" as the only legitimate principle to follow. Consequently, they articulated an ideology that glorified defiance of the existing legal system and accepted martyrdom as a result of such defiance. The true abolitionist followed God, committed himself to truth and opposed any authority except the "high law" of his conscience. This commitment might end either in mob lynching or upon the gallows of a tyrannical authority, but the abolitionist reformer was ready to undergo such a fate.

Abolitionists therefore resorted to the martyr tradition as the main device for justifying, explaining, and giving meaning to their activities and used it as an ideological weapon in their battle to redeem America from the sin of slavery. Regarding themselves as divine instruments fighting a cosmic sin, they incorporated many of the elements that glorified the ancient martyrs into their concrete experience. Their social background, reform tactics, religious world view, and the historical context of the midnineteenth century, provided them with the potential for martyrdom. Only one factor was missing: Until the eve of the Civil War they could not present the image of a famous individual whose martyrdom was well known to the general American public. Garrison, Phillips, Theodore Weld, and John Q. Adams did not die for the cause. In fact only the Reverend Elijah P. Lovejoy died as a martyr. All the others suffered living martyrdom, which had less impact on the rest of the society. Without the rituals of persecution and trial, execution and mourning, abolitionists did not produce a famous figure whose sacrifice could inspire people outside their own ranks. Consequently, without an acknowledged martyr, the whole tradition of martyrdom that abolitionists articulated at the time had only limited impact on later generations.

Indeed only a small group of committed reformers and black leaders in the late nineteenth and early twentieth centuries extolled the legacy of the anti-slavery reformers and regarded them as an inspirational source. They stressed the social and national meaning of the abolitionists' activities more than their cosmic and eschatological significance. In a eulogy to Wendell Phillips delivered in Boston on April 9, 1884, the black leader Archibald H. Grimké declared:

The noble band of anti-slavery martyrs were tried by fire. . . . No age and no cause, neither the early Christian dying by the hand of the Romans nor the religious martyrs to the Spanish cruelty and English persecution, made so sublime a sacrifice to liberty and truth. . . . Great lights are above us. Sumner, Garrison, Phillips, and an innumerable company of anti-slavery saints and martyrs watch us from the skies. . . . They implore us by the chains which we wore two hundred years, by the struggles, suffering, and triumphs of liberty, by our duties, our rights and wrongs, for ourselves, posterity, and country, to be faithful to the high trust of FREEMEN.[38]

Likewise, in one of the rare addresses for Lovejoy, Thomas Dimmock declared that he was a "Hero and Martyr, let it never be forgotten, of that liberty of speech and of press without which there can be no genuine liberty for any man, white or black—without which government of, for, and by the people is a miserable snare and sham, liable at any time to be bought by the purse or crushed by the sword."[39]

In memory of his grandfather, Garrison's grandson wrote that "there enters into the soul of the reformer a divine desire to serve, no matter what the price, if only thereby the world can be made an advance by as much as the fraction of an inch."[40] Lucy Stone's remark at Garrison's funeral, Wendell Phillips Stafford's centennial oration on Wendell Phillips, and Ernest Crosby's biography of Garrison, all noted that abolition was a step in the long march of humanity toward more progress and freedom.[41] To a committed reformer such a fervent belief in a better future justified suffering in the present.

Scorn for the present, combined with a true belief in a glorious future, was an essential element in the ideology of the antislavery movement. In challenging the conventional order and refusing to accept things as they were, abolitionist reformers were often viewed by contemporaries as the enemies of law and order. Later admirers of the abolitionists quoted Garrison's statement that "he who commenced any reform which at last becomes one of transcendent importance, and is crowned with victory, is always ill judged and unfairly estimated."[42] In other words, a true reformer was, by definition, a martyr, since his vision of a better and more enlightened future put him in advance of his own generation.

The career of a true reformer resembled the fate of the biblical prophets who suffered persecution in their own societies while preaching their message of redemption. Those who praised the legacy of the abolitionists made such an analogy while explaining the fate of antislavery reformers.[43] In a later period, John Jay Chapman, who considered himself a reformer and admired martyrs for the cause, elucidated the role of the martyr prophet to his contemporaries. In his biography of Garrison he gave a dialectic explanation of the fate of a true reformer:

An evil reaches its climax at the very moment that the corrective reform is making a hidden march upon it from an unexpected quarter. The prophet . . . is not so much an individual as a part of the consciousness of all men. . . . His understanding of his own function is uncertain and there have been many plain-minded prophets who could suffer martyrdom, but not explain. These men see the suffering of the world and they . . . feel the relation between the suffering of one man and the selfishness of the next.[44]

As prophets the real reformers could not compromise with evil and thus suffered persecution and martyrdom.

Later generations who looked at the abolitionists for inspiration, were able from a different time perspective to counterpose the abolitionists' gloomy present with an inevitably glorious future. In an introduction to one of many popular biographies of Garrison, the famous poet John G. Whittier, himself an antislavery sympathizer, wrote, "The verdict of posterity in his case may be safely anticipated. With the true reformers and benefactors of his race, he occupies a place inferior to none other."[45] Addresses on Garrison and Phillips emphasized this splendid verdict of posterity, which stood in contrast to the reformers' miserable fate in the present.[46] In a memorial book, *The Martyrdom of Lovejoy,* Dr. Samuel Villard, a Chicago historian, wrote of Lovejoy's assassination, "When the decisive struggle of the Civil War came, the sons of those who had persecuted the prophet a quarter of a century before, took their place in the ranks to fight and die for liberty; and Alton sent her quota to sustain the grand cause for which Lovejoy had died."[47]

In fact, the Reverend Elijah P. Lovejoy was killed twenty-three years before the Civil War, and when the war created more martyrs, most Americans forgot the murder of an abolitionist in Alton a generation before and did not include him in the gallery of Civil War heroes. While his death provided abolitionists at the time with a martyr figure, he never became a national martyr whose sacrifice could inspire other members of the society. It was only on December 2, 1859, when the authorities of Virginia executed John Brown, that the first famous martyr who died for the cause of slavery, came into being.

2

John Brown's Body— And Spirit

John Brown was born on May 9, 1800, in Torrington, Connecticut, one of the sixteen children of Owen Brown, whose father had served as a captain in the Revolutionary War. John grew up in the Western Reserve frontier of Ohio and at the age of eighteen intended to become a Congregational minister, yet he did not finish the religious schools in Massachusetts and Connecticut he attended. He married Dianthe Lusk who bore him seven children, and after her death Mary Anne Day who born him thirteen more. He never had a permanent profession and was engaged in many enterprises without success. John Brown worked as a drover, tanner, stock grower, wool merchant, and farmer. He moved frequently, and lived at different times in Ohio, Pennsylvania, and Massachusetts. In 1849 he settled with his family in a black community founded in North Elba, New York, on land donated by an antislavery philanthropist, Gerrit Smith. Here Brown began his career as a militant foe of slavery.

In 1855 he went to Kansas and became the conspicuous guerrilla leader of the Free States groups. Settling near Osawatomie, he was probably the central figure in the so-called Pottawatomie massacre. Brooding over the killing of five Free-Soilers, he concluded that he had a divine mission of revenge. On the night of May 24–25, 1856, he led four of his sons and three other men to the cabins of suspected proslavery settlers. His followers dragged five men out of their homes and hacked them to death. Henceforth authorities put a price on his head as a dangerous criminal and he went underground, traveling from place to place to escape the law.

In the spring of 1858, John Brown held a convention of blacks and whites in Chatham, Canada. There he announced his intention of establishing a stronghold in the Maryland and Virginia mountains where escaping slaves might gather and defend themselves. He drafted "a provisional constitution and ordinance for the people of the United States" and was elected commander in chief of his paper government. He received moral and financial support from Gerrit Smith and from five other prominent Boston abolitionists, Theodore Parker, George L. Stearns, Thomas W. Higginson, Samuel G. Howe, and Franklin B. Sanborn—the "secret six." In the summer of 1859, Brown set up a military headquarters in a rented farmhouse near Harper's Ferry, Virginia. With a disciplined band of sixteen white men and five black men he planned to seize a federal armory in Harper's Ferry as the first step in carrying out his program.

Launching his attack on the night of October 16, he quickly took the armory and then rounded up some sixty leading men of the area whom he intended to hold as hostages. Throughout the next day and night he and his men held out against the local militia, but on the following morning he surrendered to a small force of U.S. Marines, led by Colonel Robert E. Lee, after they had broken in and overpowered him. Brown was seriously wounded and ten of his followers, among them two of his sons, were killed. Six others were captured and later executed, and five escaped. Jailed in Charleston, Virginia, Brown was tried for murder, slave insurrection, and "treason to the Commonwealth." Refusing to permit a plea of insanity on his behalf, he was convicted, and on December 2, 1859, hanged. He was buried in North Elba, New York.

If John Brown had been killed at the engine house at Harper's Ferry, he would have been forgotten. However, the six weeks from his capture until his burial, during which he was the constant center of national attention, transformed him into the first famous martyr for the cause of abolition. John Brown himself leapt at the opportunity to fulfill his need for martyrdom. In a vast correspondence from jail as well as in a speech before his judges he portrayed himself in mythical terms as a martyr and saint willing to die for a glorious cause. He conveyed the impression of being a celestial figure and gave national and even cosmic meaning to his fate. The Charleston gallows became the cross of his martyrdom and the Charleston court became the "Seat of Pilate." His friends and sympathizers continued to reinforce this image up to the Civil War. In the South, however, he was depicted as the incarnation of the devil.

First and foremost, John Brown portrayed himself as a disciple of Christ. He claimed that his entire life, and especially his last mission, had represented an active commitment to God's command and considered his coming death as the necessary consequence of this commitment. He wrote to a Quaker lady on November 1, 1859, "You know that Christ once armed Peter, so also in my case I think he put a sword in my hand . . . and then kindly took it from me."[1] To Mr. McFarland he wrote on November 23, "To me it is given on behalf of Christ not only to believe in him but also to suffer for his sake."[2] To his aged cousin the Reverend Heman Humphrey of Massachusetts, he wrote on November 25, "I have . . . a strong impression that God has given me power and faculties . . . whether my death may not be vastly more valuable than my life is I think quite beyond all human foresight."[3]

Like Jesus and his followers, John Brown knew that his death would promote the cause and, indeed, expressed joy at being permitted to suffer and die as God's agent on behalf of absolute justice and divine truth. Proclaiming an abstract purpose rather than the concrete goal of abolishing slavery, Brown wrote to his family and to his old teacher the Reverend H. C. Vail that death would seal his testimony for God and humanity with his blood.[4] "It is a great comfort to feel assured that I am permitted to die for a cause. . . . My whole life before had not afforded me one half the opportunity to plead for the right," Brown wrote to D. R. Tilden three days before his execution.[5]

By endowing his execution with cosmic meaning, John Brown regarded his martyr's fate as part of a divine plan. As in the famous stories of Christian martyrs, he interpreted the death of the body as eternity for the soul.[6] Brown explained his conviction by Virginia's court as an ultimate vindication before the judgment of history and wrote in a letter to his family that "posterity at last will do me justice."[7] In another letter from prison, to Mr. McFarland, he used the language of Christ on the cross: "Let them hang me, I forgive them for they know not what they do."[8] Likewise, he used biblical language to express his victory in a reply to a letter from his cousin: "I humbly trust that He will not forsake me till I have showed his favor to this generation and his strength to anyone that is to come."[9]

John Brown had a deep conviction that his death would also allow him to become the first American among the honorable gallery of Christian martyrs. As such he perceived himself as a national martyr destined to redeem the country from its sins. Looking at America as a great Christian republic that had deviated from its mission as a redeemer nation because of the sin of slavery, Brown considered his death as a necessary sacrifice designed to purge and purify the American people. "Without the shedding of blood there is no remission of sins," he reiterated to his followers, thus portraying his death as a necessary atonement for the nation's sin.[10]

Brown wrote innumerable letters from jail to Northern friends and relatives. In these letters he no longer depicted himself as a militant guerrilla but as a martyr who awaited his end with tranquility. Again and again he compared himself to Christ, stating that he was glad to die and that his death was of more value to the cause than his life could ever have been. "We may predict for these letters as long a life as for the 'Apology' of Socrates and the dying address to his disciples," wrote Franklin B. Sanborn, who financed Brown's raid and later became his admiring biographer.[11]

In addition to the letters from prison, John Brown stressed his role as a martyr in every statement he made after his capture. When one of his captors asked who had sent him to Harper's Ferry, the old wounded captain eventually answered, "No man sent me here. It was my own prompting and that of my Maker." When another officer asked whether he considered his whole operation as a religious movement, John Brown answered that it was the greatest service a man could render to God. "Do you consider yourself an instrument in the hands of 'Providence'?" asked the officer. "I do," replied John Brown.[12]

At his trial John Brown stated that the whole raid had been right and moral. He declared to his judges, "I believe that I have interfered . . on behalf of His despised poor. . . . Now if it is deemed necessary that I should forfeit my life for the furtherance of the end of justice, and mingle my blood further with the blood of my children and the blood of millions in this slave country . . . I say, let it be done."[13] The trial itself provided John Brown with ample opportunities to portray himself as God's suffering servant battling the forces of darkness.

After his conviction John Brown continued to interpret his fate as a glorious martyrdom: he had been sentenced to the gallows for the crime of the nation. He refused to discuss plans to escape, rejected any plea for amnesty, and even refused to have a Southern minister next to him when he marched toward the gallows. When asked by the *Charleston Independent Democrat* if he was ready to meet death he replied, "I am entirely ready so far as I know. I feel no shame on account of my doom. Jesus of Nazareth was doomed in like manner. Why should I not be?"[14] His last statement was believed to be a prophecy of wrath. Standing on the gallows he pro-claimed, "I, John Brown, am now quite certain that the crimes of this guilty land will never be purged away but with blood."[15]

From the moment of the execution his real transformation into a martyr figure began. Abolitionists and Northern sympathizers as well as free blacks began to turn Old John Brown into a myth. The Civil War, which seemed to fulfill Brown's prophecy, added another dimension to his martyrdom. Brown's supporters and admirers immortalized his image and—in the con-text of the war and its results—gave America its most prominent and consummate martyr to die for a noble cause.

Under the initials P. P. P. an anonymous article was published in the *Liberator* of December 1859 commemorating John Brown:

Martyrdom . . . was but the blossom of a life intent upon the liberation of those that are in bondage. The scaffold has raised and elevated his memory to the notice of the humane world. . . . His death was a two-fold birth—the one immortal into the world of light the eternal abode of the spirit; the other, the spirit of his life, the essence of his actions, . . . into the hearts of philanthropists . . . where it will be cradled and cherished from generation to generation far away down the stream of time.[16]

This short statement encompassed in essence the importance of martyrdom to a reform movement. By fusing a personal fate with social or national history, martyrdom endowed both the individual and the society with uni-versal and cosmic meaning of their existence.

In the crucial period between the execution of John Brown and the outbreak of the Civil War, avowed abolitionists and other Northern sympa-thizers found in him an American parallel to Jesus Christ. He immediately appeared as a symbolic figure who had purified a universal cause with his sacrifice. At a memorial meeting in Melodeon Hall in Cleveland, the motto on the banner was I Do Not Think I Can Better Honor the Cause I Love Than to Die for It. Another famous slogan at many meetings of Brown's admirers was He is Dead, Yet Speaketh.[17] Brown's willingness to die and sacrifice himself made him appear unique and superhuman. According to his supporters, he overcame his human existence through his martyrdom.

None of Brown's admirers doubted that he was a divine instrument. Many speakers depicted him as a Christ-like redeemer. Henry David Thoreau declared in Concord that "some eighteen hundred years ago Christ was crucified, this morning . . . Captain John Brown was hung. These are the two ends of a chain which is not without its links. He is not Old Brown any longer he is an angel of Light."[18] In Termont Temple in Boston, Garrison proclaimed on the night of the execution that "today Virginia murdered John Brown, tonight we here are witnesses of his resurrection."[19] Shortly before the execution Ralph Waldo Emerson asserted that his death would make the gallows glorious like the cross, and the Reverend J. M. Manning regarded him as the sword of God. "The Christ of antislavery has sent forth his 'John' as forerunner," stated the Reverend Edwin M. Wheelock in a sermon in Boston Music Hall. "The gallows from which he ascends into heaven will be in our politics what the cross is in our religion."[20]

This denial of death by identification with Christ allowed the victim to fit the religious and cultural climate of the midnineteenth century. Such a transfiguration of the dead body into immortal soul corresponded with a basic belief in the morality of the universe, the existence of a benevolent God, and an optimistic faith in the future. Such a view was defined later as the "genteel tradition." Under such a tradition any tragedy was interpreted only as an apparent suffering, any death only as mundane demise of the body, any failure only as a temporal step on the way toward ultimate success. Martyrdom was among the cultural manifestations of such an optimistic worldview. When people turned a convicted criminal into a martyr they in fact asserted their conviction in the triumph of the ideals for which he had died. Some transcendental existence, hidden from the concrete reality, required the death of the martyr for the real benefit of mankind. Thus, when they claimed that John Brown had not really died but that he had joined God in the battle against the sin of slavery, his admirers in fact denied the existence of tragedy and suffering.

Both Emerson and Thoreau explained the martyrdom of John Brown within the context of transcendental thought. In an address delivered in Salem on January 6, 1860, Ralph Waldo Emerson emphasized the Puritan background of John Brown. "His enterprise to go into Virginia was . . . but keeping the oath he made to Heaven and earth. . . . As a farmer and orthodox Calvinist [Brown] . . . had learned that life was a preparation, a 'probation' for a higher world, and was to be spent in loving and serving mankind."[21] Thoreau explained the higher sphere John Brown had reached in his life and death. In *The Last Days of John Brown*, which he read in

North Elba on July 4, 1860, Thoreau praised Brown's martyrdom as an event which made the living North transcendental. "It went behind the human law. It went behind the apparent failure. . . . They [Northern people] saw that what was called order was confusion, what was called justice—injustice, and the best was deemed the worst." At the end of his lecture Thoreau addressed his audience directly:

Look not to legislatures and churches for your guidance, not to any soulless incorporated bodies, but to inspirited or inspired ones. . . . He was not to be pardoned or rescued by men. That would be to disarm him, to restore to him the material weapon . . . when he had taken up the sword of the spirit—the sword with which he has really won his greater and most memorable victories. Now he has not laid aside the sword of the spirit, for he is pure spirit himself, and his sword is pure spirit also. . . . John Brown was the only one who has not died. He is more alive than ever he was. . . . He is no longer working in secret. He works in public and in the clearest light that shines on this land.[22]

In verses, sermons, speeches, and articles many Northerners popularized this transcendental interpretation that denied John Brown's death.[23] William Dean Howells, who later became the intellectual leader and guardian of the American genteel tradition, wrote in December 1859:

Death kill not. In later time
(O, slow but all-accomplishing)
Thy shouted name abroad shall ring
Wherever right make war sublime.[24]

George William Curtis, himself an abolitionist, declared in a lecture in Rochester, Massachusetts, on December 12, 1859, that "John Brown was not buried but planted. He will spring up hundredfold."[25]

By stressing the spirit of John Brown, his supporters succeeded in transforming a specific human being who had resorted to violence into a spiritual saint. While avowed abolitionists, nonetheless, did discuss the problem of violence, the enormous power of martyrdom helped them to overcome their misgivings in this case. Although Garrison remained ideologically committed to nonresistance, in practice he adopted a more militant antislavery attitude.[26] In the *Liberator,* for example, he wrote ambivalently, "We think he [Brown] is as deserving of high-wrought eulogy as any who ever wielded the sword or battle-axe in the cause of liberty; but we do not and cannot approve any indulgence of the war spirit."[27] Henry C. Wright, a devoted nonresistant abolitionist, found a way to cope with the violence of John Brown. For him the importance of Brown's action lay not in military success or failure but in his symbolic personal confrontation with sin. "The nation is to be saved not by the blood of Christ but by the blood of John Brown which . . . will prove the 'Power of God and the wisdom of God' to resist slaveholders and to bring them to repentance," he wrote.[28]

Adin Ballou was a perhaps the only radical abolitionist who expressed overt reservations about the adventures of John Brown. He also spoke out against the general mood of glorification on the part of his fellow abolitionists. "If these laudations had held up John Brown . . . as a generous . . . though unwise military adventurer for the liberation of the downtrodden slave . . . soldier-like martyr to the cause; they would have been truthful, just, and unexceptionable," he wrote in the *Practical Christian* on December 10, 1859. "But when they characterized his enterprise and conduct as preeminently Christ-like and canonized him as a Christian saint, and some of them as a self-sacrificing redeemer more to be honored than the Christ of Calvary; they are untruthful, unjust, and utterly absurd."[29]

Abolitionists who merely paid lip service to the doctrine of nonresistance had no difficulties endorsing, justifying, and even praising John Brown's violent fight against slaveholders. Wendell Phillips expressed his disbelief in the "age of bullets" but defined the military operation in Harper's Ferry as an act of reverent self-sacrifice. In the burial oration in North Elba Phillips declared that "If any sword ever reflected the smile of Heaven surely it was those drawn at Harper's Ferry." Thus he implied that a temporal weapon could have spiritual meaning and that Brown's war was a holy war, and as such, totally justifiable.[30] A month after the execution Phillips defended John Brown's violence on the basis of the Puritan commitment to action in the name of divine justice. "Plato thought—nobody cared. . . . Socrates acted and they poisoned him. It is when a man throws himself against society that society is startled to persecute and to think."[31]

In a similar way Henry David Thoreau proclaimed that John Brown was unique and superior because, unlike other human beings, he not only refused to recognize unjust human laws but resisted them.[32] Theodore Parker, the abolitionist minister, explained in a letter from Rome why he justified Brown's military action. To a sickly minister who always yearned to use something more than words and moral suasion, Brown's raid gave a whole new meaning to the cause:

A man against his will as a slave has a natural right to kill everybody who . . . prevents his enjoyment and liberty. A freeman has a natural duty to help the slaves to the enjoyment of their freedom and liberty, and as means to that end, to aid them in killing all such as oppose their natural freedom.[33]

For most antislavery advocates the benefit of martyrdom overshadowed the shortcomings of engaging in violence. "That single hour of death granted him a higher than the soldier's place," declared Wendell Phillips at Brown's burial address. "The echoes of his rifles have died away in the hills—a million hearts guard his words."[34] Thus, John Brown's sacrifice increased the militancy of those who had already devoted their lives to abolishing the sin of slavery and weakened the doctrine of nonresistance as an effective channel of reform. The Reverend J. C. White in a memorial service in Cleveland explicitly declared that "the great and sinful system of American slavery will never be overthrown by pacific means. Without the shedding of blood there can be no remission of such a sin."[35]

In order to symbolize the ultimate sacrifice for a reform cause, it was not enough that John Brown be depicted as martyr only for a negative goal such as the abolition of bondage; he had to be portrayed as a martyr for a positive and new ideal. The positive goal abolitionists and their sympathizers found worthy to die for was the most cherished American ideal of liberty. It was difficult, however, to create a martyr for liberty-as-yet-unachieved in a country whose popular ideology affirmed that liberty already existed. Abolitionists therefore worked hard to question this American ideology by demonstrating the absence of liberty in three different areas: (1) Four million slaves were oppressed human beings, regarded as property and thus deprived of any true liberty; (2) the South created a political tyranny of slaveholders that legalized and institutionalized arbitrary laws without the consent of the people; (3) the whole nation refused to guarantee freedom of expression for the abolitionists' ideas. From this perspective, liberty was still an ideal to be struggled for. Accordingly, the first official reaction of abolitionists to John Brown's execution, known as the Lawrence Resolution, stated that "he had given his life for the liberty of man."[36] In poems John Brown was depicted as a great liberator whose death would hasten the liberation of man from the slaveholder's tyranny.[37] The following phrases from John G. Whittier's "Freedom's Martyr" demonstrate the link that was forged between the specific goal of the abolition of slavery and the general ideal of liberty:

> When the fetters shall be broke . . .
> And the SLAVE shall be a MAN . . .

In the evil days before us
And the trials yet to come
In the shadow of the prison
Or the cruel martyrdom
We will think of thee O brother!
And thy sainted name shall be
In the blessing of the captive
And the anthem of the free.[38]

Even though black followers of Brown, such as John Henry Kagi, were also executed in Virginia, for blacks, John Brown became the most famous martyr for their freedom.[39]

Indeed, John Brown was not only seen as a martyr for the liberty of an oppressed race, but also as a liberator who had fought a tyrannical regime and died on the gallows of the wicked and despotic government of the state of Virginia. His supporters in the North compared his fight to the struggle of early Christian martyrs like John the Baptist who had been convicted by the corrupt court of a despotic regime.[40] Others made analogies with the Greeks in Thermopylae, who had fought oriental despotism, Joan of Arc and William of Orange, who had resisted foreign powers, Protestant martyrs, who had defied wicked Catholic authority, or even George Washington, who could have died on the gibbet for breaking the law of his sovereign had he been caught before 1783.[41]

In reality, however, Virginia was a sovereign state in the Union and not a despotic tyranny, and Governor Wise was not a usurper but a legitimate executive elected by the citizens of the state. In order to present the government of Virginia as a tyrannical foe its legitimacy had to be undermined. The *Radical,* a Bostonian paper sympathetic to abolitionism, wrote in such a tone.

We have learned that government, because it had after some fashion got established is not for that reason the standard of an absolute right. . . . Governments are not sun but earth. . . . The moral sense of mankind holds governments as it holds individuals, amenable to the laws of equity. . . . Brown believed in America as she ought to be and did not hesitate to undertake on his own responsibility the "vast big job" in constructing her upon that basis.[42]

Such an explanation was in fact redundant to the Northern sympathizers of Old John Brown, and ineffective with regard to his bitter opponents. Yet when Lincoln was elected, Southern secessionists challenged the legitimacy of the federal authority on similar grounds, asserting that a tyrannical power had interfered with their domestic affairs and had thus forced them to rebel.

The Civil War enlarged the context of John Brown's martyrdom. The bloodshed that the country experienced in that war, and the assassination of President Lincoln at its end, turned the Harper's Ferry raid into a meaningful event that presaged the sectional conflict. The war, indeed, saved John Brown's image from the fate of Lovejoy: His figure emerged as part of the national consciousness, and he became more than the martyr of the abolitionists and their supporters alone.

At the time of the Harper's Ferry raid the mass of white Americans condemned John Brown as a madman, radical, and fanatic and certainly did not glorify him as a martyr. Politicians sympathetic to the antislavery cause regarded the whole enterprise in Virginia as counterproductive and immoral. National politicians like Abraham Lincoln, Stephen Douglas, and William Seward viewed slavery as a moral evil and advocated its restriction, but they condemned John Brown's action and, in fact, justified his execution. Douglas, a Democrat, blamed the Republican party for the violent raid, and Seward, a Republican, reacted to Douglas's accusations by denouncing the unlawful attack and denying any connection with it. Lincoln himself said that "that affair in its philosophy corresponds with the many attempts related in history at the assassination of kings and emperors. An enthusiast broods over the oppression of people until he fancies himself commissioned by Heaven to liberate them."[43]

For their own ideological purposes, only the radical secessionists in the South claimed that the Northerners considered Brown a martyr. The *Baltimore Sun* asked how the South could afford to live under a government in which the majority of its citizens regarded John Brown as a martyr and Christian hero rather than a murderer and a robber.[44] The *Baltimore American* wrote that Brown's willingness to die calmly as a martyr proved nothing in itself, since many pirates and criminals played such a role before they were executed.[45] In general, when Governor Wise declared after the execution that this would be the fate of all the enemies of the Republic he expressed the feelings of most white people in the South as well as in the North.

Less than two years later, the Republic fought a war against Southern rebellion and John Brown was transformed into a mythical soldier who had preceded the Union soldiers in fighting Southern tyranny. Three years later Lincoln emancipated the slaves, following the path that John Brown had outlined in 1859 and destroying a vicious institution by force of arms. Weapons rather than political means had brought an end to slavery. The war turned John Brown into an inspirational source for many Northerners who had disapproved of his actions in 1859. He became a martyred figure not only to radical abolitionists but also to Union soldiers and prisoners, to emancipated slaves, and to Northerners in general. During the war John Brown became a legend. Many poems were written on his life and death, many popular biographies depicted him as a universal martyr and in 1864 the *Liberator* sponsored and advertised a special event—award of the John Brown medal.[46]

The best known example of the "nationalization" of John Brown was the famous song "John Brown's Body," which became the new anthem of Union soldiers. Like many popular songs it had little significance when it first came out. According to some later research, soldiers in the Massachusetts Seventh Regiment made up some nonsense rhymes about a small ridiculous sergeant named John Brown.[47] Yet these origins were forgotten and only the lines related to John Brown's death became popular. To the music of the famous hymn "Say Brother Will You Meet Us," the soldiers sang the following words:

John Brown's body lies mouldering in the grave
But his soul is marching on.

Popular historians like Oswald Garrison Villard, himself a descendant of famous abolitionists, wrote that regiment after regiment sang that song and that the soldiers identified themselves not with Brown's feeble sword but with his soul.

They too were giving up all that was dear to them, their wives, their children, the prospect of useful lives, to march and suffer; to see their brothers . . . fall by their side. . . . Their's too was an ennobling experience of self sacrifice. How great, then, must have been their inspiration, to feel that he who was the first in the highest form of devotion to an inspired cause, was marching on in the realm above.[48]

Villard did not support this statement with any empirical information. Yet in itself Villard's explanation showed how an ideological supporter of abolitionism used the war and its consequences to enlarge the significance of

John Brown's martyrdom. First he pictured Brown's figure as a spiritual inspiration and used a popular song to validate this picture. Then he identified Brown's suffering and death with the soldiers' death, thus creating a sacrificial connection between the fighters of the Civil War and the old hero who had died on the gallows in Virginia.

The Civil War not only enlarged the social and national context of Brown's martyrdom but also provided a cosmic meaning for his sacrifice. Many abolitionists portrayed the war not as a fight between human beings who represented conflicting interests but as a purifying act of God. Even Lincoln referred frequently to the war as a divine scheme. Thus John Brown was depicted as one who had started the whole battle between the forces of Good and Evil. He had been the first victim of an apocalyptic war designed to redeem the country from the sin of slavery. Two years after his sacrifice many other just and pure souls died for remission of this sin. Five years later, Abraham Lincoln—the great martyr—sealed the whole apocalyptic era with his blood, thus ending the reign of Satan and inaugurating a new stage for the coming of the kingdom of God.

Indeed, many people saw a significant link between the fate of John Brown and the death of Abraham Lincoln. Both figures had a strong appeal to the popular imagination in the tragic yet heroic period of the Civil War. Henry C. Wright viewed John Brown, the dying soldiers, the slaves, and Abraham Lincoln as supreme examples of "self-abnegationism." He praised them as individuals who had deliberately chosen to "suffer rather than to inflict suffering, die rather than kill."[49] Of course this statement did not apply to John Brown's career. European freedom fighters, such as Garibaldi and Victor Hugo, called both Abraham Lincoln and John Brown redeemers of humanity. In reaction to Lincoln's assassination Hugo wrote, "Let not the American people weep for Lincoln. This martyr has his place between John Brown and Jesus Christ as the third redeemer of humanity."[50] Many ex-abolitionists and Northern liberals also sought similarities between the two figures, arguing that both had grown up on the Western frontier, were self-educated, hated slavery, and died in a tragic way which nevertheless assured their victory.

The Civil War helped to emphasize what we can call, using Bruce Rosenberg's term, the "binary contrasts" of John Brown's martyrdom. The explicit message of binary contrast is that the essence of a situation is the reverse of what it appears; the ultimate result is the opposite of the apparent plot. The hero dies but he lives forever; he is apparently defeated but reaches supreme victory through his martyrdom. It is these binary contrasts that give form and sometimes meaning to the narratives of martyred heroes.[51] Indeed, the war made Brown's failure to liberate the slaves a glorious triumph. It turned a villain into a hero and lawful judges into villains. Colonel Lee, who enforced law and order and led the marines to capture John Brown, became the commander in chief of the rebels. Law and order was violated by those who hanged John Brown as a criminal. The traitor became the true patriot, while the executioner turned into a great traitor in the eyes of the North.

The verdict of posterity, another essential element in the martyr tradition, was also reflected in the results of the Civil War and came even faster than most abolitionists had expected. Horace Greeley, an avowed opponent of slavery, wrote in 1860 that "the present effect of John Brown's business is bad . . . but the ultimate effect is to be good . . . and I think the end of slavery . . . is ten years nearer than it seemed a few years ago."[52] The ultimate good manifested itself even earlier than Greeley had prophesied, because of the Civil War.

The war ended in an emotional climax only in mid-1865 when the mourning ceremonies for President Lincoln were completed. Around that time Henry I. Bowditch visited John Brown's grave and wrote a letter that demonstrated how the war had imbued Brown's destiny with universal and even cosmic significance and brought about the ultimate victory.

Here was a man especially allowed to appear to the appointed hour a sort of John the Baptist mission and who sealed this mission with his blood. I thought his design foolish and wrong and how foolish and wrong was my thought. . . . And how ennobling is such an example as Brown to all the race.[53]

The war itself was now over and the nation had the task of building upon the war's legacy. Brown's supporters and admirers attempted to incorporate him into this legacy as the first soldier who had fallen in the war that had redeemed America from its sin. Not only did they describe him as the most prominent martyr of the sin of slavery, but also as the ultimate idealist and selfless reformer, whose martyrdom would be forever a source of inspiration to future American reformers. Thus they aspired to elevate the legend of Brown to a national level and create an enduring martyr whose image would have meaning and relevance for later generations.

In order to become a national martyr, John Brown had to be depicted as an American national archetype. Indeed, many sympathetic writers and spokesmen emphasized his Puritan background, his kinship to the Founding Fathers, his pioneering experience on the Western frontier, his humble yet independent work as a self-made man, his love of liberty, and his simple and authentic religious faith. All these features demonstrated his simple and democratic nature, rooted in the American national experience.[54] Herman von Holst, a well-known German historian whose biography of John Brown (1888) was very popular in the United States, described him as "an American through and through, nature had formed him for rigorous work, and the vicissitudes of his life had developed his natural inclination to a high degree."[55] Similarly, Oswald Garrison Villard wrote in his vast biography that Brown "came of a simple, frugal, hard-working folk deeply interested in religion . . . imbued with a strong love of liberty."[56]

Through the numerous comparisons that were made between John Brown and the early Christian martyrs, Jewish prophets, and Protestant saints, he became part of the American religious heritage. Some biographers stressed Brown's attachment to the Bible and his literal interpretation of biblical stories, especially those of the Old Testament.[57] Using the analogy of the biblical prophets, Brown's adherents praised his American penchant for nonestablished religion that undermined the importance of religious bureaucracy. They portrayed him as a religious clergyman applying a strict religious standard to himself and his family.[58] "He knew the Bible better than many ministers of the Gospel," wrote Herman von Holst.[59] "Like the early Puritans," argued historian James Ford Rhodes, "he drew his most impressive lesson from the Old Testament. . . . As the old puritan was doing God's work, he felt that God would not forsake him."[60] Referring to John Brown's letters from jail, many biographers and sympathizers continued to emphasize the analogy to Christ.[61] Frederick Douglass, an escaped slave and prominent antislavery leader, viewed Christ's and Brown's deaths as the inevitable fate of true reformers. "Like the great and good of all ages —the men born in advance of their times, the men whose bleeding footprints attest the immense cost of reform . . . must wait the polishing wheels of after-coming centuries to make their glory more manifest."[62]

Another important theme in John Brown's martyrdom was his commitment to the American ideal of liberty. The rhetoric of former slaves emphasized this ideal frequently. "He began the war which ended slavery," declared Frederick Douglass,[63] and to most blacks this meant that he had begun the war for liberty. Yet for blacks the fight for liberty ended neither in 1863 nor in 1865. Subjected to legal discrimination throughout the nineteenth century and until the mid-1960s, blacks continued to see liberty as a future ideal. Thus John Brown became for black Americans the first martyr for the ideal of liberty—an ideal that would require further sacrifice. The first major black historian, George Washington Williams, wrote in 1883 that "John Brown was the forerunner of Lincoln, the great apostle of freedom."[64] Later, black leaders would emphasize in their tributes to John Brown that he had merely started the long battle for freedom.[65] The Reverend C. Ranson, a black pastor and leader of the Social Gospel movement, declared that "before race hatred and class distinction are abolished, many others will be called on to wear the martyr's crown."[66] W. E. B. Du Bois concluded at the end of his biography of John Brown that his message had been very simple but universal: The cost of liberty was less than the price of repression. "He [Brown] said: 'Now is the day to strike for a free nation. It will cost something—even blood and suffering, but it will not cost as much as waiting.' And he was right."[67] John Brown died for the liberation of slaves and he undoubtedly became a major source of inspiration for black people in America to continue the struggle and sacrifices for the sake of true freedom.

Most Americans who had perceived themselves as a priori free did not, however, share this image of John Brown as a martyr for liberty. They did not view the Civil War as a war for their national liberation and consequently did not regard him as another freedom fighter. Therefore Brown's sympathizers made a conscious attempt to elevate his image to the level of myth that would help to transform him into an enduring national martyr.[68] They hoped to achieve this by replacing his real career and activities with an imaginary and inspirational plot. This task of mythologizing gathered further momentum as years passed by and Americans became less and less familiar with the real events at Harper's Ferry.

A myth embodies not only the heart of an epic story, but also inspiration and the visions, dreams, and hopes of human beings. A legend provides not only meaning to human history, but also an answer to a crisis situation. It is more than a fireside story or a fairy tale. As described by Richard O. Boyer, it springs from a specific historical situation faced by a society on the verge of destruction. The restabilization of social institutions depends later on the legend as a source for the "new birth."[69] The chaotic experience of the Civil War therefore enabled contemporaries to create the legend of John

Brown for later generations; it helped to turn Brown's raid into a holy war, his execution into a sacrifice and his whole person into a martyr for the cause, expiating for Americans the sin of slavery and, on the cosmic level, promoting the coming of the millennium. A wide variety of literary devices contributed to the legend of John Brown. A later historian noted that before the turn of the century he had counted 14 biographies, 250 poems, 11 short stories and 58 novels on John Brown.[70] Though not all of that material depicted John Brown in mythical terms, and some probably condemned him as a criminal, the amount itself is impressive and can be compared only to the literature dedicated to Lincoln.

A fictionalization of John Brown's last moments helped to build the image of a mythical martyr.[71] Immediately after the execution John G. Whittier wrote a poem entitled "Brown of Ossawatomie":

> John Brown of Ossawatamie, they led him out to die
> And lo! a poor slave-mother with her little child press nigh
> Then the bold, blue eye grew tender, and the harsh face grew mild
> And he stooped between the jeering ranks and kissed the Negro's child.[72]

The poet based this description on an erroneous newspaper report. This incident did not really occur, yet that did not prevent Wendell Phillips from declaring in Brown's burial oration that "everyone saw him stoop on his way to the scaffold and kiss that Negro child."[73] Phillips's statement was correct as a prophecy for the future: A painter painted this scene of John Brown kissing a Negro child and this picture appeared in almost every biography and text book on John Brown.[74] Nothing was more appealing than this legendary last act of John Brown, and it inspired a black poet to write a "Negro Mother's Lullaby."[75]

"Classical" iconography constituted another device for creating a legendary figure. Frank Paterson Stearns praised Mr. Brakett's famous marble bust of John Brown:

The bust of John Brown compared well with any of the heads of Greek divinities. . . . The sculptor has been most fortunate in moulding a face with strong Roman-like features . . .[which] are united with perfect classic repose. It seems as if thus Constantine must have looked, and the great Christian emperors. . . . A pose of the head and the aspect of great moral force led Sumner to compare it to Michelangelo's Moses. Mr. Brakett [the sculptor] writes: "I can only say that I intended it a physical and mental likeness of man."[76]

By creating a general Greek figure of man iconography served to transform a concrete person into a general embodiment of the ideal human being.

Paintings, monuments, sculptures, medals and other figurative artefacts were indeed numerous and well known in the case of John Brown.

Dedication ceremonies also provided perfect occasions for elevating a person to a mythical sphere by giving universal meaning to his action. Charles Robinson, the first governor of the free state of Kansas, demonstrated this when on August 30, 1877, he dedicated the John Brown monument commemorating the Ossawatomie battle. "The soul of John Brown was the inspiration of the Union armies in the emancipation war and it will be the inspiration of all men in the present and the distant future who may revolt against tyranny and oppression; because he dared to be a traitor to the government that he might be loyal to humanity."[77] President Theodore Roosevelt himself paid tribute to John Brown in the ceremonies dedicating the John Brown Park in Kansas on August 30, 1910.[78]

The sacred aura surrounding John Brown was also enhanced by the cosmic significance with which his grave was endowed.[79] The more his grave became a shrine and site of pilgrimage, the more his figure acquired universal and legendary characteristics. Contemporaries ascribed certain cosmic qualities to the fact that John Brown was buried at the foot of a huge boulder in an open area amid vast mountains. Thus he emerged forever with the authentic forces of great Nature and was transformed from a human being into a cosmic force.[80] Thus, in reaction to Wendell Phillips's proposal to transfer the remains of John Brown to Massachusetts, the *New England Magazine* wrote:

Let it never be. Let them stay beside the great boulder, itself a relic of ancient glacial age. . . . Here Nature's own hand has built for his lasting monument the great watchtowers of the mountains, and they lift their hands far into the sky and gaze ever upward and around to see if the judge of the world came not.[81]

Rhetoric that stressed the sacrificial ties between John Brown and other people also aimed to turn him into a universal and sacred figure. When the act of sacrifice becomes the focus of attention, the hero transcends the confines of his time, place, and specific historical context. He becomes a universal example not because he fought for a valuable cause, which may not exist a generation later, but because of the way he conducted his activities. "Just as John Brown has sacrificed himself," declared W. E. B. Du Bois, "so must we sacrifice our work, our money, and our position in order to beat back the evil of the world."[82] Describing a chain of sacrificial heroes, the Reverend Charles Ranson wrote in the *Colored American Magazine,* "Like the ghost of Hamlet's father, the spirit of John Brown beckons us to arise and seek the recovery of our right. The soul of John Brown goes marching on in those black men and women who aggressively fought for equality despite the opposition of the press and the public."[83] Thus a hierarchical relationship between the hero and his followers according to the degree of sacrifice served to build a vague legendary martyr from a specific human being. Obviously such sacrificial ties were meaningful only to black activists and not to the public in general.

Statements that focused upon the last stand, the classical archetype of man, the cosmic significance of the grave, and the sacrificial ties between a hero and his followers intended to turn the concrete John Brown into a legend and a myth. Yet without a general will to believe in the myth, the force of these devices is very limited. Certain interests supply people with the will to believe a mythical story, a belief that later will serve these interests. Ex-abolitionists, Union veterans, Northern liberals, and, certainly, blacks had a sincere interest that motivated their will to believe in John Brown's martyrdom. But John Brown acted against large segments of American society and provoked hostility that did not wither over time in the white South. The critique of his activities and personality no doubt undermined the efforts of Brown's followers and later sympathizers to turn his figure into an enduring martyr.

When John Brown's raid first occurred it provoked general opposition both in the North and in the South. This opposition endured over time. John Brown's foes made a huge effort to destroy his martyr image by portraying him as a mere villain, a criminal, and as un-American. They challenged all the mythical qualities that his sympathizers had ascribed to him, and even constructed a countermyth in which John Brown figured as the incarnation of the devil.

Early in 1868, Rushmore G. Horton, a Southerner, published *A Youth History of the United States.* The first picture in the book showed John Brown receiving money and rifles "for his Kansas work." The second picture portrayed him stabbing a person with a bloody dagger. In the chapter on Harper's Ferry the author wrote, "A notorious murderer went into Virginia with a posse of assassins, for the purpose of getting up an insurrection among the negroes, to murder the white men, women, and children."[84] This textbook probably reflected the way the South envisioned John Brown. Even a moderate Northern magazine like the *Nation* viewed Brown's activities as criminal. In an article in 1885 the journal criticized Sanborn's biography asserting that "a divine inspiration of Brown does not justify his murders."[85] "Brown was neither a statesman nor a warrior, only a simple fanatic," wrote the *Atlantic Monthly* in another book review of Sanborn's biography.[86] Famous historians with a pro-Southern bias like Woodrow Wilson and John W. Burgess also regarded John Brown as a fanatical madman with a price on his head. They viewed the Harper's Ferry raid as one of the chief crimes in American history.[87] Descriptions of Brown as an outstanding failure, a horse thief and an insane fanatic were added to the accusations of murder by those who justified his execution at Charleston.[88] For these opponents, John Brown would take his place in history not as a revered martyr, but as a dangerous adventurer. "He will rank among adventurers as Napoleon ranks among marshals, as Captain Kidd among pirates, as Jonathan Wild among thieves."[89]

Such passionate hatred, however, was not enough to ruin John Brown's image for later generations who had no connection with the events of the 1850s. He had to be portrayed as the antithesis of American values. Therefore his opponents interpreted his whole character and career, even prior to his activities in Kansas and Virginia, as "alien corn" of the American experience. The simple biographical data used by Brown's supporters to demonstrate his typical Americanism became proof of his deviation from the American way. In his famous monograph, *The Civil War and the Constitution,* John W. Burgess gave a negative description of John Brown:

He was a notorious dead beat himself, had never succeeded in any legitimate business, had never earned any money, had two wives and some twenty children, and left them to shift for themselves in penury and misery while he was careering around reforming things.[90]

According to these hostile portrayals, John Brown's religion was also strange and dangerous to the American religious tradition. "He was religious but not Christian," wrote the Reverend Abner Hopkins to Thomas Hughes in 1882, "Religion was the church on which his fanaticism walked. It was the 'Higher law' religion [which] found further development in the assassination of the Czar of Russia, the Emperor of Germany . . . and of our own president [James A. Garfield]. . . . Both John Brown and Guiteau

[Garfield's assassin] claimed to be 'God's men.' "[91] An article in the *Catholic World* described Brown's Christianity as a savage version of the Old Testament in which God was portrayed only as a God of wrath and destruction. The article criticized Sanborn's argument that Brown was not bound by common laws of human morality as un-Christian prophanity and pagan idolatry. "Milton's doctrine is that *God* is not the slave of the laws which He made to men. Mr. Sanborn's doctrine that heroes are not subject to the laws which God made for other men . . . but the hero himself is the only witness to a divine commission." Such a doctrine, assumed "that the final standard of right and wrong is every man's own fancy."[92]

The theory that some heroic figures were subject to some "divine light" that released them from submission to human laws received fierce criticism from a legal perspective. In a free society only law determined what was tolerable and democracy had no room for activities that defied law on the basis of some higher ethical code. Rebellion was justified only under oppressive regimes, but any attempt to compare John Brown to Spartacus or Toussaint l'Ouverture was an absurd fallacy.[93] The *Dial* asserted that such a theory of a great man contradicted the American belief in progress.

Sanborn wrote within Carlyle's theory of Great men namely that the world runs down . . . through the deficiencies of merely common men, and would go to the bad entirely only it is so arranged that just in the nick of time the Lord sends down a Hero . . . so . . . that we can then get along for . . . a generation or two.

An a priori acceptance of such a theory explained why Sanborn wrote that heroes like John Brown had the right to take the law into their own hands. Yet Americans who believed in progress rather than decline did not need heroes to redeem them and consequently would not justify breaking the law. "The theory is unsound, un-scientific and has little hold upon the minds of young Americans anywhere," concluded the article.[94]

Ironically, the change in the image of the Civil War provided Brown's foes with appropriate material to depict him as a national traitor and villain. After the failure of radical reconstruction more and more Americans looked upon the whole conflict as a tragic mistake that could have been avoided. Many believed that if only the North and the South had resorted to the traditional mechanism of peaceful compromise in 1860, the bloodshed probably could have been prevented. John W. Burgess, a supporter of this interpretation, viewed the war as a disaster and pointed at specific villains who had instigated the fight. John Brown was the extreme example of a traitor whose raid had frightened the South and whose execution had seduced the North. The holding of "prayer meetings for the soul of John Brown . . . in the North, should appear to the people of the South to be evidence of the wickedness which knew no bounds," he wrote.[95] Two Northern historians, William Cullen Bryant and Sydney Howard Gay, asserted in their book, *A Popular History of the United States*, "From this time [the Harper's Ferry raid] the intention to divide the Union at any moment became a universal Southern idea."[96] Both the Northern and the Southern versions agreed that John Brown's operation was crucial in creating a belligerent atmosphere and destroying the mechanism of compromise between the sections.

Thus the Civil War and its anticlimatic aftermath had contradictory effects on the legacy of John Brown. During the war it provided a heroic and positive context to his activities, and people in the North viewed him as herald of the emancipation, the first martyred soldier for the Union, and the forerunner of Abraham Lincoln. Ex-abolitionists and blacks continued to look upon the war as a blessed consequence of John Brown's sacrifice. But during the late nineteenth century many whites in the North expressed severe reservations concerning the war. Such a change of attitude served John Brown's enemies who used the context of the war to depict him as a bloody traitor. Oddly enough, a very favorable article on John Brown, written by E. N. Vallandigham in *Putnam's Magazine* in December 1909, asserted, "It is by no means certain that the attack on Harper's Ferry hastened the Civil War."[97] The transformation of the Civil War from a holy crusade into a tragic fraternal conflict deprived John Brown of part of his heroic context and undermined his image as the forerunner of national redemption.

Brown's literary enemies refuted his mythical qualities and stressed his worldly horrors. Many of them simply ridiculed the image that many biographies had created. Most of the critics argued against any mythical analysis, which could no longer be treated seriously in a modern scientific age. "More than a quarter of century has passed since Captain John Brown of Kansas was hanged on Virginia gallows and his soul began it's wonderful march toward the Valhalla of mythical heroes and demi-Gods," wrote the *Dial* in 1885. "But an age of voluminous printing is unfavorable to myth making."[98] Likewise the *Atlantic Monthly* wrote that as a legend John Brown "grows a more vivid, real and living-image with each year which removes into future distance his life in the flesh."[99] "His soul is marching on," asserted the *American Mercury*—a debunking magazine of the 1920s—"But it was not the soul of any John Brown who really ever lived."[100]

Brown's foes made a significant attempt to deny the story of the last stand. In 1885 the *Southern Historical Society Papers* published a letter from Captain John Avis, the jailer and executioner of John Brown. He wrote that the story of the kiss John Brown had given a black child in its mother's arms was incorrect and that nothing of this sort had happened. He refuted the story of Brown's cheerfulness as he walked to the scaffold and denied that Brown had ever thanked God for allowing him to die for a cause.[101] While Captain Avis undermined the myth of the last stand on the basis of being an eyewitness, Hill P. Wilson in his biography and Leland H. Jenks in the *American Mercury* denied it on the basis of their own interpretations. For Wilson, Brown's quest for martyrdom in his letters from jail was just another device to acquire "pecuniary assistance for his family whenever a favorable opportunity presented itself."[102] Jenks asserted that Brown changed his mind frequently in order to capitalize on his failure. He wrote also that after Brown's first bankruptcy he had planned to operate a plantation in Virginia.[103]

At least two famous monographs created a countermyth of John Brown. They depicted him as a revolutionary traitor aiming to build a new United States under his dictatorial tyranny. "He met and established confidential relations with men who plotted against the life of the nation and planned how to provoke a revolution," wrote Hill P. Wilson, "Out of his negotiations with them came money, munitions of war, mutual planning for revolution, and a dream of an empire."[104] John W. Burgess extended the conspiracy of Brown to a cosmic level by regarding him as the incarnation of Satan on earth, defying the divine order. Assuming certain predeterministic developments in the history of the world, Burgess stated that man determined only the nature of the means in this process.

It is from this point of view that the event at Harper's Ferry must be judged. . . . It was a crime . . . that made violent and destructive means possible and actual and seemingly necessary for the attainment in the United States of the principle of the world's civilization which had decreed the personal freedom of all men. . . . It is an affront to Divinity itself to assert that the world's civilization cannot be realized except through violence and destruction, blood, crime and sin. . . . It is the passionate hate of sinful man which dares to hurry the plans of Providence by employment of means which rob the plans of their glory and their divinity."[105]

This statement not only condemned John Brown personally but also accused his contemporary supporters, as well as his later sympathizers who had turned him into a myth. By applying a cosmic plan of history, Burgess depicted Brown's violence as a tragic and sinful intervention in the cosmic plan of civilization, violence that had produced only suffering and misery.

Richard Realf, a declared abolitionist whom John Brown nominated as foreign minister in his provisional government in Canada, later dissociated himself from the whole adventure. Yet, as a poet he remained committed to values of heroism and sacrifice in his poems. In the annual encampment of the Pennsylvania Department of the Grand Army of the Republic, on January 26, 1876, he read his poem *In Memoriam*:

> Great Greece hath her Thermopylae
> Stout Switzerland hath her Tell
> The Scott his Wallace heart—and we
> Have saint and shrines as well . . .
> Altar of sacrifice perfumed
> Our hot, sulphuric air;
> And Sidney's shining manhood bloomed
> Around us everywhere . . .
> Sweet saints in every home
> Through whose dear helping stood revealed
> The joy of martyrdom.[106]

The poem is very long and full of graves, blood, and tragic-heroic deaths. But the name John Brown is missing. True, poems tend to express emotions in abstract terms. But such an emphasis on war heroes without even mentioning the well-known sacrifice of John Brown raises the question of whether he ever fully became a revered martyr for the sin of slavery.

John Brown had enormous potential for becoming such a martyr. He committed himself to a specific ideal—the abolition of slavery—for which he fought and sacrificed his life. He had six whole weeks in prison to develop, refine, and articulate the meaning of his death and he exploited this opportunity to the fullest. He was not a political seeker but rather a nonconventional individual who imposed his leadership on committed and fanatical followers. A central reform group—the abolitionists—immediately adopted him and turned him into a martyr. Abolitionists who had used martyrdom as a central ideological weapon found in John Brown a perfect example of the martyr. He was not a member of the rank and file of the movement, but rather an eccentric nonconformist, depicted as a unique figure who sacrificed his life for one reform goal—to abolish the sin of slavery.

The historical context also favored John Brown. The "sin of slavery" had become a national issue in the late 1850s. The abolitionists, though hated and despised by many Americans, appeared to be the central reform movement in America shortly before the Civil War. Then came the war, which sent John Brown's spirit "marching on" with the soldiers of the Union and finally with the declaration of emancipation. The end of slavery made the martyrdom of Brown an ultimate success story. People could really interpret his sacrifice as a fate of the "suffering servant" whose role was to reform and redeem the society through personal suffering and personal confrontation with sin. Thus J. J. Ingalls wrote in the prestigious *North American Review* of 1884:

Carlyle says that when any great change in human society is to be wrought, God raises up men to whom that change is made to appear as the one thing needful and absolutely indispensable. Scholars, orators, poets . . . play their part, but the crisis comes at last through someone who is stigmatized as a fanatic by his contemporaries, and whom the supporters of the systems he assails crucify between thieves or gibbet as a felon. The man who is not afraid to die for an idea is its most potential and convincing advocate.[107]

As we have seen, American culture in the nineteenth century was receptive in general to the idea of martyrdom. People took religious symbolism seriously and believed in the cosmic structure of fall, sin, sacrifice, and redemption. Rhetoric that described sacrifice for the sin of slavery in order to purify America and to promote the kingdom of God made sense to many Americans. A description of John Brown as the ultimate altruist who sacrificed his life for such a purpose appealed to people who basically believed in the morality of the universe and the inevitability of linear progress. Such a worldview denied suffering by interpreting its temporal existence as having ultimately positive consequences. "The best portion of the people," wrote E. P. Stearns in an epilogue to Herman von Holst's biography of John Brown, "were pervaded and thrilled by the conviction that a martyr had laid down his life as an offering for the sins of the nation. . . . This seed sown in blood must . . . bring forth a mighty harvest."[108] This is an example of the genteel tradition, which, in fact, refused to accept suffering in a moral world and used the concept of martyrdom as a rationale for its apparent existence. The ultimate success of the cause for which the martyr had suffered not only uplifted him as an individual but also helped others to believe in the morality of their universe. Glorification of a martyr figure through the use of binary contrasts served to deny the existence of suffering in a moral universe created by a benevolent God.

Nonetheless, despite this enormous potential John Brown neither became an enduring national legend nor an American martyr for the cause of reform. The request of the state legislature of Kansas to place Brown's statue in the National Hall of Fame in Washington, D.C., was never granted.[109] In 1959, a famous black paper in Chicago complained that "the centennial of John Brown's raid passed almost without notice. Only conspicuous few see him . . . as a martyr of human freedom."[110] Indeed, only blacks continued to immortalize his image and to view him as a martyr for reform. To the average white American John Brown remained a very controversial figure. While worshipful biographers tried to build a national legend of the martyr-reformer, hostile writers portrayed him as a worthless villain. Even modern historians who deal with him in a more objective state of mind reach ambiguous conclusions. Many of them describe him in polemical or apologetic terms. Stephen B. Oates, one of the best biographers of John Brown, has demonstrated this ambivalence in his article "John Brown and his Judges."[111] Indeed, John Brown was never awarded a widely accepted crown of martyrdom for his reform activities.

One possible explanation for this phenomenon derives from the fact that John Brown was a sectional figure who fought the other section. He did not save the whole nation from an external enemy, and himself was the enemy of all the white South. Even for people who rejected slavery, John Brown's activities in Kansas and Virginia were far from completely valiant. Rather than providing national cohesion, John Brown's blood intensified national strife and ultimately led to war. After such a costly war Americans found it difficult to depict him as a national martyr unifying the whole nation behind the cause of reform.

The changing attitude toward the Civil War after the failure of Reconstruction also undermined the martyrdom of John Brown. Juxtaposing the war's horrors and suffering with its limited achievements, Americans began to doubt whether it had been altogether worthwhile. Certainly, they emphasized new commitments to internal peace, compromise and reconciliation. In such an atmosphere, even devout supporters of John Brown had to limit their praise. J. W. Winkley, who wrote an extremely favorable biography of Brown in 1905 based on his personal reminiscences, concluded that "John Brown belonged to the 'Old Order' which is passing away. Heaven speed its end! He was a man of war whatever else he might be. . . . While we glorify the spirit he was of, we must turn our higher ideal—to those of the 'new order,' to men of peace. Their spirit—the same, their methods are as opposite as the poles."[112]

It may be possible that the very abolition of slavery weakened John Brown's image for further generations. Americans had no more reason to glorify and remember the martyr of reform when reform became part of the status quo. This was especially true with the slavery issue, which had long made many Americans uneasy. They expressed their relief when it was legally abolished, but they saw emancipation as the end of the process and not as the beginning. Only blacks regarded the emancipation as a first step toward becoming full citizens in American democracy. Their specific experience of legal discrimination in the South and racial hostility all over the country for a century after the emancipation, verified beyond doubt such a view. Thus, for blacks, John Brown's spirit kept marching on and his martyrdom only inaugurated the battle for freedom and equality. "The spirit of John Brown moves on in social reform," declared a black historian late in 1959 during the centennial commemoration of the execution. "Does not the spirit of the Grangers, the Populists, of Eugene V. Debs, of the Muckrakers, of Robert La Follettes, of Huey Long and Henry Wallace suggest the ghost of John Brown?"[113] Most white Americans in the Gilded Age and Progressive Era would not have agreed to include John Brown's ghost in this gallery of national heroes.

What most directly barred John Brown from the acknowledged title of *martyr for reform* was his enthusiastic reliance upon overt violence in order to promote his ideals. John Brown not only defied unjust laws, but he also killed innocent people in his various activities. Had he been only a victim of the violence of his opponents he might have become a distinguished martyr, but he initiated the violence and was executed in punishment for murder. Furthermore, he had a reputation as a fanatical murderer even prior to the Harper's Ferry raid. In his monumental book *History of the United States,* James Ford Rhodes wrote:

What infinite variety of opinions may exist of a man who on one hand is compared to Socrates and Christ, and on the other hand to Orsiniad and Wilkes Booth. . . . Yet the comparison to Socrates and Christ strikes a discordant note. The apostle of truth and the apostle of peace are immeasurably remote from the man whose work of reform consisted in shedding blood—the teacher who gave the injunction, "Render unto Caesar the things that are Caesar's," and the philosopher whose long life was gained by the breach of laws deemed sacred by his country.[114]

Clearly, the application of extremely violent means to gain his goal prevented John Brown from achieving a widely accepted martyrdom. His enemies depicted him as a wicked criminal and Americans in general evaluated him with a very split voice of praise and condemnation, laudation and scorn.

Therefore, while he certainly was a very significant martyr to abolitionists, blacks, and perhaps also to some later radicals and reformers, John Brown fell short of becoming an enduring national martyr. It was quite a different figure who was killed about the same period who achieved this status. A national crown of thorns was awarded by the American public to Abraham Lincoln, the Civil War president, assassinated on April 14, 1865, at the end of the war. The image of a martyr for reform, which abolitionists perpetuated and John Brown exemplified, became nationally accepted and enduring through the figure of Abraham Lincoln, the first assassinated president of the United States.

3

Abraham Lincoln—
The National Martyr

On Good Friday 1865 Abraham Lincoln, the sixteenth president of the United States, was shot by an assassin. He died hours later. This event profoundly shocked the country, sealing the tragic period of the Civil War with both a catastrophic and sublime climax. Americans had never experienced an assassination of their chief magistrate before, and the event immediately led to unprecedented public mourning and grief. The context of the Civil War provided a unique and heroic dimension to this national bereavement. Yet the tragic event reached far beyond the ceremonies of sorrow and rites of national affliction in that it stimulated public leaders, clergymen, journalists, and various writers and orators to give meaning to the American national experience in the face of such a tragedy. On the one hand, this tragedy questioned the basic beliefs and values of the American democratic culture, while on the other it forced Americans to explain it within the context of these same values and ideals. Above all, it provided the people of the United States with their prominent and enduring national martyr.

Congressman James A. Garfield—who would become the second assassinated president—reacted to the shocking event eloquently and emotionally:

Oh Sir, there are times in the history of men and nations when they stand so near to the veil that separates mortals from immortals, time from eternity, and men from their God, that they can almost hear the beating and feel the pulsations of the Infinite. Through such time has this nation passed . . . when at last . . . that martyred president [joined] . . . the company of the dead heroes of the Republic, the nation stood so near the veil that the whispers of God were heard by the children of men.[1]

Public leaders in and out of the religious establishment, interpreted the assassination and death of Lincoln through religious ideas and symbols. They often used the concept of martyrdom, and Lincoln immediately was defined as our martyred president. Such an image helped to explain the terrible event to many Americans at the time of the assassination. It also added a legendary dimension to the Civil War president thus creating an inspirational hero for generations to come.

Underestimating the fact that Lincoln had been elected to office by ordinary political procedure in 1860, public tributes referred to God's invisible hand as the instrument by which Lincoln had become president. The Reverend Phineas Densmore Gurley claimed in the funeral sermon in Washington, D.C., that "God raised him up for a great and glorious mission, furnished him for his work and aided him in his accomplishment."[2] In his famous burial oration, Bishop Matthew Simpson said, "By the hand of God Lincoln was especially singled to guide our government in this troublesome time."[3] Not only religious officials but also political leaders referred to God as the ultimate cause of Lincoln's election.[4] Some used biblical terminology such as "God's gift to the people" when they characterized Lincoln's election, while others compared him to famous Old Testament leaders like Abraham the Patriarch, Moses, or King David.[5]

According to many addresses, God had removed Lincoln from the presidency when He thought his mission was done. Some of Lincoln's contemporaries questioned this divine decision.[6] Others admitted that they could not understand the logic of Providence since "God moves in a mysterious way His wonders to perform."[7] But most addresses did emphasize the fact that Lincoln had been removed exactly at the moment when he had accomplished his mission.[8] It seemed almost natural that at their first annual memorial convention on February 12, 1866, members of the United States Congress listened to Dr. Boyton, the chaplain of the House, appealing to God in the following words: "We bless Thee that he did not die until assured of victory, until he knew that his great work was done and he received all the honor that earth could bestow and then we believe Thou didst give him a martyr's crown."[9]

Lincoln figured as a divine instrument in many obituaries, and such an image prevailed over time in various commemoration addresses. Later writers and spokesmen explained to the public that God had selected Lincoln as His agent to save the country in time of crisis and removed him from life when his mission was done.[10] Few of Lincoln's contemporaries attempted to provide evidence of this celestial relationship; the announcement itself by a famous preacher or writer was enough. But later generations drew upon Lincoln's life and quoted from his speeches in order to substantiate this relationship historically. Thus they argued that on various occasions the president himself had discovered the fact that God was directing his activities. Carl Holliday, dean and professor of English at the University of Toledo, quoted from Arnold's *Life of Lincoln* to persuade his audience that time after time Lincoln had spoken of the guidance of God in his own affairs.[11] In an address delivered at the University of Illinois at Urbana on February 12, 1896, Andrew S. Drapper informed the audience that early in 1860 Lincoln had said to his friend Newton Bateman, "I know there is a God. . . . I see a storm coming and I know that His hand is in it. If He has a place and a work for me—and I think He has—I believe I am ready." [12]

A historical perspective also helped to support the view that the assassination had been the result of divine intervention. It became apparent that a distinctive heroic period of war, violence, emancipation, reunion, and victory characterized the historical context of Lincoln's presidency. This crucial period had significantly changed the life of the nation and thus Lincoln could be depicted by later generations as the great reformer, responsible for this new birth of the American nation through a purging baptism of blood. Following the assassination, Americans entered the anticlimactic period of Reconstruction, characterized by corruption, disappointment, and failure. This interpretation of the period, common on many levels of American historiography at the turn of the century, helped to place the martyrdom of Lincoln on historical foundations. He lived long enough to complete his mission of reunifying and reforming the nation in the heroic time of struggle, but not beyond this period.[13]

How did the description of the martyred president as a semidivine figure accord with a political culture that placed a high premium on the popular foundation of government and considered the people as the only source of the leader's authority? A direct answer to this apparent contradiction was given by the Reverend Mr. Crook in his eulogy at the Seventh Street Methodist Episcopal Church in New York in June 1865:

A new theory has arisen and it might be designated as Caesarism. It assumes that great men are representatives of Providence . . . that they are Messiahs of the race.

. . . It followed as a corollary of this theory that a great man was a law to himself and he was bound to obey nothing but his own impulse. . . . Just the hour which had given us a clear exposition of Caesarism was the hour which completed the career of lowly Abraham Lincoln whose life was a refutation of this monstrous error. . . . We then had an opposite theory of the function of great men. It was that great men are exponents of the people. . . . Abraham Lincoln . . . [was] the power which drank in its inspiration from the hearts of the common masses. [14]

Indeed, most contemporary tributes did not portray a Caesarlike figure, despite the emphasis on the divine connection of the president. They depicted a human being whose election to office and removal from the human world had been determined by Providence, but who in his life had never been more than a popular servant and an integral part of the common people. His career, his nature and his death were therefore both celestial and mundane. He was unique as well as typical, both a divine instrument and a typical human being. Some contemporaries even suggested that Lincoln would be remembered as the servant of the people and that no marble column or memorial statue would be erected to honor him. They asserted that a memorial hospital or asylum for poor soldiers and sailors would represent Lincoln's real spirit. [15] "The name of him . . . and his conviction that 'if slavery is not wrong nothing is wrong' will endure without the help of stone and bronze," wrote an anonymous journalist in 1865. [16] However, later generations did not implement such modest suggestions. Through various commemorative artefacts they portrayed a unique and even super-human image of the president who stood above ordinary human beings and aloof from the people's day-to-day affairs. [17]

Yet since they operated within a democratic political culture even those later glorifications used a variety of rhetorical devices in order to describe the martyred president as both a unique and a popular hero. As a result, such prose sometimes seems contradictory and ambiguous, but this stems from the necessity to glorify an individual leader in a democratic culture that ideologically rejected "Caesarism." A few examples will illustrate the logic some speakers used to depict Lincoln in these ambivalent terms. "To be the first man of the people in a land where every citizen is a king, is to be the manliest of men and the kingliest of kings," said Rabbi S. Shulman in an address on Lincoln and the American democracy, delivered in New York at the centennial celebration of Lincoln's birth. [18] Woodrow Wilson in a Chicago centennial celebration viewed Lincoln both as apart from and part of the people.

What is a man of the people . . . a man with his rootage deep among the people . . . of no class . . . but lifted above the narrowness and limitations of the view of the mass by the insight and study which enabled him to see what they did not see . . . and to speak . . . for them as if released from what holds them back from his leadership.[19]

Similarly, in the first broadcasted sermon on February 11, 1928, William E. Barton declared that Lincoln was a representative both of God and of the people.[20]

The figure of the martyr as both human being and divine spirit appeared in early religious literature. In the struggle within oneself the act of sacrifice constituted the final victory of the spirit over the flesh; thus the martyr purged himself of his own human sin.[21] Such a concept of martyrdom was part of the Hellenistic tradition. Clement of Alexandria in the *Martyrdom of Polycarp* asserted that martyrs such as Mucius Scaevola, Heraclitus, Empedocles, and Dido, had not been affected by torture, because they were no longer human beings but angels.[22] Other examples are found in Jewish literature of the Hellenistic period such as the *Book of Maccabees,* which depicted the martyr Elazar as one who had overcome pain and passion by his reason.[23] The Jewish book, *The Wisdom of Solomon,* conveyed the message that the righteous were forged and purified through suffering and tortures. "For Lord tried them and found them worthy . . . accepting them as sacrificial offering."[24] Christianity adopted this idea of the purification, victimization, and spiritualization of the martyr. The New Testament expressed the idea that by suffering the Christian faithful were disciplined, tested, purged, and purified.[25]

The idea of spiritualization through martyrdom appeared in a modified version of the case of Abraham Lincoln, particularly in religious sermons delivered immediately after his assassination. The Reverend Henry Ward Beecher asked in one of his famous sermons, "Is a man that was ever fit to live dead? Disenthralled of flesh, risen to the unobstructed sphere where passion never comes, he begins his illimitable work."[26] The sermons that stressed the theme of Abraham Lincoln's spiritual purity lacked, however, two central elements: they did not view suffering and pain as a necessary step toward the final stage of pure spirit, and they did not interpret Lincoln's death as an act of self-sacrifice that had enabled him to purge himself of his own sin.[27] The explanation for the absence of suffering was somewhat trivial: Lincoln did not suffer physically in his last hour on earth since he lost consciousness immediately and died twelve hours later. The absence of personal sin to be purged through martyrdom was explained by the perception of Lincoln as an a priori pure and sinless person. "He was a man without vice," said Emerson, thus expressing that part of American ideology that challenged the Christian dogma that every human being was an innate sinner.[28] Although Lincoln's death changed his mode of existence, the transformation according to the various sermons was not from a sinful person to pure soul, but rather from an innocent person to a pure soul.[29]

The theme of suffering became more frequent over time. While it was impossible to show that Lincoln had suffered in his death, later generations could easily portray him as a melancholic leader who had suffered for his people under the burden of office throughout his career.[30] Julia Ward Howe's centennial poem presented an elaborate version of this same theme:

> No throne of honor and delights
> Day of distrust and sleepless nights
> To struggle, suffer and aspire
> Like Israel led by cloud and fire . . .
> A teacherous spot, a sob of rest
> A martyr's palm upon his breast
> A welcome at the glorious sea
> Where blameless souls of heroes meet.[31]

In general, later generations used the historical context of the Civil War in order to depict Lincoln as a unique leader, personally suffering for the people who had not fully understood his entire vision. His fate resembled that of a prophetic reformer who found rest in heaven after a troubled life of struggle and suffering.

Lincoln the individual was portrayed as a martyr who had experienced divine revelation, thus bearing testimony to a perfect divine world. Yet according to most addresses commemorating Abraham Lincoln, he had not been a mere passive witness of the transcendental world but rather an instrument of reform, chosen by God to perform actively in the mundane and imperfect world at a time of crisis, in order to take it one step further toward perfection.[32] Therefore he had been removed from the world when his mission had been accomplished. As a hero, he was above ordinary people, but as a democratic hero, he was also a typical human being. According to most religious preachers Lincoln's life and character refuted the pessimistic assumption of innate human sin, and his assassination transformed his being into pure spirit. It ended the active and somehow tragic life of a visionary reformer in this world and opened before the martyred president the gates of eternal rest in the heavenly world.

But Lincoln's image as a national martyr transcended his personal career. He emerged as a martyr for a certain collective who gave new ideological significance to the whole American experience. He was depicted as one who had sacrificed his life for the cherished American ideal of liberty, for the Union and its republican government, and for the "newborn" American nation. Many spokesmen and writers argued that Lincoln had died not only to keep alive these ideals and institutions, but to improve, reform, rectify, and fortify their existence forever.

The commitment to the inalienable right of liberty constitutes a cornerstone of American democratic ideology. In order to incorporate Lincoln into this ideology many people depicted him as the chief martyr for liberty. His activities in the Civil War, and particularly his Emancipation Proclamation, provided concrete proof for such a view. The struggle for black liberation was thus placed in the general context of the struggle for the victory of freedom. Consequently, Lincoln, the Great Emancipator, was portrayed as the Great Martyr for Freedom.

At the center of the struggle between North and South was the issue of slavery. Lincoln's life and death were clearly related to this problem. Though not a declared abolitionist, Lincoln found himself the leader of the new Republican party, which ideologically opposed the expansion of slavery. Reluctant to abolish the "peculiar institution" at the beginning of the war, Lincoln issued the Emancipation Proclamation in 1863, which freed the slaves beyond the confederacy lines. Thus legally as well as symbolically he attacked the system of bondage by presidential action. Lincoln's assassination was interpreted at the time as a slaveholders' plot in which John Wilkes Booth, the assassin, had been sent to kill their chief enemy. Lincoln, therefore, had the potential for becoming a martyr for black emancipation.

Most contemporary addresses that referred to the role of Lincoln as the emancipator of blacks explained his action in a strictly concrete way: He had freed an enslaved race. A Jewish rabbi compared him to Moses who had redeemed Israel from the bondage in Egypt.[33] Such analogy served to give meaning to the president's premature death and imbued him with the image of a liberator: Moses had been sent by God to free the people of Israel and died on Nebo mountain when he had accomplished his mission, yet without entering the promised land. An enthusiastic reporter for the *New York Evening Post* wrote that, according to Father Chinquy who had come to Washington to warn the president against possible assassination, Lincoln himself had referred to the example of Moses. "I have a clear presentiment," Lincoln had noted, "that God will take me away by the hand of an assassin. . . . As Lord had Moses upon the Mount of Pisgah and pointed out to him . . . the holy land, but told him that he would not be allowed to enter, so I have a presentiment that I will not see the fruits of my labor." [34]

Senator Charles Sumner praised Lincoln as one who had fought a good fight for black emancipation. His eulogy, like many others, did not extend beyond the specific humanistic result of Lincoln's emancipation act. [35] "We are all grateful to the good man whom we are burying," wrote the *Harper's Weekly* in May 1865, "but if we had all been Carolina slaves what eternal gratitude would ours be! As time passes by, they will learn that . . . slavery not Lincoln is dead." [36]

The Reverend Richard Edward's address delivered before students at the University of Illinois on April 19, 1865, expressed an unusual version of Lincoln's significance as an emancipator. He could not have been aware that precisely this version would prevail over time and by far eclipse the narrower interpretation, that of Lincoln as liberator of four million blacks in America. "The oppressed millions of every land will catch the glitter of our triumphant bayonets," declared the minister. [37] Indeed, less than a decade after Lincoln's assassination the emancipator of American slaves was transformed into the figure of universal emancipator. As early as 1870 Bayard Taylor wrote a ballad about Abraham Lincoln:

> Wherever men are sore oppressed
> Where hearts in bondage bend
> All mourn for him in East and West
> For they have lost a friend. [38]

Confederate veteran, poet Maurice Thompson in his poem "Lincoln's Grave" (1890) declared that his figure inspired the oppressed all over the world:

> He is not dead. France knows he is not dead
> He stirs strong hearts in Spain and Germany
> In far Siberian mines his words are said
> He tells the English Ireland shall be free
> Aye! calls poor slaves about him in the night. [39]

The tendency to substitute the abstract for the concrete, and the universal for the specific in order to give broad meaning to particular events, is, of course, characteristic of poetry. However, the theme of Lincoln as a universal emancipator of the oppressed people of the world became prominent in prose tributes as well.[40] Senator Cullom, for example, in a eulogy before the U.S. Congress in 1888, declared, "Wherever men were struggling to be free, wherever the rights of men have been invaded, wherever the iron hand of despotism fell with violence upon the oppressed, there would the heart throb to the memory of Lincoln."[41]

Both during and immediately after the Civil War, good Northern liberals praised emancipation and saw it as a valuable action. It soothed the consciences of many American patriots by eliminating the contradiction between democratic ideology and a social system based on bondage. Slavery was conceived of as a sin, and as such it had created a grave sense of guilt for many white Americans.[42] Lincoln abolished slavery, thus relieving the consciences of many liberal Northerners from that burden of guilt. "Our country stood redeemed and bright with not a slave on all her soil," wrote the *Chicago Tribune* in April 1865.[43]

When the act was done, it declined in value. To the generations who never knew slavery, the Emancipation Proclamation provided no inspiration for the future but was regarded simply as a rectification of past error. To the people who grew up after the Civil War, Lincoln belonged to the past and it was hard to use him as a model for emulation. But if Lincoln's act became a model for the potential emancipation of all oppressed people, he might transcend his concrete historical significance and enter the sphere of perpetual inspiration. Thus, his martyrdom would remain meaningful to later generations, as long as oppressed nations, classes, or other groups existed all over the world.

White Americans in the North had also changed their attitudes toward blacks as a result of Reconstruction. Jim Crow regulations and antiblack terror in the South, as well as blatant racism throughout country, eroded the value and significance of the Emancipation Proclamation. Liberation of the black race ceased to be an outstanding virtue in a society that believed in the innate inferiority of blacks. Thus, writers and speakers preferred to use more general rhetoric and less defined goals in order to portray Lincoln as a martyr for all oppressed peoples rather than specifically for blacks in America.

The universalization of the Emancipation Proclamation went hand in hand with the change in America's self-image that occurred around the turn of the century. Until the Civil War, American culture had been in general an escapist culture: the flight from the sinful Old World to a new and pure existence in the uncivilized new continent. In the last decade of the nineteenth century, the American government abandoned this tradition in its conduct of foreign policy and turned toward a policy of intervention, which culminated in its military activities in Europe in World War I. American politicians, businessmen, and missionaries developed a belief in the superiority of their system over the Europeans'. This new stage of American foreign policy was justified and strengthened by the new ideology of democratic imperialism—the belief that the United States was the avant-garde for the liberation of the world. In this ideology Lincoln became the leader of the liberation movement, and his martyrdom acquired universal significance.[44] The Emancipation Proclamation became significant only as a preamble to the liberation of all oppressed people in the world, according to the American model.[45]

Clearly, the image of Lincoln, the martyr for the oppressed, needed to be fused into the general American belief in liberty to make it meaningful beyond its specific historical circumstances. But the idea of liberty is a more diverse and complex component of American political culture than the emancipation of slaves. Liberty is a vital element of the ideological rationale for the existence of America as a nation apart from Europe. In time, it provided the main explanation for the American Revolution. Not surprisingly then, the most common interpretation of Lincoln's death derived from his relation to the state of liberty. "The blood of the martyrs of liberty, like that of the martyrs of the gospel, has ever strengthened the cause for which it was shed," declared the Reverend Samuel J. Niccolls in a memorial sermon to Lincoln in St. Louis.[46] "As he died to make man holy, let us die to make man free," wrote Julia Ward Howe in "The Battle Hymn of the Republic." Lincoln's death could be interpreted as an outstanding example of a national leader who literally followed this moral call.

Philosophically, there is at best a nonlogical relationship between the classic liberal concept of freedom and the figures of martyrs. Freedom as a theoretical concept stems from John Locke's theory of the social contract. As perceived by Locke and his followers in Europe and America, freedom is a negative concept—freedom from intervention in the individual's life.[47] Every human being was free from the intervention of the other according to natural law. Politically, this meant that all individuals should be free and immune from any tyrannical and arbitrary intervention. Hence, every historical struggle in the name of liberty is a struggle to preserve the natural law against arbitrary power, and not a struggle to pursue a future-oriented teleological purpose. Martyrs, on the other hand, had a revolutionary potential. They were extraordinary people who gave their lives in order to change, reform, and improve their society and to elevate their people to a higher mode of existence. They were seen as an avant-garde of the coming new stage and not as guardians of the existing status quo. They were the heralds of a new utopia, not the representatives of the existing natural order.

In the historical context of the Jews' Second Temple, liberty had been a revolutionary and teleological goal. Thus, the Maccabees promoted through their sacrifice this new state of national freedom. Early Christianity was a revolutionary stage in pagan society, thus Christ and his imitators used the device of martyrdom to promote a new stage of liberty that would free the world from superstitious worship. In the European context of the Old Regime, freedom was the desirable ideal of the coming future for many nations, classes, and other social groups. Thus, Europe produced martyrs like Joan of Arc, William the Silent, Protestant clergymen, French Revolutionary leaders, Socialists and Anarchists. But in a country that accepted an ideology of a priori free-born citizens, how could someone promote a new stage of freedom by his sacrifice? Lincoln may be viewed as a martyr for freedom in the strict context of the black population of the South, but for the rest of the American people he simply fought a war designed to restore the status quo that the South had violated by secession.

Perhaps this was the reason for the abstract and vague way in which the term *martyr for liberty* was used, despite its frequent recurrence in many addresses. Some writers labeled Lincoln as "champion of liberty," "sacrifice upon the altar of freedom," "martyr to the cause of human liberty," and so on, but most of the time they did not elaborate on these designations.[48] Others described Lincoln as a martyr to the cause of liberty and justice, liberty and truth, liberty and peace, using the term *liberty* as a general cliché to express desirable ideals.[49]

Some of the addresses on Lincoln that mentioned the relationship between Lincoln's death and the cause of liberty used the term *liberty* not in its meaning of "freedom from intervention" but rather as an everlasting and infinite goal. They defined liberty as God's gift to the people, thus arguing that Lincoln's death had furnished a great service to the world by revealing that divine justice was connected to human liberty.[50] Such an interpretation mingled Locke's individual liberalism with Calvin's religious pietism, substituting the freedom of Emerson for the freedom of Locke. In these addresses, which were mostly made at the funeral ceremonies, liberty was viewed as a final stage of human history.[51] The speakers followed the romantic rather than the Enlightenment version of the term and located the state of liberty at the end of a universal development of human history, rather than at the starting point of a free-born nation. It was therefore seen as a teleological ideal subjected to further amelioration throughout the course of history, rather than as an inalienable right that Americans had already achieved by their Constitution. In this teleological interpretation, Lincoln's martyrdom became a necessary stage for the inevitable promotion of universal liberty, and the Emancipation Proclamation became only the first example of further reform activities that would expand and increase the existence of liberty all over the universe.[52] "By the same act he freed my race," said Booker T. Washington in an oration at Lincoln's centennial ceremonies in New York. "He said to the civilized and uncivilized world that men everywhere must be free, and that men everywhere must be enlightened, and the Lincoln spirit of freedom will never cease to spread and grow in power till throughout the world all men shall know the truth, and the truth shall make them free."[53]

While liberty is a fundamental ideal in American democracy, a republican form of government is that democracy's main institution. President Lincoln embodied the institution of a republican government by being elected to the presidency both through popular will and according to lawful procedure. He also embodied another more specific institution of the American republic —the federal union. When Southern secession violated both the integrity of the Union and the legitimacy of republican government, Lincoln defended and restored the Union and its government. When an assassin's hand put an end to Lincoln's life, his martyrdom strengthened the Union and reinforced republican government. His death at the end of the struggle could be interpreted as the price he had paid for the concrete purpose of keeping the Republic together.

The reunification of the Republic resolved the sectional conflict, and contemporaries argued that Lincoln's death forever sealed the new political structure of one inseparable union.[54] "From Maine to the Southwest boundary on the Pacific it [Lincoln's assassination] makes us one," declared the historian George Bancroft. "He was happy in his life for he was the restorer of the republic; he was happy in his death for his martyrdom will plead forever for the Union of the States and the Freedom of Man."[55] Such an interpretation presented Lincoln's assassination as an advantage to the Republic and to the federal union. His martyrdom not only demonstrated the victory of the Republic and the Union, but also provided them with a sanctification they had previously lacked.

But the assassination per se seriously challenged the American republic's political institutions because it demonstrated the vulnerability of the head of the Republic to criminal actions. Paradoxically, however, the immediate consequences of the murder proved the basic stability of republican government, thus giving additional legitimation to its existence. The Reverend J. R. W. Sloan of the Third Reform Presbyterian Church in New York used the absence of any serious attempt to seize the reins of power to argue for the superiority of the American republic as a political system.[56] "Such an act would probably overthrow the throne of any European power today. But it will not inaugurate anarchy here," wrote the *New York Times*.[57] On the first celebration of Lincoln's birthday, the chaplain of the House of Representatives thanked God that "such was the enduring strength of our institutions that they received no perceptible shock from the death even of such a man and in such an hour."[58] This theme appeared in many addresses and tributes following the tragedy of April 1865: Lincoln is dead, but the Republic lives.[59]

Thus, Lincoln's martyrdom proved the stability and endurance of republican institutions. The American republic had been transformed from a mere political regime into a system that had undergone a baptism of blood and therefore was confirmed by Providential authority. "President Lincoln is dead," declared A. P. Rogers in a sermon in Brooklyn, "but the republic lives—aye! God lives, and is sovereign on his throne."[60] Contemporaries emphasized that the aftermath of Lincoln's death not only demonstrated the stability of the republic and the integrity of the Union, but also showed that no violent revolution or criminal action could overthrow a legitimate, divinely ordained, political system. Yet such an idea offered no inspiration to later generations who considered the integrity of the Union and the legitimacy of a republican form of government as a self-evident phenomenon. When no serious event undermined the federal union and the lawfulness of the government, Americans ceased to portray Lincoln as a defender of republican government.

If there was a challenge to republican institutions around the turn of the century, it came from the men of power and influence: it derived from the concentration of capital in the hands of the few in the Gilded Age, from the use of the government as an instrument to promote special interests. Thus many speakers and writers used Lincoln's name as an example of one who had never abused his power and remained a real representative of the people. According to various memorial addresses, despite the emergency situation that had given him power to act beyond the popular will, he had been reluctant to do so.[61] "The profound lesson of Lincoln's career is not that he rose from the people," wrote the *Chicago Tribune,* "but that he did not rise away from the people, that his triumph was by them and through them."[62] This emphasis accorded with the ideology of many reform movements at the turn of the century. From a legal defender of the Republic and the Union in time of peril, Lincoln emerged as a real exponent of republican institutions. To contemporaries his death sanctified the Union and the Republic and demonstrated their stability and legitimacy. Later generations simply used Lincoln's image as a normative example of a democratic leader who represents the people rather than the powerful few: "Identified with the humblest of us, transcending the best of us, he led us by the genius of his mind and the warmth of his heart," declared Robert E. Brown in Oakland, California, on February 10, 1927.[63]

In his career as president, Lincoln freed the blacks from slavery, restored the integrity of the Union, and manifested the basic stability of the government. His tragic death consecrated these actions, giving them a universal and eternal meaning. Yet the significance of Lincoln's death reached beyond these concrete activities: it also came to symbolize the sacrifice of the many Union soldiers who had died in the Civil War, thereby bestowing new emotional meaning on American nationality.

Religious leaders, immediately after the assassination, used "the blood of Lincoln" as an essential part of their rhetoric. The Reverend Samuel J. Niccolls of the Second Presbyterian Church of St. Louis asked rhetorically, "Is it not remarkable, and a proof that God has, in a measure, purified us, that he who was called a 'sectional' president, should be carried to his grave, mourned for as a father by the whole land?."[64] Protestant, Catholic, and Jewish leaders invariably referred to "the blood of Lincoln," stressing the fact that his sacrifice would consecrate the Republic and thus would create "a real nationality."[65] They usually extended the significance of the martyr's blood beyond a strict reunification between South and North. Charles Robinson's sermon in Brooklyn exemplified this broader interpretation. After the assassination he noted that "a martyr's blood had sealed the covenant we are making with posterity. . . . The republic is secure. . . . Our cause is eternally secure."[66] Speakers and writers apart from the professional clergy also mentioned in their obituaries the martyr's blood theme.[67] Thus, the historian Frederic De-Peyster Hitchcock, in a memorial address before the American Historical Society, argued that the blood of Lincoln had been given as a sacrifice to the continent. "Before we were bound by the memory of our fathers—now the blood of the martyred president binds us."[68] Yet the South at the time certainly did not share this view.

Nonetheless, except for the defeated South, there is no doubt that the shocking tragedy—which triggered a general outpouring of grief demonstrated by the various rites around Lincoln's coffin—created a new sense of solidarity among the mourners. The funeral train of eight black coaches passed from Washington, D.C., to Philadelphia through many little towns and was visible to thousands of people. Huge crowds participated in the ceremony in New York City. An estimated 150,000 people viewed Lincoln's body in the city hall. Along the Hudson River crowds of country people lined the tracks with lanterns and torches. From Albany westward, arches and tableaux were erected on hills. Cleveland and Columbus offered Chinese pagodas to house the casket as it lay in state. Indianapolis built a catafalque of black velvet and gold stars in the state house. In Chicago 125,000 people viewed the body within twenty-four hours. In Springfield, after the funeral, the red, white, and blue blanket on "Old Bob," Lincoln's horse, was torn to pieces by relic seekers.

In all, an estimated seven million people saw the coffin on the funeral train, and one and a half million viewed the corpse. Ninety funeral marches were composed and played, and more than four hundred sermons were delivered during the funeral week.[69] The tragedy became an act that consecrated the Republic and cemented the nation. Such an attitude preserved the name of the national hero beyond the concrete action of restoring the integrity of the Union or liberating the blacks.

Yet the various addresses that used "the blood of the president" in their rhetoric, as well as the rituals around the president's casket, were designed not only to commemorate and preserve Lincoln's name; they also invested new meaning in the American nationality as a whole. Lecturing on the death of Abraham Lincoln, Walt Whitman noted that battles, martyrs, agonies, blood, and even assassination were the elements that should lastingly condense a real nationality: "I repeat it—the grand deaths of the race—the dramatic deaths of every nationality—are its most important inheritance—value—in some respect beyond its literature and art."[70] Whitman was here touching upon the complicated question of defining nationality. Common territory, a unique history, particular religion, one language, a specific legal system, and a distinctive ethnic origin cannot provide a complete answer to this problem. Some nations have a defined territory, others do not. Some nations have a unique religion, others have various congregations. For a more conclusive understanding of the national phenomenon we must examine these various factors at the level of human mentality: Nationality is part of group awareness, not a neutral fact in empirical data. Thus, a group of people who consider part of the above ethnographic data as a common and identifiable value can be viewed as a national entity.

The United States in the midnineteenth century was a relatively new country with a short national history. The country underwent constant geographical changes through expansion and experienced enormous demographic transformations through immigration. Although predominantly Protestant and Anglo-Saxon, American people were without a religious or an ethnic center and had their cultural roots all over the world. The earliest common denominator that contributed to the building of the American nationality was not ethnographic, but connected to a common ideology: Americans perceived themselves as a unique people who experienced freedom in the only free and democratic country in the world. Although the United States was not a completely representative republic, the republican political system constituted a normative value for most Americans.

That ideology, which viewed citizenship as the main characteristic of American nationality, lacked an emotional dimension. A nation is more than a group of people who rationally express their consent to participate in a republican political system. Nationality has some additional, irrational dimension, which Walt Whitman specified in his address. In that sense traumatic events shared by a large group of people, such as wars, battles, the assassination of a leader, and so on become important raw materials in the everlasting process of nation building. Some political figures who can be convincingly shown to have suffered for other members of the community become national martyrs. Thus, many individuals develop a sense of brotherhood and fellowship with other individuals who share the agony of the dead or suffering leader. Rev. Edwin A. Bulkley expressed this feeling in his sermon at the First Presbyterian Church of Plattsburgh, New York:

> When I saw the universal bereavement of friends and foes I was strengthened. And when there followed from the public press of every variety of conflicting opinion, so unanimous an outburst of lamentation and appeal for consolidated and preserving support of the government, my faith in my mind, my faith in the republic was greatly renewed.[71]

Many people mourned Lincoln; his death as a common tragedy aroused the sense of a common destiny. If in his life Lincoln represented specific segments of American society (Northerners, blacks, Unionists, Republicans), after his assassination he began to embody the nation as a whole. Unlike John Brown, who remained a sectional martyr, most spokesmen portrayed Lincoln as one of the main figures who had built the nation, as well as one who had exemplified Americans' common ideals and shared heritage.

One way to portray Lincoln as a national hero was to view him as a leader of fallen soldiers. Indeed, immediately after the Civil War many addresses portrayed the president as a war hero who had fallen in battle. In these discourses, however, the term *martyr* was mostly used in the sense of *hero* rather than *witness* or *redeemer*. This definition suited the context of the terrible war that had cost more than 600,000 lives. Lincoln as the head of the army was thus perceived as the last warrior to sacrifice his life in this bloody war. In the summer of 1865 the *Atlantic Monthly* published a long poem written by H. H. Brownell that portrayed Lincoln as the leading martyr of the army of martyred soldiers. Imagining the host of fallen warriors, the poet wrote,

> The bee hums in the clover
> As the pleasant June comes on
> Aye, the wars are all over
> But the good father is gone
> There they all in his side
> The noble hearts and true
> Winthrop and Ellsworth and

Baker . . . and Douglas . . .
All such and many another
(Ah! list now long to name!)
That stood like brother to brother
And died on the field of fame . . .
Close round him hearts and pride
Press near him side by side
Our father is not alone!
For the Holy Right ye died.[72]

Lincoln's death at the end of the most traumatic war in the nation's history embodied the tragedy of the war in its clearest form. Many families had lost fathers and many mothers mourned their sons. Herman Melville who invoked sacrifice and stressed martyrdom in many of his works, expressed this theme clearly in the poem "The Martyr" which he wrote to commemorate the president: Lincoln became both the lost father and the fallen brother and son of the nation as a whole.[73]

Abraham Lincoln himself was the first president to have glorified fallen soldiers explicitly as martyrs for their country, in his famous Gettysburg Address. He viewed self-sacrifice in war as the ultimate virtue. It seemed only natural that after his tragic death, contemporaries would add his name to the list of martyrs he himself had acclaimed.[74] The historian George Bancroft made this link between Lincoln's death and the dead soldiers at Gettysburg in his congressional address: "The heroes who led our army . . . and fell in service did not die in vain," argued the historian. "They, and he —the chief martyr—gave up their lives willingly, that government of the people by the people and for the people shall not perish from the earth."[75]

While contemporaries emphasized Lincoln's sacrifice as a fallen soldier who had sealed with his blood the American nation, later generations tended to underestimate this theme. People mourned for "a man who believed in his brother-man; they longingly gaze not upon a warrior, though it was in war, but upon the face of a giver of peace," wrote Frank W. Z. Barrett in a memorial book that appeared on the centennial of Lincoln's birth.[76] The figure of Lincoln the warrior martyr faded over time, since Americans did not consider war per se as a state of glory and honor. The fascination with battles, blood, and violent struggle and consequently the glorification of death on the battlefield constituted an essential ideological ingredient of extreme national movements in twentieth-century Europe. Americans, however, were still reluctant to endorse an ideology that valued death more than life and venerated a sacrificial act more than the pursuit of happiness. Therefore, Lincoln's image as a fallen soldier, so meaningful to his contemporaries, did not persist over time.

Other images of Lincoln as the American national martyr did prevail. Many addresses described Lincoln only in terms of an American ideal type. George Bancroft, for example, described the president as "a man born west of the Alleghenies, in the cabin of poor people of Hardin County, Kentucky. . . . His education was altogether American. . . . He lived the life of American people, walked in its light, reasoned with its reason . . . and so was in every way a child of nature, a child of the West, a child of America."[77] Although such portrayals hardly contributed to a better understanding of Lincoln the individual, they do give us an insight into the collective images that make up the American political culture. The ingredients of Lincoln's life were distorted in order to construct an inspirational ideal identified with the society he represented. Since he had significance only as a normative example, he had to be portrayed according to the normative values of the national American ideology. The addresses that depicted him as "the American" reflected these normative values of American culture. He thus became the very incarnation of all that was just and valuable in the American experience.

The first characteristic that Lincoln exemplified derived from the uncultivated natural Western frontier, which was viewed as the basis for an authentic American culture. This culture preferred the West to the East, the rural environment to the urban setting, the hard and simple life to the refined and sophisticated. Many Americans shared the belief that uncultivated Western citizens were the fittest for pure democracy. They had a better ability to identify corruption and they were more sensitive to injustice than the people from the urban East. "A voice from the savage wilderness, now fertile in men, was inspired to uphold the pledges and promises of the declaration," said Charles Sumner in an address delivered in the least "Western" of all American cities—Boston.[78] Ralph Waldo Emerson specified this Western and authentic American characteristic of the slain president in his funeral oration at Concord. "He was thoroughly American, never crossed the sea, had never been spoiled by English insularity or French dissipation."[79] In many addresses at the time of Lincoln's assassination, Kentucky, Indiana, or Illinois, symbolized the young, semicultured and entirely pure environment. Here was the new soil that produced the typical nature of Lincoln.[80]

This image of Lincoln endured. The ideal of Western simplicity survived even when the society experienced a rapid process of industrialization and urbanization. The centennial celebration indicated that the frontier that had perhaps disappeared as a geographical reality, remained an essential ideological element in the American national culture. Economic and demographic changes did not automatically produce a cultural change at the beginning of the twentieth century, and the rural environment of the "unexhausted West" was still viewed as superior to the new urban setting.[81] The *Chicago Tribune* devoted a substantial part of its centennial edition to the subject of "Lincoln the Railsplitter and Boatman."[82] A memorial poem written by Edwin Markham stressed the fact that "the great West nursed him on her knees."[83] Even an advertisement that urged people to buy land in Florida used the Lincoln centennial to announce that "Lincoln was a farmer . . . a pioneer who blazed the trail that the civilization which came after him might flourish."[84] This image continued to be relevant to later generations and even became more attractive to Americans who experienced the processes of industrialization and urbanization around the turn of the century.

Another element that made Lincoln so American was his individual history. His contemporaries noted that he was a typical American because he had been born in poverty and had succeeded through his own efforts until he had become the president of the United States. His career exemplified the American dream of success. Some addresses mentioned that the assassinated president had started his career as a rail-splitter, a typical American with no fortune and no advantages of fame or dignity.[85] Thus, Lincoln's birthplace and the belief in his rise from lowly status identified him with the uniqueness and vitality of America.

These themes, however, were not fully elaborated until later in the twentieth century when the "rags to riches" career of the martyred president became part of the national ideology. "He was an impossibility in any other country," declared Edward Pierpont, a wealthy businessman. "If Lincoln had been born to a million he should never have been the man he was. A good governor of other men must have known something of the sorrows and trials of this life."[86] Lincoln's great school was his poverty and the difficulties to which it had accustomed him. This training, many addresses stressed, had provided him with the necessary strength to overcome obstacles and consequently with the love and support of the people.[87]

Yet Lincoln's career exemplified more than a personal success story. It reflected American uniqueness and proved the superiority of the New World over the Old. "The heroes of the old world are linked together in one vast dynasty of greatness. . . . But Columbia begins a new order," argued William G. Frost Oberline in an address in Ohio in 1891. "The shadow of the pyramids falls upon every European but it does not cross the sea."[88] When Walt Whitman wrote that kings and queens had sent their condolences and sorrow in memory of one who had risen from the most common and average life, he implied that Lincoln's death proved to the world the uniqueness of American institutions.[89] "He belongs to the aristocracy of America," said the Reverend D. Hattsock on February 12, 1911, "whose inquiry was not 'how much are you worth' or 'who was your grandmother' but 'who are you and what can you do!' "[90] Lincoln's personal career, then, as president of a new democratic nation revealed the differences between the Old and the New World. Most addresses that stressed this theme were written in the beginning of the twentieth century at a time when the actual differences between the Old and New Worlds were beginning to narrow significantly.

Prominent speakers who represented the elite of the new industrial society used Lincoln's supposed rags-to-riches career as an ideological weapon against popular criticism. They argued that Lincoln's life proved that America was the land of open opportunities. William McKinley declared after his 1896 victory in the Vermont primaries that

his life and career put to shame the false doctrine that there are class divisions in America. Humble to birth, surrounded by poverty, forced by circumstances to acquire unaided whatever education he had, he forged the way to the front reaching the highest place in the gift of free people and the greatest place in the world.[91]

Journalists, religious leaders, and many politicians echoed this argument, particularly during the centennial celebrations.[92]

In an era when American politics were becoming increasingly bureaucratized, the quest for a personal and direct relationship between the leaders and the people created a nostalgic myth. Lincoln's memorial addresses provided speakers with the opportunity to convey that nostalgic message to their audience. They depicted Lincoln as head of a coherent and organic community, able to communicate in a human and unalienated way with the people. "In talking with him you were listening to your neighbor whom you loved to hear in business associations, or the village store, or the farmers gathering when you were at home," said Senator Chauncey M. Depew in his centennial address.[93]

Thus Lincoln came to symbolize the ideal America. To stress this notion, later obituaries selected relevant data from Lincoln's life, such as his Western-frontier birthplace, his humble beginning and his lack of formal education, his personal career, and his simple conduct and style. They tended to ignore other features of his life such as the period when he worked as a lawyer, how he became wealthy, his political affiliation with the Whigs, his moderate reputation as a politician, and so on. "It makes little difference whether our estimate of him is historically accurate," explained the *World of Today* in its centennial edition:

Whether idealized or not, the real Lincoln is now this portrait. For in him the American people find the personification of democracy. . . . Unsentimental loyalty to ideals, unpretentious sacrifice in the interest of the community, simple and unquestioning devotion to those forces which from the chaos of today we feel, are to make the better world of tomorrow—all these ideals which after all constitute the real America are found in him.[94]

Lincoln's assassination supplied the American nationality with the emotional dimension it had lacked from the beginning. He was the first president who "sealed the covenant with his blood" and became after his death an important component in the process of forging a national identity. In April 1865, immediately after the assassination, the *New York Times* wrote that "it may be that one purpose of that strange manner of summoning him to the skies, was to signalize his character all the more, and to engrave his traits all the deeper into the memories of the coming generations."[95] Indeed, future generations ceased to emphasize the tragic death of the president as a meaningful event that might strengthen the unique spirit of the nation. They rather regarded his assassination as serving primarily to commemorate and perpetuate his life, character, and career. Here, in the life story of their national martyr, Americans were able to demonstrate, inspire, and justify their democratic creed. The *World of Today* clearly stressed this notion: "Slavery would have perished, the Union have grown united without him, but our national life would have been poorer."[96]

The martyr is essentially part of a religious symbolic system. Despite certain relations to the ideal of sacrifice in pagan and archaic religions, the martyr became a fundamental figure primarily in monotheistic theology. In Christianity the martyr is not only a unique individual or a savior of his community, but also has cosmic significance. He atones through his suffering and death for the sins of all other members of his society, he appears as a redeemer of mankind, and his sacrifice is an inherent part of the cosmic order.

Although Americans had officially separated church from state, they never abandoned the monotheistic worldview, and especially in the nineteenth century used biblical symbols, images and archetypes to explain, justify, and invest meaning in their historical experience. Thus American political culture was saturated with religious terminology. Lincoln himself used religious concepts and symbols in his main speeches throughout his political career. He viewed the Civil War as a redemptive event designed by God both as punishment and atonement for the sin of slavery, as well as a necessary step toward national salvation. In his Lyceum Address, the debates with Douglas, First and Second Inaugural Speeches, and Gettysburg Address, Lincoln enriched this religious dimension of American political culture, providing it with a "theology" of sin, suffering, sacrifice, atonement, and redemption.[97] Following his assassination Lincoln personified all these sacred concepts of the American political culture through his martyr image. Indeed, in their various eulogies, his contemporaries interpreted Lincoln's entire life and death in religious and cosmic terms, using such concepts as sin and millennium, and making analogies with biblical redeemers such as Christ and his followers.

Human sin and atonement are part of a cosmological order, according to the biblical religions. Sin was the first event in the historical stage of the world, an event that caused the separation of the mundane from the celestial sphere. Total atonement and expiation will lead to the end of historical time and to a reintegration of the divine and earthly worlds into the eternal cosmos. The martyr's death and suffering, like Christ's crucifixion, further this process of redemption, since through his sacrifice he atones for his community, expiates the people's sins, and propitiates God's wrath.[98]

Indeed, some preachers described the existence of sin as an inseparable part of the human condition that required expiation through a mighty sacrifice. Thus they explained Lincoln's death as part of a divine program and urged the members of their congregation to share symbolically the president's baptism of blood through extensive prayers and personal confession of repentance.[99] Other sermons incorporated the religious concept of sin into the more concrete context of a redeemer nation. They asserted that like the biblical Chosen People, the American people had deviated from its mission and committed such sins as indulgence in pleasure and entertainment, national pride and folly, atrocities against the native tribes of the land, and so on. Hence, Lincoln's fate was perceived as a punishment of the American people.[100] "We have been a sinful and proud people and the black catalogue of our crimes can scarcely find anything darker than itself," said the pastor of the First Presbyterian Church of Fort Wayne, Indiana, on April 16, 1865.[101] Though predominant in religious sermons, this idea appeared in some nonreligious addresses as well.

At the time of the assassination, however, many obituaries related the tragedy to the sin of slavery.[102] "The savior of the world died for the sins of man, while the savior of the nation died for the sins of the South," declared the Reverend Charles Cook in Smyrna, Delaware.[103] In a discourse delivered on April 23, 1865, the Reverend Henry Ward Beecher discussed the themes of sin and atonement in their broadest universal sense. For him, Lincoln's death had a cosmic significance as "the most acceptable sacrifice offered by the nineteenth century in expiation of the great crime of the seventeenth. . . . Above all the anguish and tears, will appear the shade of Lincoln as a symbol of hope and pardon."[104] Looking for the significance of Lincoln's martyrdom Robert H. Mewell wrote that it vindicated the sovereignty of God, humbled the arrogance of man, released the guilt of slavery and atoned the people's sin, since "the pardon of sin is with suffering brought."[105] Two years later in October 1867, the poet Edward Grenier wrote in the *Harper's Weekly*: "A nation's crime to expiate thy life the great soul offered as a sacrifice."[106] He depicted Lincoln as a sacrifice for the national, not sectional, sin of slavery, echoing Lincoln's second inaugural address, which had described slavery as a sin of both North and South.

Over time, the concept of sin virtually disappeared and even came under attack. In the book review section of the *Atlantic Monthly*, Herndon and Weik's *History and Personal Reflection of Abraham Lincoln* was criticized as being based on folklore rather than on historical records. Therefore, according to the magazine, it portrayed a false picture of Lincoln's fate as a sacrifice for national sin.[107] We have already seen that many obituaries and addresses constructed an image of Lincoln more out of tradition than historical fact, some even arguing that the idealistic traditional figure was more important and "correct" for the American national ideology. Hence, the image of Lincoln as a martyr who had atoned for the people's sins through his sacrifice did not decline because of its fictitious nature, but because, for various reasons, sin simply ceased to be a meaningful concept to later generations.

First, the image of the sinful South became irrelevant to the American national tradition. After the failure of Radical Reconstruction, the tendency was to forget the sectional conflict and, in particular, the problem of black discrimination. Lincoln became a national figure and ceased to be associated with the sin of slavery or rebellion. Second, something in the culture of the late nineteenth century had changed. The culture of the Gilded Age stressed the human potential for wordly success, thus undermining the previous Christian ideology of the limits imposed by man's innate sin. The rigid and pessimistic Calvinistic worldview of a sinful people had lost its relevance even before the Civil War. But with the tragedy of war and the shock of assassination, the theme of a sinful people regained its meaning, especially in the pulpits of the North and among abolitionists. Later, under more peaceful conditions and within the new cultural atmosphere of a more optimistic belief in human capabilities, the Christian notion of original sin lost its significance. Consequently, the previously very popular concept of the Christian martyr, who atoned for the sins of his people through sacrifice, became less relevant to the American experience in the Gilded Age.

Lincoln emerged, nevertheless, as a martyr redeemer, even though not as a redeemer of a sinful people. Contemporaries incorporated his image into a cosmic order and even compared him to biblical redeemers from the Old and New Testaments. According to biblical belief the world's redemption is the ultimate divine purpose. At the "end of time," God would redeem mankind and the kingdom of Heaven would reign upon Earth. The unified and eternal mode of existence would then replace the dualistic and temporal present world. Despite the diverse millennial visions of the monotheistic religions, the structure of the future-oriented cosmology (named eschatology) remained similar. The mechanism of salvation has a very precise form in Judeo-Christian tradition: God would reveal Himself to certain individuals during the historical period, finally transmitting the gospel of world salvation through His selected individual—the Messiah. Salvation through messianic martyrdom constitutes part of the biblical eschatology, a necessary step toward the millenium. According to the Jewish tradition the Messiah has yet to appear. In Christianity, Jesus was the Messiah, but he was killed by a sinful and undeserving mankind. As the embodiment of messianic sacrifice, Christ symbolizes redemptive martyrdom in Western religion more than any other biblical figure.

Indeed, numerous analogies with Christ served to tie Lincoln's martyr-dom to the cosmic process of redemption.[108] It was not only by giving his life that Lincoln seemed like Jesus; the very date of his death touched upon beliefs and superstitions of a great army of pastors as well as lay people. "Oh friend," preached the Reverend C. B. Crane of the South Baptist Church of Hartford, Connecticut,

on the evening of Good Friday, the memorial day of the crucifixion of our Lord, our . . . good president was smitten down by the hand of an assassin. . . . It is the after type of the tragedy which was accomplished on the first Good Friday more than eighteen centuries ago. . . . Yes, it was meant that the martyrdom should occur on Good Friday. It is no blasphemy against the Son of God and the Savior of Men that we declared the fitness of the slaying of the second father of our Republic on the anniversary of the day on which He was slain.[109]

The tributes that stressed this point seldom, however, mentioned the fact that Lincoln himself had chosen not to pray but to attend the theater on that holy day.[110]

Some eulogies used the phrase "Father forgive them they know not what they do" or the term *savior* in order to deepen the analogy between Lincoln and Christ.[111] Other tributes painted a vision of how Christ had accepted Lincoln and assigned him a role in the Second Coming.[112] H. H. Brownell ended his poem "Dirge" in the *Atlantic Monthly* with such a picture of providential fraternity:

Close round him hearts of pride!
Press near him side by side—
Our father is not alone!
For the Holy Right ye died
And Christ the crucified
Waits to welcome his own.[113]

The image of Lincoln as Christ's close disciple resembled that of the Christian martyrs who followed Christ's path. According to the New Testament, God chose the Messiah, Jesus, whose crucifixion was a divine way of carrying out the world's salvation.[114] His close followers gave their lives and died to proclaim the eternal truth of his message. Through their sacrifice and martyrdom, they conveyed to the sinners the true message of Christ.[115] For these followers, *Imitatio Christi* meant real death and the perpetuation of His ideas by their martyrdom.[116] Indeed all Christians were obliged to work out the meaning of dying with Christ by sharing His suffering through liturgical acts such as baptism and the Last Supper.[117]

The fact that Lincoln died on Good Friday inspired contemporaries to elevate his image to the level of Christ's follower-disciple. He was portrayed as a mediator between the Messiah and the people, as a human being who had literally imitated Jesus and had thus risen above the rest of the community, to become a "soldier of his captain Christ."[118] But he was transformed into neither a dying God nor a new Son of God. The various addresses never endowed Lincoln with a new divine status like many heroes in archaic or pagan cultures. He had risen only to the level of Christ's messenger and follower and thus fulfilled on important function within the monotheistic eschatology. Such a figure accorded with the American political culture, which never turned its tragic heroes into dying gods.

The analogy between Lincoln and Christ did remain meaningful well into the twentieth century. Speakers continued to emphasize the fact that on this tragic day the president had followed the man of Galilee.[119] The humble background of both figures and their roles as saviors contributed additional validity to the analogy.[120] Thus, John Wesley Hill wrote in his book *Lincoln—Man of God* that the president in his last hour on earth had been eager to follow in Christ's way.

A yearning had come over him to tread those holy fields over whose acres walked those blessed feet . . . nailed for our advantage on the bitter cross . . . there was no place he wished so much to see as Jerusalem. . . . Mary [his wife] heard him whisper Jeru. . . . The man of God started for Jerusalem but it was Jerusalem the golden, the home of God's elect.[121]

Yet, paradoxically, Lincoln did not belong to any particular church during his life. If this fact meant that he was a deist or freethinker, how could he be portrayed as Christ's follower? Indeed, shortly after his death Lincoln's religion came to be at the center of a popular as well as scholarly debate. In a famous lecture delivered in Springfield in 1873, William H. Herndon, Lincoln's law partner, discussed this subject. First, he attacked all those clergymen who described Lincoln as a Christian and as a defender of the faith. Then he distinguished between religion as a form of belief, and Christianity as a particular set of doctrines.

I have said that Mr. Lincoln was . . . a deeply religious man, and now I repeat it. . . . He was not an unbeliever in religion, but was as to Christianity. Mr. Lincoln was a Theist. A Theist does not necessarily deny revelation. . . . Mr. Lincoln never joined any church. He was a religious man always as I think . . . [but] Mr. Lincoln was not a technical Christian.[122]

Herndon's version of Lincoln's religion was far from being the last word on this subject. Henry Whitney, Lincoln's riding friend, wrote: "The conclusion is inevitable, that Mr. Lincoln was practically and essentially, though not ritualistically a Christian"[123] Isaac Arnold, a congressman from Illinois and a close friend of the president, shared this view: "For creeds and dogmas he cared little. But in the great fundamental principles of religion, of the Christian religion, he was a firm believer."[124] Noah Brooks, Lincoln's personal secretary, asserted that the martyred president was at his heart a Christian man, believed in the Savior and even seriously considered the step of becoming a church member.[125] Nonetheless, Lincoln had never affiliated himself with any particular church and was not an orthodox Christian according to the standards of his day.

Later, in the twentieth century, historians and biographers continued the debate. John E. Remsbur in his *Six Heroic Americans* (1906) agreed with Herndon that Lincoln had not been a Christian in the formal sense. Other studies, however, such as Ervin Chapman's *Latest Light on Lincoln* (1917), William Johnson's *Abraham Lincoln: The Christian* (1913), John Wesley Hill's *Abraham Lincoln—Man of God* (1920), and W. Barton's *Soul of Abraham Lincoln,* stressed that Lincoln had accepted the Christian faith. They all underscored the biblically rooted faith of the president and rejected the interpretation of his religion as creedless and free from any doctrine.[126]

While historians tried to substantiate their arguments concerning Lincoln's religion with evidence from Lincoln's life, other commentators simply accepted the belief that the president had been a devout Christian despite the fact that he had not been a church member. "If the platform of Christian religion is not broad enough to furnish standing room for one so pure and lofty as the Great Emancipator then the Christian religion is fatally weak," argued the Reverend Dr. Eaton of New York Presbyterian Church. "They are many who hold that to be a Christian is to follow the example of Christ. . . . Among this class was Abraham Lincoln."[127] Many addresses depicted the martyred president as the most Christian president in American history precisely because he had never been affiliated to any specific church. He had extended the essence of Christianity far beyond a specific doctrine and a particular denomination.[128]

The noninstitutional character of Lincoln's religion had created some problems for certain ministers and preachers of his time. For later generations, however, it was an advantage, not only because the definition of Christianity became more liberal—accepting Christian devotion without specific creed—but also because it accorded with the more general American culture. Like Christ's disciples, who had not belonged to a particular denomination but had been more Christian than the rest of the people, Lincoln did not belong to any particular church but embodied the essence of Christian principles by his total commitment to love, forgiveness, and justice. He had also carried these principles into the realm of politics and imbued the democratic creed of the good society with the religious values of Christianity. Reinhold Niebuhr elaborated upon this notion in *The Irony of American History* by writing that Lincoln's religious insight gave moral significance to the political dilemma of his days.[129] Other generations, in portraying Lincoln as both a democratic and a Christian martyr, immortalized this religious insight and thus continued to give religious meaning to the American political experience.

In biblical millennial tradition, the suffering and martyrdom of the messianic figure was part of the cosmological order. According to the common interpretation of the book of Revelation, the period of an apocalypse—the terrible days of Satanic domination of earth—will clear the way for the final millennium. The death and suffering of the righteous and innocent logically stems from this terrible final stage of history. The martyr is thus the herald of redemption and his death is part of the divine scheme regarding the messianic community. This community had to endure a certain quota of suffering before the purpose of God would be fulfilled. The death of the innocent is part of this quota.[130]

Most Americans as Christian people were familiar to a certain extent with this millennial vision even if they interpreted it in diverse ways. The Civil War and the president's assassination as its climactic aftermath were events that lent themselves to an apocalyptic interpretation. The war—the most tragic and costly war in American history—could be viewed as a holy war between the forces of Good and Evil that would end in the final victory of heavenly forces but at an enormous cost. Abolitionists as we have seen, resorted to such an analogy. Lincoln himself—though reluctant to compare the Civil War to a struggle between Good and Evil—drew upon a Christian interpretation of the war as a conflict that had rescued the nation from a bleak tragedy and given redemptive meaning to its suffering.[131] Indeed, some sermons stressed the analogy to a holy war and depicted Lincoln's death as the costly but necessary sacrifice prior to the coming of the millenium.[132]

Yet, this apocalyptic vision did not last over time. First, a reconciliatory attitude toward the South, which Lincoln himself conveyed in his last speeches, became the dominant Northern attitude after the failure of Radical Reconstruction. Many Americans in the North and the South viewed the war as a tragic conflict between brothers rather than a holy war. Consequently Lincoln's image became more of a national reformer and peacemaker rather than a sectional crusader. Second, the American perception of sacrifice began to change. In order to portray Lincoln's death as martyrdom in the stage of apocalypse, people had to attach importance to the sacrificial gesture. Toward the end of the century, however, less tragic and more positive versions of Christianity were gaining ground, which made the act of self-sacrifice seem less and less acceptable to Americans. The belief in inevitable progress toward a better order on earth, was fortified by new evolutionary dogma, which undermined the belief in a tragic apocalypse at the premillennial stage of history, considering it a myth that contradicted the scientific laws of evolutionary progress. American theologians did not abandon the religious faith in the millennium at the turn of the century, but they no longer emphasized either the virtue of self-sacrifice or the necessity of an apocalypse as part of the cosmic order.

"Self-sacrifice for its own sake is not good," argued the Reverend Josiah Strong, the general secretary of the Evangelical Alliance for the United States and one of its leaders of the Social Gospel movement. "To teach that God required it or is pleased by it is to caricature Him. . . . What is needed today is . . . more costly martyrdom—that of the LIVING sacrifice, the SUSTAINED resolve, the REDEEMED self-giving, the DAILY consecration."[133] Walter Rauschenbusch, the most famous intellectual leader of the Social Gospel movement, wrote in *Christianizing the Social Order* that the scientific evolutionary theory had freed the kingdom of God ideal from the catastrophic setting and its background of demonism, and thus adapted it to the climate of the modern world.[134]

While the necessity of sacrifice as a prerequisite for redemption made sense in the early and gloomy version of Christianity, it lost some of its significance in this more liberal and optimistic version. Nevertheless, Lincoln continued to be interpreted within the context of Christian eschatology as a martyr redeemer who had lived and died in this world in order to promote the stage of redemption. His death remained significant because it perpetuated his actions and character and thus paved the way for a better world in the future, closer to the stage of redemption. In that context American people had a specific role as a republican messianic community, chosen by God to hasten the coming kingdom.[135] This community had deviated from its mission, but Lincoln had reformed it through suffering and martyrdom.

The Civil War ceased to be a holy war, but—as Daniel Aaron concluded in his book *The Unwritten War*—some writers still portrayed it as a religious event leading to national redemption.[136] Both North and South were "right" as well as sincere and neither wholly to blame. The war became an episode in the people's progress toward coalescence, directed by a divine hand as another step toward the millenium. In that context, Lincoln's martyrdom remained an essential component of the American eschatology and a crucial part of the mythical-religious explanation of the American experience.

Lincoln's image as a national martyr reflected the need to interpret a political assassination in religious terms and demonstrated the degree to which American political culture in the midnineteenth century drew upon religious—mainly Christian—symbols, images, and concepts, as ideological components. These symbols invested sacred meaning to Lincoln's tragedy and anchored it in the whole heroic context of the Civil War. Walt Whitman predicted that Lincoln's image as a martyr would endure for the future as a significant element in the historical consciousness of the American nation.

When centuries hence . . . the leading historians and dramatists seek for some personage, some special event, incisive enough to mark . . . this turbulent nineteenth century of ours . . .—something to identify with terrible identification, by far the greatest revolutionary step in the history of the United States . . .—the absolute extirpation . . . of slavery from the States—those historians will seek in vain for any point to serve more thoroughly their purpose than Abraham Lincoln's death.[137]

Over time, many elements of Lincoln's martyrdom changed but did not disappear. The various memorial addresses showed that even those generations that had not experienced the Civil War and the assassination viewed Lincoln as a national martyr. His image as an individual witness of a divine sphere, as well as a national hero and a religious redeemer, persisted over time, while his martyrdom was interpreted as a crucial stage toward the democratic salvation of the country.

Certain circumstances enabled Lincoln to become an enduring martyr of American society. First, he had been a national figure, the president of the United States, and not a marginal minister, like Elijah Lovejoy, or a rebel, like John Brown. Second, it was easy to demonstrate that during his life Lincoln had resorted to sacred rhetoric and stressed concepts such as sacrifice, suffering, and redemption, and even envisioned himself as a potential martyr.[138] Third, a concrete historical event combined the personal tragedy with a collective trauma as well as a collective triumph. The Civil War provided an outstanding context for turning Lincoln into a martyr for the cause—the chief magistrate who sacrificed his life together with more than half a million innocent souls to redeem the whole country from a terrible sin, thereby reforming the whole nation through a baptism of blood. "Without the shedding of blood there is no remission of sin, and the blood shed for such a purpose is always that of the innocent," wrote Frank W. Z. Barrett in 1909. "And the moving lights and shadows and growing gloom of the mourning days of 1865 were the somber settings behind which God the Artist was to paint, with one last illumination stroke—a struggling soul in triumph."[139]

Lincoln's emphasis upon forgiveness and reconciliation with the South permitted later generations to portray him as a national figure. At the time of the assassination the majority of the South had remained calm. Only some of its leaders had condemned the murder and called against blaming the South for such a crime.[140] Later generations, however, emphasized this Southern reaction.[141] Frank W. Z. Barrett described, for example, how General Johnson of the defeated Confederacy had told General Sherman that Lincoln's assassination had been the greatest calamity that had happened to the South. "They began to understand that he [Lincoln] was their earnest friend. . . . So the South, as well as the North, mourned at the death of their truest friend."[142] An emphasis on Lincoln's racist rhetoric enabled many Northern conservatives and even Southerners to accept his heroic image. On the other hand, liberal whites and certainly blacks stressed the Emancipation Proclamation and always regarded Lincoln as a liberator.

Most addresses, however, ignored Lincoln's conservatism or radicalism and rather portrayed him as a great martyr-reformer whose tragic death shed a glorious light upon his whole career, turned his image into an inspirational example, and thus spurred the American nation toward further progress and perfection. "For him, when the nation needed to be raised to its last dread duty, we were prepared for it by the baptism of his blood," declared Wendell Phillips in a speech in Tremont Temple.[143] I shall now examine whether under different circumstances other assassinated presidents also became such enduring national martyrs.

4

Sacrifice for Law and Order

Two American presidents besides Lincoln fell victim to an assassin's bullet within less than forty years. On July 2, 1881, James Abraham Garfield, the twentieth president of the United States, was shot by a disappointed office seeker in Washington, D.C., and died eighty days later on September 19, 1881. Twenty years later, on September 8, 1901, William McKinley was shot by a self-proclaimed anarchist in Buffalo, New York, and died on September 14, 1901. These two presidents belonged to the dominant Republican party, which represented the legitimate and conservative political establishment of the Gilded Age. As political leaders killed while representing the existing order, they had the potential for becoming celebrated martyrs for the American established elite. But unlike Lincoln their martyr image was very short-lived. For reasons this chapter will explore, Garfield and McKinley never became national martyrs for later generations. Their tragedy was a traumatic and meaningful event to their contemporaries, but it never transcended the conservative social milieu of the Republican party.

When President Garfield died after a long period of suffering, Charles Henry Parkhurst, a Presbyterian clergyman and social reformer, declared "We do not understand it. . . . We have got to feel that in it God teaches us and stand face to face with Him."[1] Henry Ward Beecher; Dr. Hinsdale (the president of Hiram College where Garfield studied and worked), and the editor of the *Chicago Tribune*, all expressed a similar sense of wonder at the mystery of divine ways.[2] Twenty years later, when President McKinley was killed, John Wanamaker, a wealthy businessman, also turned to God's mysterious design for an explanation.[3] This sense of wonder, however, was also accompanied by a more bitter and indignant reaction. Many members of the political elite asked how such a terrible event could happen three times, in the only free country in the world that had never experienced tyranny or repression. The recurring political assassinations generated anxieties and fears in the hearts of many public figures. While contemporaries expressed deep concern regarding the endurance and well-being of the United States in the face of such assaults on their presidents,[4] they also sought to make sense of the tragedies through rhetoric that turned the assassinated presidents into celebrated martyrs.

Immediately following President Garfield's death, various spokesmen compared his character and career to those of Abraham Lincoln.[5] William M. Thayer, a popular writer of success stories, summed up the similarities between the two presidents in his book *From Log Cabin to the White House*: Both had been born in a log cabin, had grown up as poor but talented orphans, become farmers and woodchoppers, and dedicated themselves to self-education through extensive reading. They had started their careers as teachers in the backwoods, then studied law while engaging in other occupations to make a living. Both had been army officers, attained national prominence as compromise candidates, and achieved popular support as a result of their election. "Both died in presidential office by the shot of an assassin. History has no parallel for such an amazing fact. . . . Beginning life in the obscurity of the wilderness and ending it on the summit of renown! Their first home—a log cabin! Their last—the White House."[6] When McKinley died some speakers also stressed previous political assassinations,[7] but most of them ignored Garfield and emphasized the similarities between McKinley and Lincoln alone.[8] According to Bishop Andrews who delivered the funeral sermon for McKinley, William of Orange, Cromwell, Washington, and Lincoln were the heroes with whom McKinley's name would be compared.[9]

Despite the analogy with Lincoln, the addresses and tributes to Garfield and McKinley lacked the mythical dimension of the individual martyr. While Lincoln was seen as both a witness to divine truth and an embodiment of human devotion to duty, the other martyred presidents were portrayed only as faithful and virtuous human beings. Most speakers and writers depicted them as typical Americans and interpreted the significance of their career in terms of human experience. They remained human also in their suffering and death and lacked the unique status of Lincoln, whose figure often appeared to loom above ordinary persons.[10] By using the term *martyr* without its transcendental significance, contemporaries actually misinterpreted the exact meaning of the word. Instead of divine testimony to the superhuman world, the martyred figure bore witness to the existence of pure life in the mundane world. Unlike the case for Lincoln, it was hard to claim that Garfield and McKinley had experienced any divine revelation. No one could quote from their speeches, remarks, dreams, or personal diaries, to show that they had viewed themselves as divine instruments or had attached any supernatural meaning to their political careers. They did not give any sublime and mythical interpretation to their position and had no Civil War to dramatize such an interpretation. The relative decline of the presidential office as the country's tone-setting institution in the late nineteenth century, also impaired the mythical superhuman images of these two presidents.

Though not superhumans who bridged the divine and mundane worlds, Garfield and McKinley were depicted as extraordinary figures. *Great, pure, stainless, perfect,* and *virtuous,* were among the adjectives spokesmen used to extol these dead presidents.[11] Many praised the virtues of the assassinated presidents in their private lives, glorifying their attitude toward their wives and relatives and stressing the affection and love they experienced in their last moments on earth from their family members.[12] The Reverend L. W. Brigham of La Crosse, Wisconsin, devoted his whole tribute to Garfield's domestic life, arguing that he had made home the most sacred spot on earth. "His tender heart and Mrs. Garfield's wifely devotion have sanctified every home in the land."[13]

Various explanations account for such a disproportionate emphasis on the domestic lives of Garfield and McKinley. Under the influence of Victorian culture, Americans wanted their presidents to be not worldly and ruthlessly ambitious men, but rather pure and domesticated. Even in the case of Lincoln, the American print industry showered the country with sentimental family pictures of the martyred president. He appeared reading the Bible to his son, studying in his library, riding in front of his house, resting with his family in the backyard, or taking a walk hand in hand with his wife. Popular prints of Lincoln and his family were sold all over the country after 1865.[14] But Lincoln had also been a great liberator, a brave warrior, and savior of the Union, all of which demonstrated how exceptional and extraordinary he really had been. Since Garfield and McKinley lacked this dramatic dimension to their careers, the only way to demonstrate the purity and uniqueness of their personalities was to concentrate upon their honest and peaceful family lives in a Victorian context that placed great value on domesticity.

Another reason for this emphasis may have been that, just as every assassinated leader is transformed into a symbolic father figure, so the dead president was turned into a lamented patriarch of the entire community; although he had been killed by members of that community, his death had sanctified the community's existence. According to this interpretation, a rhetoric that focuses on the family lives of the martyred presidents helps to build the collective archetype of a father figure that is necessary to any national ideology. This explanation does not, however, take into account the specific historical context in which such a figure is created.

Garfield and McKinley were both part of the political establishment of the Gilded Age, which emphasized family as a cornerstone of the moral and socioeconomic order. As legitimate leaders of their society, they all had to demonstrate their virtues through perfect domestic lives. Consequently, the assassins were portrayed as emotionally disturbed people who had suffered in their domestic lives and thus affiliated themselves with the destructive forces of society. The identification between pure domestic life and stable political and social order was essential to the ideology of the Gilded Age. Elizabeth Stuart Phelps Ward, the famous sentimentalist author, visualized in her popular literature a domestic heaven as the final stage of human redemption.[15] Eulogizing President McKinley, she asserted that the domestic example of McKinley's life was very important "in a day when . . . the great national danger is the abandonment of the home idea."[16]

An emphasis on domesticity and family life might also provide a broader popular identification with the dead figure. Most American voters were not professional politicians; they were, however, fathers, husbands, and children. By stressing this familiar realm, members of the political elite provided a means by which the plain people could identify with their leaders. If not through political affiliation or social status, emotional identification with the dead president could be aroused via the individualistic domain of family life. The Reverend J. A. Cruzan pointed out that after Garfield had been shot and throughout his suffering "a sense of kinship for the sufferer has grown into the hearts of fifty million Americans."[17] In an address in Cincinnati commemorating the one hundredth anniversary of McKinley's birth, Harry Kelso Eversol, a distinguished and rich enterpreneur, said that "to Americans it seemed as if someone very near and dear in family life had been snatched away. Every home shared in grief for everyone felt the sense of personal loss."[18] But personal loss was not enough to turn the deceased presidents into enduring martyr figures. Lacking the superhuman and redemptive dimension of their personality, these assassinated presidents could not enter the pantheon of the nation's mythical heroes. Later generations who did not experience the shock of the assassination hardly remembered their names and never viewed them as inspirational martyred figures.

As in Lincoln's case, speakers and writers described the deaths of Garfield and McKinley as sacrifices upon the altar of human liberty. Yet unlike Lincoln's case, nothing in their political careers demonstrated any particular commitment to extending freedom in America. They had not initiated any new Emancipation Proclamation and were reluctant to implement the one signed by Lincoln. Since Hays's administration, blacks had suffered a decisive setback in implementing the rights and liberties they seemed to have been granted by the Emancipation Proclamation. In the late nineteenth century other segments of American society felt that their freedom was in jeopardy. Many farmers and workers discovered that impersonal forces and specific plutocrats deprived them of their ability to exist as decent citizens in the land of liberty. The government was not inclined to promote their economic well-being and even seemed to join forces with strong corporations against the poor farmer or workingman. Ethnic groups like the Chinese were deprived of their legal rights and basic freedoms. Women in general could only demonstrate their freedom outside the political arena, which remained closed to them.

Thus, most addresses that defined Garfield and McKinley as martyrs for liberty avoided any concrete example to support this title. The assassinated presidents became martyrs for liberty in its abstract and negative sense. Insofar as liberty remained an already-achieved ideal, they could be depicted as its defenders. As an a priori and immanent ideal, liberty needs only protectors not promoters. In that sense liberty became part of the conservative ideology of the Gilded Age, which identified every attempt to reform or change the society as an assault against the sacred principle of freedom.

Hence, rather than reformers who expanded the realm of liberty, Garfield and McKinley were generally portrayed as defenders of a static and long-standing ideal of liberty. Many obituaries asserted that while the statesmen had died, freedom as an ideal would stand forever and would even be consecrated by their deaths.[19] "We offer him as an example of the products of Freedom," said Senator George F. Hoar in his eulogy of Garfield, "thus he made the Constitution which granted freedom to all citizens more sacred."[20] McKinley too was eulogized as one who had joined the martyrs for Constitutional liberty, "whose blood was poured upon the altar of liberty."[21]

Contemporaries implied the Lockean version of freedom in which an individual is free insofar as he is protected from the arbitrary intervention of others. Republican leaders in the Gilded Age viewed freedom as a cornerstone of order, designed to immunize society against both tyranny and anarchy. Thus a condition of liberty was a strict adherence to the law, and an assault upon the law was perceived as an assault upon liberty. William McKinley himself drew this connection between liberty and law in one of his famous orations. On the Fourth of July 1894, as Governor of Ohio, he delivered a speech dedicating the Cuyahoga County Soldiers' and Sailors' Monument in Cleveland. At the end of the speech, McKinley gave his interpretation of this ideal of liberty. "Liberty to make our own laws does not give us license to break them. . . . Liberty is responsibility, and responsibility is duty, and duty is to preserve the exceptional liberty we enjoy within the law, and for the law, and by the law."[22]

Identifying liberty with the law, contemporaries portrayed the assassins of Garfield and McKinley as representatives of forces that aimed to undermine freedom in the United States. Many speakers who eulogized Garfield warned that the spoils system was such a force. They argued that a crowd of ambitious office seekers was very dangerous to the peace and lawful order of the country.[23] Charles Guiteau, the man who shot Garfield, embodied the ultimate danger of such a system. Consequently Garfield became a martyr for law and order who died while fighting the spoils system, a system that jeopardized the lawful procedure of political nomination. Many addresses described the assassinated president not only as a victim of an evil system but also as one whose death would spur the nation to uproot it.[24] "This . . . event will enable us to absolve ourselves from our party hate, self love and greed for office," declared the former governor of Minnesota C. K. Davis.[25] Obviously, no one mentioned that Garfield himself had been as much a spoilsman as the others, and that he had risen to political power through shrewd use of that very system.[26]

When McKinley was murdered, spokesmen described the assassin as the incarnation of the demonic forces that were planning to destroy liberty in the name of licentiousness. According to various addresses, anarchism was not a doctrine that advocated total freedom, but rather an ideology that opposed liberty.[27] Czolgosz, who killed President McKinley, declared himself to be an anarchist and thus embodied the dark forces of destruction. Many speakers asserted that the shot that had killed McKinley had actually been directed against any legitimate institution of authority.[28] President Theodore Roosevelt proclaimed on September 14, 1901, that this crime had been committed not only against the chief magistrate, but against every law-abiding and liberty-loving citizen.[29] Citing Lincoln's famous statement, the ex-congressman from Massachusetts John F. Fitzgerald declared that "the law and order must prevail and that a government of the people, by the people, and for the people shall not perish from the earth."[30] David Star Jordan, the president of Stanford University, argued that under democracy every act of violence was treason and the lesson from the tragedy had to be more respect for the law.[31] Archibishop Patrick William Riordan, the head of San Francisco Diocese, drew the following lesson from the assassination: "There must be government, there must be society, and these can only be held under authority."[32]

Indeed many public figures were happy to affirm that the assault on the presidents had not overthrown the government of a republic.[33] In his inaugural address, President Chester Arthur declared that "men may die but the fabric of our free institutions remains unshaken."[34] Senator Hoar explained in his tributes to both Garfield and McKinley why the assassinations had not shaken the American institutions and why they had failed to generate any kind of chaos and revolution. "All Americans must be slain to slay a Republic. . . . The anarchist must slay 75 million Americans before he can overthrow a Republic."[35]

Yet unlike the period of Lincoln's assassination, Garfield and McKinley died in a relatively peaceful time when there was no apparent menace to republican institutions. Therefore, in order to make the leader's death meaningful, contemporaries had to point to something beyond the mere existence of the republican form of government and the federal union. Some of them argued that the tragedies had not only proved the stability of the republican government, but also consecrated it as a sublime institution.[36] But the sanctification of republican institutions without the concrete example of a struggle that had saved the Republic and the Union in time of trial, provided little inspiration for later generations.

Thus the term *martyr for liberty,* when applied to the assassinated presidents of the Gilded Age, meant primarily martyr for the status quo, for law and order. The Constitution and the legal-political institutions of the country were the concrete and lawful manifestations of the ideal of liberty. The leaders who died by criminal action became martyrs for liberty according to such a worldview. They did not promote freedom in a country that already enjoyed it, but they embodied the law and the legal institutions that upheld this freedom.

The various spokesmen who defined the presidents as martyrs for law and order simply transformed law and order from a means of control into an ideal in and of itself. They turned the basic need of any political regime into the ultimate value of democracy. Such an ideology, which sanctified the status quo, had no appeal to later generations. Only close friends and relatives of the assassinated presidents as well as very conservative politicians continued to pay tribute to the ideal of law and order; the public in general forgot the presidents who died while defending that law and order. With their deaths, the assassinated presidents did not transform law and order into a new ideal for a democratic culture in general. Lincoln, who had fought secession and fortified the Republic, inspired further generations both as a savior of the existing order and as a political pioneer for reform who had enlarged freedom and thus strengthened the moral foundation of the American political system. But Garfield and McKinley, the guardians of the status quo, did not change any ideal or institution and thus could not become enduring sources of inspiration.

As in the case of Lincoln, the theme of building a nation through emotional identification with the leader's sacrifice reemerged in various eulogies and sermons to Garfield and McKinley.[37] The national grief and lamentation created a community of mourners. The length of time that Garfield and McKinley lay on their deathbeds, suffering and facing their inevitable deaths, prolonged the period of collective concern and sorrow. It built a sort of familiarity with the dying presidents. Newspapers brought the scenes around the deathbed into the lives of millions of Americans. For more than eighty days people followed Garfield's condition, and for six days they became intimate with McKinley's struggle against death. Many spokesmen tried to invest meaning in the long suffering of the dying presidents and used the deathbed scenes as an emotional common denominator that strengthened the national consciousness.[38] Secretary of State James G. Blaine declared that Garfield in these days had become the center of the nation's love, enriched in the prayers of the world.[39] "His suffering chastened and elevated the whole nation. The country became familiar with his wonderful story and with his unique character," wrote *Harper's Weekly*.[40]

Although Garfield's murder was merely a symptom of the strife and disorder of the spoils system, many spokesmen emphasized its significance as furthering the real unification of the nation: in their common grief, they asserted, Americans forgot their sectional affiliations and really became one nation.[41] "Alabama and Massachusetts, South Carolina and New York, Georgia and Ohio . . . the seal is set by the cold and emaciated hand of our dead President," declared Dr. De-Witt Talmage in New York.[42] "No North, no South, no East, no West," exclaimed the Reverend Charles H. Parkhurst. "We all became in an unusual way members of one another."[43] Other speakers asserted that Garfield's death in a dialectic way had ended once and for all the factional strife that had motivated a mentally disturbed individual to shoot the president.[44] They noted that sectional conflict, party hatred, and factional strife had prevented America from being a nation and were happy to declare that these sectional and party lines had been obliterated and that the whole nation stood as united mourners.[45] "We have been fused into one nation," said Mr. Parkman from the city council of Boston. "Party lines vanished before the assassin's blow and political differences were forgotten in our common grief."[46] "Now when South and North, Democrats and Republicans, Radicals and Conservatives lift their voices in one unbroken accord of lamentation . . . we are nearer a united people than ever before," wrote the poet and author John Greenleaf Whittier.[47]

Twenty years later, when Americans mourned William McKinley, his death was again portrayed as adding an essential dimension to American nationality. Contemporaries declared that universal sorrow bound the nation together and undermined any particular affiliations.[48] "Thank God, there is no division in the people today," declared Senator Hoar. "Rich and poor, Democrats and Republicans, Protestants and Catholic, native born and foreign born are mingling their sorrow."[49] William Jennings Bryan, the "Great Commoner," who embodied more than any one else the popular opposition to President McKinley, affirmed this statement in a memorial service in Lincoln, Nebraska.[50] Again, contemporaries stated that the tragedy had bridged sectional conflicts and created a new sense of patriotism common to North and South.[51] This was expressed in a poem written by James R. Hewlitt, a Civil War veteran from Chicago:

> A Nation no longer divided
> No North no South, but at call
> We are brethren forever united
> With one God, One flag over all.[52]

Nothing in the actual careers of Garfield and McKinley accounted for such an emphasis upon their roles as national figures who had reunited the North and the South. As Republicans and Northerners they associated themselves with industrial interests and were never endorsed by the South. Garfield delivered some speeches with a conciliatory tone toward the South and McKinley even made a well-publicized trip to the South, but overall they were Northerners and Union veterans. Insofar as religion, ethnicity, class, or political orientation is concerned, both Garfield and McKinley remained partisan figures. Very much a part of the Protestant and Anglo-Saxon upper middle class, these presidents served very well their particular social group. The overwhelming emphasis upon their roles as nation builders, therefore, had nothing to do with their concrete careers as politicians, but rather with their tragic assassination, which provided the American establishment with the "emotional cement" necessary to build a national consciousness.

Political martyrs, even in a pluralistic society that accepts conflict and diversity, provide a kind of national unity. The universal mourning tends to submerge conflicts and real divisions and stresses a common national destiny. Whether Garfield and McKinley promoted such national unification in their political careers was not so important to their contemporaries who wanted to endow their death with meaning. In the long run, however, this was a crucial factor. While Lincoln continued to be remembered as national unifier, the new level of nationality that Garfield and McKinley had supposedly created remained emotionally shallow to those who had not experienced the ritual around their deathbeds. In the case of Lincoln, his martyrdom at the end of the Civil War was perceived as the baptism of a nation reborn. In the cases of Garfield and McKinley, this moment of national rebirth was lacking. Inasmuch as they were remembered at all, these two presidents remained partisan figures. The career of Lincoln and especially his leadership in war accounted for his sustained image as a national martyr. The absence of such a career turned Garfield and McKinley into very short-lived national martyrs.

A new theme appeared in the eulogies to Garfield and reached its peak in the various addresses to McKinley: The dead presidents had not only brought together parties, sections, factions, religious beliefs, and classes, but they had also created a new sense of unity and solidarity between the United States and Europe. When Garfield died many speakers stated that the world reacted with great sorrow. His long suffering strengthened mankind's fraternity around the deathbed.[53] Newspapers published Queen Victoria's letter of condolence, described the expression of sorrow in England and stressed the solidarity of the Anglo-Saxon race.[54] The universal mourning on the other side of the Atlantic proved, according to many American public figures, the importance of Garfield's martyrdom to the civilized, English-speaking, world.[55]

This vague emotional identification with the civilized world in the case of Garfield became more concrete in the various addresses to McKinley. Contemporaries explained the death of the president in the context of his foreign policy, which had aimed to "Americanize" the rest of the world by exporting capitalism and democracy beyond the boundaries of the New World. Writers and journalists stressed the significance of the universal mourning, praising the fact that political differences and international jealousies had been forgotten.[56] "Though he has gone," wrote the *Chicago Tribune*, "the cause of commercial expansion and of the trade supremacy of America surely will find other champions . . . who, like him will be willing to sacrifice selfish and personal considerations to promote the welfare of the republic."[57] Thus McKinley's martyrdom sanctified his foreign policy and enabled patriotic politicians to glorify imperialism as a new component of the American national character. Later in the twentieth century, conservative politicians commemorated McKinley as martyr for this new nationalism,[58] but it is doubtful whether the public in general shared such a view.

Contemporaries depicted the assassinated presidents as the embodiment of Americanism. As in the case of Lincoln, many tributes emphasized the uncultivated Western frontier as a unique and blessed environment for building a leader's career and character. Many writers discussed in detail the log cabin story of James A. Garfield, describing the difficult physical conditions of the orphan boy in the wilderness of Cuyahoga County and emphasizing his heroic efforts as a canal-boat driver.[59] "The poverty of the frontier," declared James Blaine, "is but the beginning of wealth, and has boundless opportunities."[60] The frontier provided its residents with freedom and direct contact with nature, something that Americans had always admired in their national experience. Thus, Colonel Townsend asserted that McKinley had "this contact with mother Earth which falls to the lot of the farmer's son."[61]

Yet not everybody extolled the frontier as solely responsible for building the American character of the assassinated presidents. Many addresses stressed ethnic roots, family sources, and racial affiliations as the foundations of Garfield's and McKinley's characters.[62] They were blessed with purely democratic and freedom-loving ancestors, hence heredity, as well as environment, accounted for their "American" natures. Charles F. Warwick expressed this new dualism in his address in Fairmount Park, Philadelphia, while unveiling a monument to James A. Garfield. "The Garfields were sturdy God-fearing people, they were of that stuff that in a new country opens a way through the forests . . . makes a stony land yield up harvests, and the desert to bloom and blossom like a rose."[63] A moral and decent family background combined with the frontier environment produced such a unique and noble national figure. The Reverend W. C. Bartlett discounted the significance of environment and declared that "blood, not environment initiated the long struggle for supremacy." He elaborated this point, arguing that Garfield had drawn his blood from two distinguished sources: Huguenot and Puritan.[64]

This new emphasis on family heritage as well as the Western frontier derived from the historical context of the Gilded Age. Toward the end of the nineteenth century Americans reached their last frontier on the continent. The open West actually was closed in the 1880s. On the other hand, the country had experienced more than a hundred years of national history which had become a distinctive ingredient in building national consciousness. Hereditary factors such as family background, connections with colonial ancestors, and relationships with historical figures, became more important in this new context of a collective national history. The emergence of social Darwinism as the conservative ideology of the economic and political elite of the Gilded Age permitted contemporaries to use factors such as Anglo-Saxon background as signs of the presidents' superior character. The frontier in and of itself could not produce such an elite-oriented character. It could help, though, those individuals who by virtue of their background were already endowed with a noble character.

The most common theme that demonstrated the Americanism of the martyred presidents was their personal rags-to-riches story. According to most eulogies, such a career proved the viability of the American dream. Regardless of their real biographies, the assassinated presidents were portrayed as poor boys who rose by their own efforts from poverty and obscurity to greatness and fame. Garfield's rags-to-riches story was the most popular theme in the various discourses written and delivered after his death.[65] James D. McCabe wrote in his introduction to his popular biography of Garfield that "it is the pride and boast of America that this is the country of self-made men. . . . No career in all our history furnishes a more brilliant example of this, than that of General James A. Garfield."[66]

It was hard to demonstrate any poverty in the early career of William McKinley. Unlike Lincoln and Garfield, he was not a poor orphan but rather the son of a wealthy enterpreneur. Nevertheless, contemporaries described him as a man who had started life in humble conditions and who, through sheer effort and hard work, had made his way to the presidency.[67] "Born on the American farm he started barefooted in the furrow. . . . Marching in the ranks of Lincoln and Garfield to the solitude of the martyr's throne."[68] John Hay, the secretary of state, provided a more moderate version of the president's career in a speech before the U.S. congress on February 27, 1902: "The life of William McKinley was from his start to his death typically American . . . neither rich nor poor, neither proud nor humble . . . knows no hunger . . . no luxury which could enervate mind and body."[69]

As in the case of Lincoln, the rags-to-riches story characterized the "Americanism" of the martyred presidents. But around the turn of the century and in face of the Progressive critique of the industrial and political establishment of the Gilded Age, this story became an ideological device for the elite. Conservative politicians and businessmen used it as a response to the attack upon the new corporate structure. Republican newspapers like the *New York Times* and the *San Francisco Chronicle* wrote immediately after McKinley's death that he exemplified the possibilities open to poor boys in this country. Ignoring the fact that McKinley had never been a poor boy, they asserted that such a career made him a typical American. He rose in the only place in the world that did not put obstacles in the way of success.[70]

Thus, the American political establishment of the Gilded Age distorted the personal careers of the martyred presidents for ideological purposes.

Garfield and McKinley served to affirm the existence of the frontier, the advantage of noble and virtuous family background, and the persistence of open opportunity in new industrial America. Yet unlike the case of Lincoln, later generations did not attribute these characteristics to the second and third assassinated presidents and never viewed Garfield and McKinley as simple, Western, self-made men who exemplified American democracy. On the contrary, later generations identified these presidents as being part of the financial and corporate elite of their time. Unlike Lincoln, Garfield and McKinley represented the establishment, strove to maintain the status quo and opposed any significant change or reform. Such a political career reduced their prospects of becoming national martyrs for those who had not experienced the trauma of the assassination.

I have examined in previous chapters how, as a religious archetype, the martyr suffered and died to atone for human sin and consequently to promote the coming of the millennium. Indeed contemporaries often referred to this biblical cosmology in order to give meaning to the assassination of the presidents. Whereas the concrete sin of slavery enhanced the image of Lincoln as martyr redeemer, such a clear evil did not exist in the cases of Garfield and McKinley. Nevertheless, religious preachers found some national sins for which the presidents' deaths had provided atonement. Deviating from the theological and cosmic meaning of human sin as an inherent part of human existence, they identified sin with certain social shortcomings of American society. When specific groups or individuals pointed to concrete foes as sinners, they in fact undermined the Christian meaning of original sin, which is immanent and universal.

A combination of widespread religious blasphemy, immoral behavior, such as drinking and gambling, and social injustice, such as corruption in business and politics, provided many spokesmen with an explanation for Garfield's tragedy.[71] Some clergymen added to these national sins an explanation based on the immanence of human sin.[72] "As the tallest pine of the forest is sought by the savage to light up and burn down as a signal, so Garfield, the majestic and peerless chief magistrate, was selected that the whole world might see our country's sins and her sorrows," declared the Reverend Thomas N. Haskell in a memorial address in Denver.[73] "The shot fired in the depot at Washington was God's voice calling the nation to order," declared Charles Parkhurst. "Guiteau's case simply publishes the possibilities of evil that lurk in every man. . . . The precious blood has been shed, may it be applied by us to the end that we may be cleansed."[74] Yet not everybody regarded the assassination as a consequence of national or original sin. Professor Swing, who delivered a sermon in Chicago, asserted that, while the previous history showed that leaders died for some sin or wrong, "our new history points us to two great leaders who were the unhappy victims, each of a single wicked heart."[75]

Sin was an ambiguous subject in the obituaries to McKinley as well. Many addresses mentioned the failure of religious standards, growth of luxury, decline of morals and piety, indifference toward laws and authority, and the tyranny of the rich as reasons for the tragedy. Yet these jeremiad-style addresses mainly focused upon social injustice and deviation from righteousness, rather than upon the existence of a flawed humanity.[76] They never viewed the death of McKinley in biblical terms as a sign of expiation and atonement for human sin.

Despite the absence of the theme of atonement, contemporaries made analogies between Garfield or McKinley and Jesus Christ who had died on the cross to save humanity. As in the case of Lincoln many speakers used "empirical" evidence from the life and death of the presidents to make this analogy. Thus many clergymen claimed that, like the Savior who had suffered on the cross, Garfield had lain on his deathbed for eighty painful days and, like Christ, had become perfect through pain and torment.[77] Arguing that some people literally imitated Christ's fate and thus became closer to the Savior, religious preachers depicted Garfield as Christ's close follower and a mediator between Him and the people.[78] Likewise, professional clergymen and devout laymen emphasized the Christian character of President McKinley and depicted him as Christ's disciple.[79] "I never knew a man in all my life," announced Senator William A. Mason from Illinois, "who carried the teaching of Jesus Christ with him every hour and every day as did President McKinley."[80] Again, speakers tried to base the analogy on "empirical" grounds. The reaction of the president to his assassin provided such a proof. According to eyewitnesses, the crowd wanted to lynch the assassin, but the wounded president called out "don't harm the boy." This phrase sounded like Christ's last statement on the cross, "Father forgive them, they know not what they do." McKinley's last words, "Thy kingdom come, thy will be done," were also used by some preachers and writers to substantiate the analogy with Christ.[81]

Garfield and McKinley were both members of a particular church. Therefore clergymen and conservative politicians who viewed religion as a cornerstone of orderly civilization declared that the assassinated leaders were not only American martyrs but also Christian martyrs. Yet most addresses focused upon the presidents' faith while de-emphasizing their specific religious affiliation. The fact that Garfield had joined a certain Baptist group (the Disciples of Christ) and that McKinley had been a Methodist Episcopalian was disregarded; the important thing was that they had been devoutly religious people with deep faith in God. Their religiosity was interpreted as a moral asset that demonstrated their commitment to justice and righteousness. Faith had been an integral part of their character and consequently affected their political behavior.[82] Some used the term *Christian resignation* when they interpreted the manner in which both Garfield and McKinley had faced the inevitability of their deaths and which had made them even more Christian in their last moments than during their lives.[83]

Various religious leaders used the martyred presidents and their devout Christianity to affirm the centrality of religion in the American political culture.[84] In a ceremony laying the cornerstone of a monument to Garfield in Golden Gate Park, San Francisco, on August 23, 1883, Henry E. Highton declared that

the Government of the United States . . . is not pagan, and not atheistic. . . . The foundation of all things material and immaterial is not abstract law . . . not self-generating independent force, but GOD . . . penetrated by the perfect attributes of LOVE, JUSTICE, and TRUTH. . . . This is the rock upon which . . . self-government can surely repose, this is the plain and massive cornerstone of the Republic.[85]

Dr. Harrison Ray Anderson from the Chicago Presbyterian Church argued that the Christian religion and its church, and the American people and their government, were related in deeper ways than many Americans realized. Eulogizing William McKinley, he stated that the president had fully comprehended this phenomenon, and that his foreign policy had aimed to bring the benefits of Christianity and the advantages of democracy to remote parts of the world.[86]

Archbishop Ryan gave extreme expression to the idea that Christianity must play a central role in American society:

We need religion that is not merely sentimental but doctrinal. . . . Because this is the land of liberty and there are fewer restraining influences from without, we need more from within. . . . Our modern unbelievers would sweep all the truth away, and with them they would sweep away this glorious young Republic. . . . We must perpetuate Christianity to defend the Republic in the name of our murdered President [McKinley] and the founder of Christianity.[87]

This call for the supremacy of the Christian religion was a significant departure from the ideology that guaranteed freedom of religious belief in America. Yet conservative politicians and fundamentalist ministers of the Gilded Age argued for a more restricted version of doctrinal religion in order to defend the fragile political institutions. They hoped to fight the dangers of pluralism with a moral orthodoxy based on Christian dogma. They used such solemn and passionate events as a president's assassination both to proclaim the dangers of pluralism and to announce the need for a new order based on Christian doctrine.

On the other hand, the mainstream of American Christianity underwent a process of liberalization in the Gilded Age. The specific dogmas of all formal religions declined, which made religion more acceptable within the American democratic culture: if religion could be regarded primarily as a moral principle without specific doctrine, in the political context, it served to prevent human tyranny. A Christian leader from this perspective, is a humble and modest leader who knows the limits of his power and therefore acts in the political arena in a very restrained way. The mere acceptance of a superior power protects democracy from tyranny since its rulers, as Christians, remain humble and obedient human beings. Insofar as the president is a Christian, his position as leader is restrained by his Christian obedience to God. Thus in his address before the United States Congress, James G. Blaine asserted that Garfield's Christian beliefs had built his character as a leader committed to liberalism and tolerance.[88] "He attained the highest place of honor and usefulness," announced Captain Henry Jackson of Atlanta, Georgia, in a memorial address to Garfield, "while he maintained his Christian virtue and kept himself in fear of God."[89] Thus contemporaries depicted Garfield's Christianity in a liberal context that enabled them to combine the political realm with the domain of Christian religion. "Let us praise God," wrote E. E. Brown, "that for once we have had a president who could shine in the most illustrious position in the nation, and yet light up for us the humblest walls of Christian obedience."[90]

Less frequently in the case of Garfield, but very often after McKinley's assassination, the murderer was depicted as the incarnation of the anti-

Christ. While Garfield's contemporaries labeled Guiteau a "half-crazy office-seeker," McKinley's eulogists portrayed Czolgotz in different terms. They viewed him not only as an anarchist foe of law and order, but also as an enemy of God. They described anarchism as a source of all moral evil, not merely as a destructive political force.[91] Some preachers and writers explicitly used infernal symbolism and defined anarchy as hell, Satan, a serpent, or a monster.[92] "Anarchy is an advance theory of Socialism," argued the Reverend James McDonald in San Francisco. "They [anarchists] deny the existence of God and the right of every authority. The anarchists would suppress religion and overturn society as it exists. In a few years if not stamped out, they would succeed in bringing the country to ruin."[93]

Since this apocalyptic vision had no basis in the reality of the time, on the whole contemporaries did not interpret the martyrdom of either Garfield or McKinley in these terms. True, immediately after their death many addresses did attach some mythical significance to the presidents' fate and, especially in texts such as poems and sermons, the concrete political leaders were transformed into celestial figures: they were seen as saints, Christian soldiers, divine spirits, and redeemers, thus entering the sacred domain of eschatology.[94] But these mythical images of Garfield and McKinley were not incorporated into the collective American experience and over time they totally disappeared. Unlike Lincoln's figure they never became a sustained part of the American civil religion. The absence of a traumatic and heroic event like the Civil War prevented them from being perceived as hero-redeemers who had sacrificed their lives for the victory of Good in its battle against Evil. The religious rhetoric many speakers adopted was limited to the short period following the assassination and at best strengthened the positions of some conservative leaders who tried to incorporate Christian pietism into the American democratic ideology.

Although, as we have seen, Garfield and McKinley were certainly depicted by their friends and followers as martyrs, posterity did not include them in the gallery of heroes and martyrs who had died for American democracy. While later generations continued to pay tribute to Abraham Lincoln, the other martyred presidents disappeared from the public consciousness. Thus, a single article appeared in the *New York Times* at the time of Garfield's centennial, and this was dedicated to explaining why no one remembered the second martyred president. The conclusion was that there had been nothing spectacular in his career as a factional politician.[95] Insofar as memorial addresses appeared later in the twentieth century, they were limited to certain interest groups mainly associated with the conservative wing of the Republican party and with certain business and social clubs.[96]

Garfield and McKinley were depicted by contemporaries as unique and almost perfect individuals, as exemplary husbands and fathers, close to the plain people, and devoted statesmen, but, on the whole, not as prophets or celestial figures. In death they defended the status quo, demonstrating the existence of lawful freedom and the stability of republican institutions. Their deaths at most reinforced the existing order but did not generate new inspiration for the future. Their tragedies served to glorify a nostalgic past, but did not promote a new and better future. The tragedy in itself created a sense of common fate among the mourners but this emotional participation was short-lived. The American people did not experience a collective baptism of blood in the Gilded Age. Thus, unlike Lincoln's fate—which was interpreted in relation to the collective bloodshed of the Civil War— the blood of the other martyred figures had no collective analogy. Therefore their deaths did not provide a new traumatic national experience that might strengthen the sacrificial ties among diverse people. As typical Americans, these martyred leaders remained partisans and elitists, and their rags-to-riches stories served primarily as an ideological device of the powerful elite, legitimizing its power and preventing reform on behalf of the less privileged. Although contemporaries interpreted the martyrdom of Garfield and McKinley in religious terms, this religious interpretation lacked a mythical aura. Christian symbolism decorated many obituaries but did not create the legendary attributes that turn such symbols into inspirational forces. Thus, the martyr image of these presidents remained meaningful only to their close friends and disciples and was never assimilated into the general American population as part of its civil religion.

The difference between posterity's view of Lincoln on the one hand and of Garfield and McKinley on the other, demonstrates that it was the leader's career that determined whether his tragic death would transform him into an enduring national martyr. Only the commitment to a better future, expressed in a lifelong devotion to an altruistic ideal, could guarantee such an enduring martyr image. Lincoln fought secession and built a new Union through this fight. He liberated the oppressed slaves and turned them into freemen. As a warrior he led the nation to defend the republican institutions and in fact he created a new Republic forever immune from the challenge of disunionists. The Great Emancipator changed the status quo of American society as a warrior, liberator, and second-founding father of the nation.

By contrast, Garfield and McKinley did not promote any major reforms during their administrations. These two Republican politicians remained loyal to the existing forces that had brought them to power and represented the conservative elements in American politics. They died as "martyrs for law and order," but as time passed, such a title seemed a contradiction in terms. Martyrs by definition promote a new order and even defy unjust existing laws that prevent the society from entering this new stage. Garfield and McKinley did not intend to change the status quo and their deaths resulted in no significant reform activities. They had no cause to which they could commit their lives. Consequently, while Abraham Lincoln gained the title of *national martyr* immediately after his assassination, James A. Garfield and William McKinley vanished into oblivion shortly after their tragic deaths.

The decline in the martyr image of the two later presidents can be explained also by another factor that is extraneous to their careers and rather reflects a change in the culture of the time. In the early and midnineteenth century American political culture was saturated with religious—basically Calvinistic—symbols, concepts, and images that gave meaning to the American political experience. Toward the end of the century, and especially in the twentieth century, the appeal of such a mythical explanation declined and religious symbols seemed to lose some of their ideological power in America. Concepts such as sin, sacrifice, and martyrdom, which explained tragedy in a traditional Calvinistic culture, had less relevance within a modern and pluralistic culture that suffered from a certain emotional poverty. Consequently, the martyr image of the suffering hero lost its prestige in the transition period between the 1880s and 1920s. This ambiguous attitude toward sacrifice and martyrdom could be found even among various reformers of this time who, unlike the reformers of the early nineteenth century, hesitated to praise automatically any "martyr for the cause."

5

Progressive Reformers and Martyrdom: Mixed Attitudes

Wendell Phillips was a renowned reformer who participated in both the early and later reform movements of the nineteenth century and was therefore defined by certain spokesmen as the last abolitionist and the first Progressive.[1] He vigorously affirmed martyrdom for the cause throughout his career, never abandoned the rhetoric of sin, sacrifice, suffering, and redemption, and used religious concepts and images when interpreting and justifying his various reform activities. In his many orations he emphasized the value of sacrifice for reform whenever he had an opportunity to do so. As a former abolitionist, Wendell Phillips celebrated the abolitionists' legacy and long tradition of martyrdom for the cause. Until his death in 1884, he dedicated his whole life to improving various aspects of American society and to fighting certain institutions of "reactionary capitalism." Not surprisingly when he died many of his friends depicted him as a martyr for the cause of reform, and praised his career as an example of ultimate altruism and continuous sacrifice. As a radical abolitionist who continued his reform activities long after the emancipation of the slaves, Phillips became an inspirational model for certain Progressive reformers, yet he had only limited appeal to the leading figures of the Progressive Era and to the public in general.

The fact that Wendell Phillips was born into a Boston Brahmin family and consciously gave up his privilege and wealth, contributed to his image as a martyr. The son of the mayor of Boston, he grew up on Beacon Hill, went to Harvard, gained a degree in law, and was automatically accepted to the Massachusetts bar. He had nothing to expect but a prosperous career. But he repudiated this future and associated himself with the radical abolitionists, which virtually barred him from the high status he otherwise would have achieved, and deprived him of the financial resources of his family. Obviously, many of Phillips's friends and admirers glorified this conscious decision and defined it as a deliberate sacrifice for the cause of reform.[2] "He had entered upon a life of self-renunciation," said the black leader Archibald H. Grimké, "and it did not matter how dear former friendships and hopes and social privileges had been, he laid them all now upon the altar."[3] On July 5, 1915, at the dedication of the statue of Wendell Phillips, the acting mayor of Boston again praised Phillips's decision to reject his aristocratic background:

Wendell Phillips had the heart and the vision and the courage to step outside the limitations of his own aristocratic, cultured, privileged class and give himself . . . to the men and women of another class . . . in order that he might improve their station in life. What we need today more than anything else . . . is men like Phillips who are sufficiently big-hearted, broad-minded and courageous to sense the difficulties and suffering of some class or race not their own and devote themselves to an improvement of their condition.[4]

Such a rhetoric certainly appealed to the reform-oriented, upper-middle-class Bostonians of the Progressive Era, who attended the ceremony.

Indeed, Wendell Phillips conceived martyrdom as the highest stage of human existence, reserved only for a few elect individuals. He pronounced this idea when he eulogized American figures such as Theodore Parker, John Brown, William L. Garrison, and Abraham Lincoln, or extolled famous freedom fighters such as Toussant l'Ouverture of Haiti and Daniel O'Connell of Ireland.[5] But Phillips did not confine himself to praising specific heroes as martyrs but rather looked upon the whole concept of martyrdom as the ultimate value that made life worth living. "None know what it is to live till they redeem life from its seeming monotony by laying it a sacrifice on the altar of some great cause," he declared.[6]

When the Anti-Slavery Society was dissolved, Phillips became a solitary agitator reformer and resorted to the ideology of martyrdom even further to justify his continued commitment to reform.[7] Phillips argued for the right of petition, spoke against racism and on behalf of Ireland's struggle for independence. He advocated women's suffrage, equal treatment for the Chinese immigrants, and enforcement of prohibition laws. Committing himself to labor issues, especially to the Eight Hour Movement, he even ran for political office in Boston on a socialist-labor ticket. Wendell Phillips continued his agitation on behalf of blacks and always found new causes for a crusade such as preserving the Old South Hall in Boston, or accusing intellectuals of being aloof from reform issues. He sympathized with farmers, workers, ethnic groups, women, criminals in overcrowded jails, city street people, in brief, with anyone who suffered in America.[8]

Phillips always integrated the value of martyrdom into a deep Christian pietism and gave his reform activities a religious interpretation.[9] Glorifying the virtue of a nonconformist Christianity, Phillips turned his reform activities into religious and moral crusades and even fought the Christian establishment of his time. He held that the nominal Christianity that surrounded him was a body without soul and he longed to imitate authentic Christians such as Paul, Luther, John Wesley, and Calvin.[10] Such figures convinced him that martyrdom was essential to real Christianity, which Phillips saw as a battle for permanent reform. In a speech on Christian faith in Boston in 1869, he asserted that sacrifice was the most important principle of Christianity. "All other religions allow that the strong have the right to use the weak. . . . Christianity ignores it in its central principle. . . . Ours is the only faith whose first teacher and eleven out of his twelve original disciples died martyrs to their ideas."[11]

Wendell Phillips frequently used binary contrasts as a rhetorical device to explain the mechanism of reform and viewed suffering, failure, death, and sacrifice as necessary steps in the ultimate triumph of any reform cause.[12] His quest for sacrifice appeared to be intrinsic to his whole performance on stage. Always ready to confront the angry mob, always prepared to challenge the conventional values of his audience, always aware that he might be killed by passionate foes, Phillips himself expected a martyr's fate. But except for one mobbing incident in Boston, he did not encounter physical violence during his life. He died peacefully and naturally in his home in Boston on February 2, 1884, at the age of seventy-two.

Phillips's admirers and supporters had to cope with this peaceful death when they tried to depict him as a celebrated martyr. Charles Edward Russell, a famous socialist writer, argued that a life of continued sacrifice was more valuable than a martyr's death: "other men have flashed into fame by the sacrifice of one moment on some altar of patriotism. This man's sacrifice was of all the years of his life—all that comfort, leisure, peace, culture, study, learning, friendship, achievement and honor, can mean to one endowed beyond almost all other men for the enjoyment of these."[13]

Yet Russell did imply that Phillips had died as a result of his reform activities. He wrote at the end of his book that "the incessant attacks of more than forty years had worn down the warrior's heart under the brave and unruffled front that he presented to the world, the arrows had taken effect at last."[14] Most of Phillips's followers, however, did not make such a connection and preferred to focus upon his long career as an example of disinterested commitment to reform, which required constant sacrifice. Yet in their eulogies, obituaries, and memorial addresses, they portrayed a reformer who embodied many characteristics of a mythic martyr.

In some eulogies Phillips appeared as an individual who had witnessed an absolute truth, because of his relationship with divinity.[15] "He was called of God as truly as ever Moses and the Prophets were," declared Henry Ward Beecher. "He belongs to the race of giants . . . because he gave himself to the work of God upon earth, and inherited thereby, or reflected upon him, some of the majesty of his master."[16] Theodore Dwight Weld, the 82-year-old ex-abolitionist, eulogized Phillips in Boston. He openly stated that Phillips belonged to "these great souls [who] are God's ambassadors. . . . Alone, God-sent he lifted up his prophecy against a generation of oppressors. . . . Thus called by God he counseled not with man. . . . He bowed to its sacred baptism . . . consecrating with the anointing of a divine apostleship."[17] This divine connection, according to Weld, enabled Phillips to endure suffering and tribulations that for him were nothing but happiness. "Supernatural passion fired him, a divine magnetism lifted him exultant above all perils, loss, and sacrifice, till he counted suffering and desperate struggle all joy, a glad free-will offering . . . to the cause of humanity, freedom and the nation's salvation."[18]

Wendell Phillips was also portrayed as a national martyr whose sacrifice and devotion to reform had purified and improved the American national experience. The abolition of slavery demonstrated Phillips's achievements as a fighter for human liberty—a sacred value in the American political culture.[19] But liberty for Phillips meant more than a lack of oppression. It was a never-ending inspiration. Contrary to the conservative interpretation, which assumed that freedom was an already-achieved ideal, reformers like Phillips and his supporters regarded it as only a partly existing ideal, always subject to further amelioration.[20] He derided those institutions and laws that claimed to grant freedom to American people, by showing how these very laws deprived large numbers of American citizens of freedom. "He showed the crimes of the Republic," stated John Davis Long in a eulogy to

Phillips in Washington, D.C.[21] Justice Wendell Phillips Stafford gave a precise definition of the meaning of liberty and freedom to a reformer like Phillips. For him "a person that is satisfied with the institutions he has gained, that worships the past and refuses to go forward to larger freedom, has already ceased to be free."[22] Only a permanent quest for more liberty through commitment to reform gave Phillips a real sense of freedom.

Phillips's followers capitalized upon the fact that in his career he had refused to confine his agitation to any specific reform. In various biographies and addresses he emerged as a universal reformer whose suffering and sacrifice had more than a personal or national meaning.[23] He embodied the mission of America as a redeemer nation intent on hastening the coming of the kingdom of God.[24] He was depicted as American in his permanent quest to help the oppressed and in his commitment to democracy, welfare and liberty for everyone in the world. Even his "riches-to-rags" career was used as a sign of true Americanism: radical reformers and socialists who rejected American materialism glorified Phillips precisely because he had repudiated wordly success for idealistic purpose. Other reform-oriented speakers stated that Phillips's denunciation of his aristocratic background corresponded with the spirit of American democracy. When a famous reformer like George William Curtis eulogized Phillips before the municipal authorities of Boston, he said, "No American more truly than he purged the national name of its shame and made the American flag the flag of hope for mankind."[25]

Some contemporary biographers even described Phillips as a prophet whose message extended beyond his time. Referring to his own expressed desire to be judged by posterity, they wrote that Wendell Phillips could see where others could not and described him as a citizen of the twentieth century sent as an example to the people of the nineteenth. They explained his suffering and estrangement by the fact that he often belonged to the future and would be vindicated at a later time.[26] Being ahead of his time explained the martyr's gloomy fate in his own life and also endowed him with a cosmic message. Indeed, Frederick Douglass, the famous black abolitionist, expressed this view when he eulogized Wendell Phillips. Using an analogy with Jesus Christ, Douglass ended his address with the following poem:

> While the coward stands aside
> Doubting in his abject spirit
> Till his Lord is crucified

And the multitude make virtue
Of the faith they had denied
For Humanity sweeps onward
Where to-day the martyr stands
On the morrow crouches Judas
With the silver in his hands;
Far in front the cross stands ready
And the crackling fagots burn
While the hooting mob of yesterday
In silent awe return
To glean up the scattered ashes
Into History's golden urn.[27]

Thus Phillips's image embodied most of the elements of the martyr. His followers portrayed him as an individual who had a unique relationship with the divine sphere. As a social and national martyr, he suffered to bring liberty to any oppressed group and thus proclaimed the need for never-ending improvements both in the United States and beyond its boundaries. As a cosmic figure, he transcended any particular territory and period, in order to promote the future redemption of mankind.

Many individuals who viewed themselves as reformers regarded Wendell Phillips as an example of the martyr-reformer. For Theodore Weld, Phillips's fate was a necessary consequence of his commitment to reform.

Great moral reforms are all born of soul-travail. . . . They compel desperate struggles to wrench out false principles embedded in public sentiment. . . . To this the reformer had to undergo pains, traversing, exploring, sifting, testing, etc. The reformer must set himself apart, its sacred devotee baptized into its spirit, consecrated to necessity.[28]

Such an image of the martyr-reformer emerged again later in the midst of the Progressive Era. In a centennial address before the Woodberry Society of New York, which was committed to urban reform issues, George Edward Woodberry declared: "There is one lesson that blazes from Phillips' memory —the principle of sacrifice as an integral element in normal life. . . . He gave all . . . in order that the unfortunate might be less miserable. . . . A life of daily sacrifice. This is, as it were, our baptismal night."[29]

Specific reform groups even used this image of the martyr-reformer as an ideological device for their interests. Former abolitionists compared Phillips to John Brown and William L. Garrison.[30] Blacks incorporated his image into their struggle for emancipation and equality.[31] Julia Ward Howe, a famous figure in the women's suffrage movement, declared in a commemorative address that she had come to praise the strength of a helper and deliverer like Wendell Phillips.[32] Social Gospel clergymen such as the Reverend Minot J. Savage regarded Phillips's sacrificial life as an example of modern martyrdom that would promote, through commitment to reform and welfare, the kingdom of God.[33] A Christian Socialist such as Charles Edward Russell added his voice to that of many prominent labor leaders, especially among the Knights of Labor, who viewed Phillips as one who had "made his life one long sacrifice on the altar of righteousness."[34] Prominent Bostonians who had dissociated themselves from Phillips during his life glorified him as an example of local idealism after his death.[35]

Thus, Phillips's commitment to a better future and his enduring struggle against the existing order endowed him with the potential for becoming a celebrated martyr reformer. His deep devotion to the ideal of democracy and his religious faith made him an acceptable figure in the context of the American national consciousness. He himself aspired to martyrdom, and his close friends and admirers elevated his memory to the mythical realm of saints and martyrs. Nevertheless, despite all these attributes, he did not become a second Lincoln in the eyes of most Americans, and later generations did not view him as a national martyr figure. The reason seems trivial: Wendell Phillips lacked a tragic death to create the drama of a martyred figure. Without a battle of the last stand, without trial or scaffold, without a catastrophic end, the public did not share emotionally the sacrifice of Wendell Phillips. His description as a living martyr—who sacrificed his daily life to the cause—made sense to various reform groups in the Progressive Era but had no emotional appeal to the public in general.

The nature of Phillips's reform activities also denied him a universal crown of martyrdom. He agitated on behalf of blacks, workers, women, Chinese, Irish, Jews, prisoners, prohibitionists, deprived children, prostitutes, historical monuments, and many more. He fought against the constitution of the United States, Boston gentlemen, Southern slaveholders, plutocrats, noncommitted intellectuals, Protestant clergymen, police officers, municipal politicians, and presidents of the United States, among others. Such a profusion of reform objects and plethora of foes blurred Phillips's martyr image. The very diversity of his reform activities meant that he did not have a homogeneous body of devoted followers who might use his image as an ideological weapon and publicize it among apathetic members of American society.

Phillips's figure, however, was significant to various reformers in the

Progressive Era. In fact, his career as a pluralistic reformer seemed to anticipate the heterogeneity of reform activities from 1880 to 1920. Those who celebrated martyrdom for the cause of reform used his figure as an inspirational model; those who rejected sacrifice but affirmed commitment to improvement and progress also regarded him as a revered figure. Overall, he provided a bridge between the early and the late phases of reform and his emphasis on the martyr tradition was later echoed by certain Progressive reformers in the twentieth century.

Among the diverse reformers who affiliated themselves with the Progressive movement some particularly devoted individuals used the concept of martyrdom as part of their reform ideology. Socially oriented intellectuals, especially those who were closely related to reform movements such as the Knights of Labor, the Christian Socialists, and the Social Gospel, resorted to the martyr tradition when explaining their commitment to reform. These individuals fought to purge American society of corruption and greed, as representatives of all the good, moral, and democratic values of America.

George E. McNeill, for example, the chief propagandist and organizer for the Bay States Knights of Labor, occasionally used martyrdom as an ideological device. Himself an ex-abolitionist and of Puritan origin, he argued that the human mission was to fight "the ancient foe of *Mammon Priest* who tempted the nation to sin for gold against the Indian, the Negro, and the worker." Until his death in 1906 he conceived of himself as a servant of God, making whatever effort he could to build the earthly heaven in the New World. He was engaged in labor reforms as a newspaper editor, historian, statistician for the Massachusetts Bureau of Statistics of Labor, labor organizer, and executive of certain industrial reform groups.[36] Together with famous labor reformers such as Henry George and Terence Powderly, McNeill edited *The Labor Movement: The Problem of Today*, in which he wrote in 1887 that there was still hope for a peaceful solution based on Christ's example, rather than a violent conflict between the plutocrats and the workers.[37] After the collapse of the Knights of Labor as a workers' reform movement McNeill turned to a general quest for the millennium and used the concept of martyrdom in order to give meaning in the apparent failure of the labor movement. He also imitated Wendell

Phillips by joining many reform crusades and agitating for any oppressed group in the United States and beyond.[38]

While the martyr theme was only latent in the rhetoric of a labor reformer like McNeill, other labor sympathizers developed this theme more explicitly. Their desire for martyrdom derived in part from their abhorrence of worldly success and in part from a deep contempt toward what they regarded as the anti-Christian world of the competitive economy. The most prominent group of such reformers was the Christian Socialists. They perceived themselves as Christ's disciples who, in spite of the present failure of the Knights of Labor, would keep alive the holy war against the plutocrats on behalf of the deprived workers.

The Christian Socialists believed that as disciples of Christ they had to follow the Nazarene's example of earthly failure as a means of regenerating the people. They looked forward to their cross and were convinced that progress had resulted only from the efforts of a creative minority. In the Boston area the first Christian Socialist clergyman was the Reverend Jesse Jones. A Congregationalist minister influenced by the fundamentalism of Charles Grandison Finney, he was obsessed by millennial fervor. He always expressed an intense moral zeal to fight for the Lord as a Christian soldier, yearned to bear a personal cross, and was fascinated with the story of John Brown. After the collapse of the slavocracy he regarded the plutocracy as the unregenerated. "Wall Street and all that belongs with it surely will be cast down into the bottomless pit forever," he argued.[39]

In 1871 Jesse Jones published a popular theological book entitled *The Kingdom of Heaven,* in which he attempted to prove that the United States was identical to the kingdom of Heaven. Among other characteristics he noted: "The fundamental idea of the Kingdom of Heaven is self-sacrifice. That also is our national idea."[40] He regarded reform as the means by which the United States would come closer to full realization of its eschatological mission:

With steady flow and irresistible sweep, our nation is to move forward on its present line of progress, thrusting out from itself one evil after another, and incorporating into its organic law one principle of the Kingdom after another, until at last it becomes the complete, harmonious, symmetrical, perfect embodiment of them all.[41]

Two years later Jones repeated most of his ideas in another book, *The Bible Plan for the Abolition of Poverty and the New Political Economy Therein.* He claimed that Americans had supplanted the Hebrews as God's Chosen People in the modern age, and to complete their appointed mission of democratizing the world they must abolish poverty by sharing their wealth in common. Once established as a Christian society, America would stimulate other nations to follow its example. Then the Messiah would return as religious and secular leader of the world to terminate the woes of history and begin the glory of the millennium.[42]

By 1890 Jones's radicalism had so angered his North Abington congregation that it refused to renew his contract. "Perhaps in all the land," he wrote, "there is not a pulpit open to me." Viewing his life as similar to that of Jesus Christ, Jones embraced personal failure in the present as a means of redeeming mankind in the future. In 1907 he published a semifictional autobiography entitled *Joshua Davidson Christian: The Story of the Life of One, Who in the Nineteenth Century, "Was Like Unto Christ" as Told by His Body Servant.* The hero of this book, a descendant of Jews and Puritans, preached communism and pentacostal society and won the love of the poor. Finally a lynch-mad mob of workers led by capitalists killed him. They hanged Joshua and turned him into a modern martyr.[43]

Jesse Jones remained a relatively insignificant figure even to the Christian Socialist movement. A more important figure was an Episcopalian minister, William Dwight Porter Bliss, who in 1899 founded The *Dawn,* the movement's official paper. Aside from mundane obligations like editing *The New Encyclopedia of Social Reform,* Bliss found time to write about the ideal of martyrdom. In some of his writings he identified himself with John Ball, the English priest who had been crucified for preaching "medieval Christian socialism" in the peasants' revolt of 1381.[44] This quest for sacrifice repeated itself in a nostalgic way when in 1922 Bliss recorded with pleasure how suffering went hand in hand with his social-reform activities, how he and his wife had endured loneliness and poverty.[45] The violent strikes of the 1880s and the 1890s provided radical ministers like Bliss with proof of their apocalyptic visions. The spread of the slums, the Haymarket Affair, the Depression of 1893, Coxey's Army, the Populist uprising—all these suggested to him that Americans were fast approaching the Day of Judgment. Bliss reasoned that America had been desecrated by the original sin of plutocracy but it could turn back to God's way. The church therefore had a special mission to lead the people to salvation, by purging them of the capitalistic sin and preparing them to live like brothers in the earthly kingdom of God.[46]

Not all liberal clergymen who belonged to the Social Gospel movement embraced radical activism against the plutocrats. Not all of them identified money with sin. Yet, by calling upon every clergyman and layman to fulfill a divine duty through social service to the poor, the liberal ministers embraced the ideal of altruistic sacrifice. Many of them rejected the inevitability of martyrdom in a divine eschatology, but they welcomed martyrs who sacrificed their whole career to social justice and the elimination of poverty. Social martyrdom rather than cosmic martyrdom was for the Social Gospel ministers the path for redemption within history.

The best-known reform clergyman who advocated continual sacrifice and viewed himself as a social martyr was George D. Herron. Born in Montezuma, Indiana, on January 21, 1862, and growing up in a very religious atmosphere, he considered himself a modern disciple of Christ. After studying at a theological seminary, Herron was appointed to a congregation in Burlington, Iowa, and began to preach the Social Gospel message. He asserted that Jesus' message to everyman was to sacrifice himself by doing service to others. "We ought to suffer with our brothers, we are bound to expiate what is evil in the past," he wrote. "Our faith may, and it must, make future out of the past, through making the present a holy gift and sacrifice to progress which is the coming of the Kingdom of God."[47] Herron proclaimed his personal quest for martyrdom, stating that "I go to witness to the righteousness of society and the nation. . . . I go to suffer for the truth and the name of Christ."[48]

In 1893 Herron received a teaching position in the Department of Applied Christianity at Iowa College which became a symbolic center for the Social Gospel movement during the 1890s. By preaching extremely radical arguments against the existing establishment of the college, he alienated himself even from Progressive supporters and started upon the path of martyrdom that he had deliberately chosen for himself. Soon professors in the college were outraged by the radical tone of Herron's preaching and decided to expel him from the school.

Herron expressed the core of his ideas in eight lectures that he gave in Chicago between October 24 and December 12, 1898, to the Christian Citizenship League. He published these lectures in his most famous book, *Between Caesar and Christ*. The main theme in all the lectures was the importance of constant sacrifice for the redemption of society. In "Tragedy and Economic Problems," for example, Herron argued that "our social wrongs carry in themselves the seeds of their own regeneracy. Our economic evils are vital with the elements of their own redemption."[49] Such a deterministic yet optimistic view called for permanent service and suffering by confronting the existing evils of the system, thereby promoting its salvation. Herron characterized the modern martyrs who would be the agents of redemption in history in his lecture "The Social Sacrifice of Conscience." They belonged to "the brave and self-denying men and women who associate themselves in co-operative enterprises and colonies, or who group themselves in social settlements in order to concentrate their efforts or to educate the people by illustrating social principles."[50] He interpreted many Progressive endeavors as sacrificial acts aimed at fighting evil through personal service. "There is no ascending into heaven, save through descending into hell," he declared.[51] "Redemption through the gutters" was the only true reform according to Herron. "It is only those who toil and endure with their brethren, in the thick of wrong and struggle with which society travails, who will furnish the sympathy and dynamic able to bring forth redemption and freedom."[52]

Since Herron's ideal was social martyrdom fulfilled by a sacrificial life, he viewed the Christian martyrs as social reformers. They did not have any superhuman characteristics, did not witness divine truths, and had no cosmic role in the millennium. Herron depicted them as unyielding fighters against social wrong who always engaged themselves in the battle to improve their society: "When the historian pierces the mystic halo religious romance has gathered about these days of sanctity and martyrdom, we find the early Christian heroes involved like ourselves, learning wisdom through folly and failure, entering peace out of great pain."[53] In Herron's view reformers and martyrs were merely two names for the same thing. He reduced reformers to those who lived sacrificial lives for others whatever the concrete goal of their reform. He viewed martyrs only in their social context as those who struggled against the evil of their society to redeem it from sins and bring the kingdom of God to earth. Martyrs had neither individual qualities apart from their social context nor any cosmic role.

Throughout his lectures Herron preferred living martyrdom to the sacrifice that ended in a tragic death. He devalued the significance of death since he focused only upon social martyrdom and rejected attaching any mythical or symbolic meaning to the martyred figure. "It is not mere material sacrifice or a physical martyrdom that is required," declared Herron.

If it were only that how easy and joyful would be the sacrifice! Who cares for poverty, for the stake, for the fire, the dungeon, the gallows or the rack, if that were all. . . . But . . . in order to save others . . . in order to make possible better human future, he [the Christian reformer] must literally take part in the sins and oppression of the present. It is by this daily spiritual dying . . . by this hourly crucifixion of all one's ideals . . . that the social problem brings unique significance and suffering to the Christian conscience.[54]

Devotion to unpleasant and hard work, living in the slums, suffering with the poor and underprivileged—this was the only path for a Christian reformer in Herron's view.

Reformers like Jesse Jones, William Dwight Porter Bliss, and George D. Herron portrayed themselves as martyrs for the cause, but nobody else viewed them as martyrs. Their importance to my subject does not lie in their personal fate but rather in the way they articulated the martyr tradition within the American political culture. They revealed in their speeches and writing the central place of the concept of martyrdom in the rhetoric of middle-class reformers who viewed themselves both as Christians and as progressive Americans. By combining religious imagery, national ideology, and a commitment to reform they perceived themselves as "suffering servants" destined to reform their people and rededicate America to its mission as a redeemer nation. Such rhetoric helped to keep alive the early tradition of martyrdom and to foster the image of figures such as Abraham Lincoln and John Brown as national martyrs whose example should be followed by any progressive reformer.

Professional clergymen were not the only ones to praise the ideals of sacrifice and martyrdom when they advocated social reform. Laymen reformers also used such religious categories when they had to confront social, political, and economic problems. Some of the so-called muckrakers grew up under the influence of Christian pietism and certainly used religious symbols in their fight to correct their society. Writing about his childhood, S. S. McClure, the founder of *McClure's Magazine*—the chief muckraking journal of the Progressive Era—remembered that there had been only three books in his home: the Bible, *Pilgrim's Progress,* and Foxe's *Book of Martyrs*. Ida Tarbel, Jane Addams, George Mead, and Woodrow Wilson, all central figures in the Progressive movement, shared similar childhood environments of religious pietism. Both Jane Addams and Ida Tarbel wrote that for them Lincoln's death had been an event that had fused their religious ethics with the concrete American experience.[55] Upton

Sinclair, even when he had joined the Socialist party, never abandoned his old religious vision. In his *Autobiography* he stated, "I count myself among the followers of Jesus of Nazareth. His example has meant to me more than any other man, and all the experiences of my revolutionary life have brought me nearer to him."[56]

Frank Parsons was a reformer intellectual who deliberately chose the path of daily sacrifice in order to reform society. A brilliant student who came from an upper-middle-class New Jersey family, he had a promising future. A graduate with many awards from Cornell University and a lawyer at the age of twenty-six, he combined legal work with scholarly achievement. In the 1880s he gave up scholarship for its own sake and became a committed reformer. In 1892 he was appointed to the Law School of Boston University. He wrote many books on political economy and expressed his reform ideas in a vast number of pamphlets, newspaper articles, magazines, speeches, and reports. He joined the staff of Kansas State Agricultural College in 1897 because of its populist and liberal policy. Parsons was dismissed from the conservative Boston College and then helped to organize the Ruskin College of Social Science and the Oxford Movement in America. He became interested in settlement-house projects and organized in 1905 the Breadwinner's College in Boston's North End slums. Frank Parsons advocated many concrete reform measures such as the eight-hour day, slum clearance, public works projects, cooperatives, municipal and national ownership of public utilities, women's suffrage, initiative, referendum and recall, direct primaries, a progressive income tax, and elastic currency.[57]

When he died in 1908 at the age of fifty-four, his Progressive friends mourned his death as a serious loss to the reform movement and depicted him as a martyr-reformer.[58] "Every earnest scholar respected him," noted Edwin D. Mead, the editor of the *New England Magazine*. "We can none of us afford to forget easily the lesson of a scholar's life so simple and unselfish, so untiring and devoted. . . . He was a 'worker together with God' in the long and painful process of transforming human society on this old earth of ours into some sort of reflection and bailiwick of the kingdom of God."[59]

A very eloquent eulogy to Parsons came from Benjamin Orange Flower, the editor of the *Arena*. Himself a reformer intellectual, Flower expressed a Christlike desire to sacrifice his fortune, well-being, and reputation, in order to serve others.[60] Reacting to Parsons's early death he wrote:

He turned his back upon positions of honor and power . . . to serve the nation by popular education and awakening a sleeping people.. . . He fell in the very prime of life; fell with his armour on, battling against greed, corruption and egoism and for truth, justice, freedom and fraternity.[61]

He described in the *Arena* how contemporary America resembled ancient Rome prior to the appearance of Christ. He first portrayed the decadent life of the Roman Empire and then showed how Jesus had appeared in the middle of the decay and saved the world by his martyrdom. Flower ended the story of Christ with a picture of America yearning for its revival.[62]

Two European figures provided Flower with examples of the value of social martyrdom. Of John Ruskin, the British philanthropist and economic reformer, Flower wrote that he was one of civilization's redeemers. He described in detail how Ruskin had disposed of three quarters of his inheritance and given everything he had to the poor.[63] Victor Hugo, the French novelist who wrote about the lives of the poor and who experienced exile himself, was Flower's other example of social martyrdom. He defined Hugo as a noble worker for a better day, one who could not live for himself and felt he must give to others. Flower quoted Hugo's statement from his exile and defined them as words of fire:

Sacrifice to the mob O poet? Sacrifice to that unfortunate . . . despairing mob; sacrifice to it . . . thy repose, thy fortune, thy joy, thy country, thy liberty, thy life. . . . The mob is the greatest victim of darkness. . . . Sacrifice to it thy gold, and thy blood and thy thought and thy love. . . . Sacrifice to it everything except justice. . . . Alas! it suffers so much and it knows nothing. Correct it, warn it, instruct it, guide it, train it.[64]

Intellectuals like Benjamin Flower, Frank Parsons, and Upton Sinclair incorporated martyrdom into their reform ideology. Like Wendell Phillips, but without his abolitionist's history, they viewed sacrifice to the cause of reform as essential to achieving their goal of reform. Yet unlike the abolitionists they emphasized only the social significance of martyrdom. They placed little value on the uniqueness of the martyr as an individual who had received divine revelation and did not refer to any cosmic context that might turn the reformer into a mythical redeemer. They depicted a human being who would help to bring about the kingdom of God on earth by constant sacrifice to reform and preferred the concrete realm of American society to the abstract realm of universal metaphysics. They glorified the martyr in his life rather than through his death and in that sense did not deviate from the American liberal tradition that viewed life as the supreme value, superior to any kind of glorious death. A sacrificial life, the daily consecration of life to reform was conceived by them as the ultimate ideal.

Progressives also differed from the abolitionists in the concrete meaning that they gave to sacrifice for reform. Abolitionists extolled individuals who sacrificed their lives while fighting the existing forces of an evil establishment. Some Progressive individuals revered such martyrs but generally stressed another kind of sacrifice: they glorified and admired those individuals who sacrificed their lives by living with the mob, serving the deprived and poor, and renouncing their status in order to uplift the down-trodden and ignorant masses. These figures were the martyrs of reform to many Progressives, more than those who openly fought the existing evil establishment.

Although some Progressive reformers praised martyrs for the cause in their rhetoric, the period between 1880 and 1918 did not produce a national martyr for their movement comparable to John Brown or Abraham Lincoln. Even as an ideal, the concept of martyrdom was not as central to all Progressive reformers as it had been to the abolitionists. Certain factors rooted in the cultural context of the Progressive period undermined the ideal of martyrdom as an ideological device. Leading intellectuals of the nineteenth century, such as Ralph Waldo Emerson, Henry David Thoreau, Herman Melville and Walt Whitman, had viewed martyrs as part of their ideal and normative world. Thus they had added their voices to the abolitionists' glorification of martyrdom and even used their own talent in order to lend additional, more universal, meaning to such a concept. Poets such as Longfellow, Whittier, and Lowell, and even the early William D. Howells, had joined Emerson and Thoreau in building the martyred image of John Brown. Herman Melville and Walt Whitman had defined Lincoln as the American national martyr and thus endowed his tragic death with universal meaning. On the other hand, leading intellectuals of the Progressive Era, like William James, Oliver W. Holmes, Josiah Royce, or George Santayana, were indifferent and sometimes even hostile toward anyone who used martyrdom as an ideological device. None of these intellectuals opposed reform. They were even engaged in various reform issues in their own fields. Their negative attitude toward martyrdom was not part of a conservative position that suspected any change. It was part of a shared world view imbedded in progressive thought that can be defined as pragmatism.

The long career of Oliver W. Holmes exemplified the transformation of an enthusiastic supporter of abolitionism into a pragmatic reformer in the Progressive Era. From being a young admirer of the abolitionists who shared their quest for martyrdom, he turned into an open enemy of those who embraced the martyr spirit. In his voluminous correspondence with the British reform leader Harold Laski, he expressed this attitude again and again.[65] "I do despise a martyr," Holmes wrote. "He is a pigheaded adherent of an inadequate idea."[66] Later, when Laski became the leader of radical reform in England, Holmes supported his concrete policy but added some warnings at the end of his letter: "The only thing that I am competent to say from the experience of my youth is that I fear your getting into the frame of mind that I saw in the Abolitionists, (and shared)—the martyr spirit. It is apt to be wrongheaded."[67] In a letter to a friend and colleague, Sir Frederick Pollock, a distinguished British legal scholar, Holmes explained why the martyr spirit was so false and dangerous. "The Abolitionist had a stock of phrases that a man was either a knave or a fool who did not act as they (the Abolitionists) *knew* to be right. So Calvin thought of Catholics and Catholics of Calvin. So I don't doubt . . . [that] when you know that you know persecution comes easy."[68]

This negative attitude toward the martyred hero was not only a personal obsession of Justice Holmes's. Many other intellectuals influenced by social Darwinism expressed new opinions about the structure of the cosmos, the morality of the universe, the meaning of suffering, the nature of truth, and the essence of religion. Implicitly they rejected martyrdom both as a fictitious idea and as an ethically wrong and misleading belief. A detailed analysis of the new cultural critique of Progressive intellectuals is beyond the scope of this work. However, a few famous examples from the most outstanding intellectuals of the period provide an illustration of these new cultural tendencies of the period.

Social Darwinsim shattered many of the religious beliefs of the nineteenth century. The Edenic myth, which required martyrs in order to regenerate the cosmos and redeem mankind, had no place in the Darwinistic paradigm. Darwin's theory reduced man to mere biology and thus deprived him of a divine connection. It portrayed a world constantly moving toward improvement without a start or end, thus repudiating the whole mechanism of creation, sin, fall, sacrifice, and redemption.

Progressive intellectuals had diverse opinions concerning the social implications of Darwinist theory although, in general, they welcomed the fact that after Darwin the old genteel tradition had begun to crumble. As we have seen, under the genteel tradition the concept of martyrdom had explained suffering in the context of a moral universe. Insofar as the martyr had a redemptive purpose that would fulfill itself in the future, his present suffering was conceived to be part of a moral order. However, this view of martyrdom not only gave meaning to suffering, turning it into sacrifice for an altruistic ideal; it also rationalized the very phenomenon of suffering. Any tragedy that befell an innocent figure was interpreted as some form of sacrifice, making the tragedy appropriate and necessary. Progressive thinkers, on the other hand, refused to rationalize suffering. They searched for ways to minimize its existence and reduce its effectiveness. Hence, they had no place for martyred heroes and "suffering servants" and refused to turn an individual tragedy into a happy event by rendering the victim a martyr and his suffering a sacrifice. "When the genteel tradition forbids people to confess that they are unhappy . . . imagination is driven for comfort into abstract," argued George Santayana in a lecture at the University of California in 1911.[69] He praised William James who broke "the illegitimate monopoly which the genteel tradition had established over what ought to be assumed and what ought to be hoped for.[70]

Josiah Royce discussed the issue of suffering in his famous essay "The Problem of Job." He stated his objection to the traditional explanation, which viewed evil as a necessary part of a divine and moral order, designed to redeem the guilty and wicked by the sacrifice of the innocent and righteous. For Royce suffering was both human and divine. It was part of life, but conscious and free-willed individuals could reduce its influence.

The knowing of the good, in the higher sense, depends upon contemplating the overcoming and subordination of a less significant impulse, which survives even in order that it should be subordinated. . . . You can never clean the world of evil; but you can subordinate evil. The justification of the presence in the world of the morally evil becomes apparent to us mortals only in so far as this evil is overcome and condemned. It exists only that it may be cast down.[71]

Such an argument affirmed commitment to reform by fighting evil and reducing its existence without any rationalization of suffering. The holy mission of the martyr-reformer defined to create a perfect world and to abolish suffering in the future—which served as a rationale for his suffering in the present—was unacceptable to many Progressive thinkers.

Under the influence of pragmatism, the idea of sacrifice was criticized rather than praised. William James wrote in *Varieties of Religious Experience* that pessimistic religions took a moment of evil and woe as a gifted moment that would lead the sufferer to salvation through absorption in the supernatural good. But for him the suffering had no value per se. Everything had to be valued according to its result. "The value of saintliness is tested by its effects and what they add to human life. Purity unbalanced by social responsibility leads to selfish withdrawal from useful life."[72] William James regarded truth as dependent upon personal action rather than an absolute. He rejected the existence of an absolute truth and consequently did not believe that some gifted individuals could witness an absolute truth that would determine their activities and their fate. Precisely the lack of an absolute truth required every human being to take responsibility for his actions, according to James. "We stand on a mountain pass in the midst of whirling snow and blinding mist, through which we get glimpses now and then of paths which may be deceptive," he wrote in *The Will To Believe*. "If we stand still we shall be frozen to death. If we take the wrong road we shall be dashed to pieces. We do not certainly know whether there is any right one. What must we do? 'Be strong and of a good courage,' act for the best, hope for the best, and take what comes. . . . If death ends all we cannot meet death better."[73] Such advice was contrary to the example presented by the martyr, who knew the right road and deliberately chose death as a result of this knowledge.

In general, a culture influenced by social Darwinism and pragmatism was less receptive to the idea of martyrdom than a culture that reflected transcendentalism and the genteel tradition. Therefore, many Progressive reformers avoided using the concept of martyrdom as a central ideological weapon and even those who glorified sacrifice restricted it to the social realm of one's life career, rather then to the mythical realm of an after-life.

In addition to this intellectual climate, the political, economic, and social context of the period between 1880 and 1918 was relatively calm. There was no galvanizing event such as the Civil War to create martyrs out of individual reformers. On the surface, the period of Progressive activities (1896–1918) was one of peace, progress, and prosperity. Although in fact the peace was interrupted by the Spanish American War, progress proved to be a setback to large segments of American society, and prosperity was unevenly divided, on the national level the Progressive period was without traumatic catastrophes. Consequently, without a baptism of blood the whole reform impulse had only limited emotional significance. If some reformers suffered to some extent for their reform purpose, this suffering could not become nationally meaningful in a time of peace and prosperity. This period ended in April 1918, when the United States entered the First World War. Many historians regard this event as a turning point that killed the Progressive reform movement and ended in the fiasco of the 1920s. Yet, the short period of the war unexpectedly turned some famous Progressive figures, such as Jane Addams, Randolph Bourne, and even President Woodrow Wilson, into martyrs.

When the United States entered World War I in order to make the world safe for democracy, most Americans enthusiastically embraced this crusade. Many reformers viewed it as another progressive enterprise aimed at democratizing European governments and ending once and for all secret diplomacy, military imperialism, and international warfare. Those reformers who, like Jane Addams and Randolph Bourne, opposed this intervention in the war, suddenly found themselves being condemned by their society as unpatriotic and defeatist.

Jane Addams was probably the most renowned Progressive reformer. Aside from Theodore Roosevelt and Woodrow Wilson, both presidents, only Addams became a national and even international figure. Deeply involved in many reform activities, she was a well-informed activist and publicist for the causes of progressive education, housing reform, child-labor legislation, criminology, labor, direct democracy, feminism, fair treatment of immigrants, and more. The epitome of her work was the founding of Hull House in Chicago in 1889, the pioneer social settlement where well-known social reformers lived as residents and worked with the population of the city slums. Jane Addams worked in this large settlement, leading many reform groups and engaging in active social work. She helped poor people by advocating many welfare laws such as the first juvenile court law and the first "mothers' pensions" law, tenement house regulation, an eight-hour working day for women, factory inspection, and workmen's compensation. She was the first woman president of the National Conference of Social Work (1910) and took an active part in the Progressive presidential campaign of Theodore Roosevelt in 1912. A well-known pacifist, Jane Addams chaired the International Congress of Women at the Hague in the Netherlands in 1915, and thereafter the Women's International League for Peace and Freedom, of which she became president. She was the co-winner of the Nobel Peace Prize in 1931, four years before her death at the age of seventy-five.

Born into a pietistic Protestant family, Addams grew up in the religious atmosphere of a midwestern upper-middle-class home. After graduating from Rockford College she entered the Women's Medical College of Philadelphia, but her health failed and she realized that she would never be able to become a mother and wife. She therefore left school and decided to devote her life to social reform. It was probably inevitable that people should call her a saint—a woman who sacrificed herself to the welfare of the wretched masses. She was often compared to St. Francis of Assisi, and some people even called her Saint Jane.[74]

But Jane Addams herself had no taste for self-sacrifice. She approached her career with a matter-of-fact attitude, struggling to achieve her various goals, aiming to reduce suffering but not to sacrifice herself for it. She worked rather than fought, tried to convince others, rather than confront them, and longed for understanding and sympathy rather than for a "crown of thorns." Jane Addams shared the idealism of the abolitionists without their quest for martyrdom. In that sense she was well suited to the pragmatic atmosphere of her time.[75] Historian Christopher Lasch noted that the experience of being almost alone, tempted her more than once to self-pity, and at times, made her wish for martyrdom. But "the way in which she wrestled with these . . . dangers was in many ways her finest achievement."[76]

James Weber Lynn, Jane Addams's first biographer, noted with mixed feelings that she had not played the role of a Progressive John Brown.

Let one attain victory or martyrdom and his fame was secure; but the middle road of tolerance, sympathy, compromise, had often led into oblivion. Only by crucifixion did Jesus of Nazareth become the Christ of millions. Galileo is remembered not as a scholar but for a conviction of a single phrase 'e pur si mouve.' . . . The North triumphed and Lincoln was assassinated, therefore, and not only because he was Lincoln, is he our Great American.[77]

Then the biographer, sensitive to the spirit of his time, continued:

It is possible that the times are slowly changing. It is possible that moderation, tolerance, the desire rightly to understand and interpret human society are becoming articles of our American creed. If so, then Jane Addams has been a force; if the national imagination has actually been stirred to an interest in understanding, then history cannot ignore Jane Addams.[78]

When, however, America entered the Great War in 1917, Jane Addams experienced agony and suffering, which for a short period turned her into a martyr for peace. In her lecture "Peace and Bread in Time of War," she used the notion of self-sacrifice to explain her lonely stand against the majority of Americans. She portrayed herself as part of a moral vanguard who knew the truth and were thus subjected to harassment and hatred. "We could not, however, lose the conviction that . . . moral change in human affairs may also begin with a differing group or individual, some-times with the one who at best is designated as a crank and freak and in sterner moments is imprisoned as an atheist or a traitor." She described her struggle as a fight against the establishment and compared her fate to that of many other martyrs. "To this an estimated nine million people can bear witness who have been burned as witches and heretics, not by mobs, . . . but by order of ecclesiastical and civil courts." Yet even at that time of wrath, when Addams suffered for her pacifist ideas, and all of her friends and supporters deserted her, she stopped short of a glorification of sacrifice.

We . . . have none of the internal contentment of the doctrinaire, the ineffable solace of the self-righteous which was imputed to us. . . . Perhaps we suffered from the fact that we were no longer living in a period of dogma and were therefore in no position to announce our sense of security![79]

Precisely because Jane Addams was so rooted in the spirit of pragmatism, she lacked the conviction that made John Brown so calm and self-assertive in prison. Since she could no longer use martyrdom as a rationale for her fate, her situation during the war was especially tragic. Nevertheless, Addams admitted that the martyr figure who had witnessed some inner truth that made him aloof from his present situation, served her as an inspirational model when all her friends and followers deserted her.

We were well aware that the modern liberal, having come to conceive truth of a kind which must vindicate itself in practice, finds it hard to hold even a sincere and mature opinion which from the very nature of things can have no justification in works. . . . It therefore came about that ability to hold out against mass suggestion, to honestly differ from the convictions and enthusiasms of one's best friends, did in moments of crisis come to depend upon the categorical belief that a man's primary allegiance is to his vision of the truth and that he is under obligation to affirm it.[80]

After the war, when most Americans regarded the whole intervention as unnecessary and tragic, Addams regained her friends and her status. In that sense her martyrdom was temporary. This was not the case for another

Progressive who resisted the war—Randolph Bourne. He died at the end of the war at the young age of thirty-two. To many ex-Progressive intellectuals of the 1920s, he became the real martyr of the whole reform experience; the martyr who sealed with his death the old prewar "innocent" America. Randolph Bourne was far less known than Jane Addams, confining his reform activities to the literary realm. An extremely talented writer, he worked as an independent columnist in liberal and progressive magazines like the *New Republic* and the *Dial*. Later in his life he joined the radical *Seven Arts*. Although he never participated in any specific reform movement, Bourne conceived of himself as a radical intellectual within the Progressive tradition. Consequently, only literary intellectuals viewed him later as a martyr for the dying Progressive movement.

Randolph Bourne certainly had the potential for being depicted as a martyr early in his life since, as a result of a birth defect, he was very deformed. Fully aware of the consequences of such physical deformity, he knew that he must give up love, marriage, and family. In his article "The Handicap," full of autobiographical elements, he argued for a more sympathetic attitude toward the despised and ignored of society. Yet in his essays Bourne valued sacrifice as a way of living a meaningful life rather than dying a heroic death. The need, according to Bourne, was to learn to live, not to die, to be teachers and creators, not destroyers. As a spokesman of the younger generation he called for a new inspiration for American youth. He wrote that "the young radical today is not asked to be a martyr, but a thinker, an intellectual leader. So far as the official radicals deprecate such an enterprise they make their movement sterile."[81]

When the United States entered the war, Bourne viewed this as a tragic event that would unleash the aggressive instinct of the nation and would impose homogeneity on American pluralism. He could not compromise with such a belief and refused to support Wilson's decision to intervene in Europe. Moreover, he believed that it was his duty "to prevent the war from passing into the popular mythology as a holy crusade."[82]

By standing openly against the war when American soldiers were battling in Europe, Bourne encountered much hostility. Many viewed him as a traitor. In reaction to Bourne's antiwar essays, the *Wall Street Journal* threatened that "we are now at war and the militant pacifists are earnestly reminded that there is no shortage of hemp or lamppost."[83] The *New Republic* restricted Bourne's commentaries on the war to his book reviews and the chief editors of this liberal magazine decided to terminate Bourne's role as a major contributor. John Dewey, who had viewed Bourne as his most gifted student, openly opposed his position. In an essay entitled "Conscience and Compulsion," which appeared in the *New Republic*, Dewey suggested that it was better for the conscientious intellectual to join with the forces that moved toward democratization of the world than to play conscientious martyrs. "Then will conscience itself have compulsive power instead of being forever the martyred and coerced."[84]

Randolph Bourne replied to this criticism in two articles—"Conscience and Intelligence of War," which appeared in the *Dial*, and "The Twilight of Idols," which appeared in the short-lived magazine, the *Seven Arts*. In the second article especially, Bourne departed from Dewey and from all that he represented. He argued in the essay that antiwar sentiment was a realistic reaction to this specific war, a reaction that neither welcomed martyrdom, nor wished such a sentiment to be attached to it.[85]

Nonetheless, during the war Bourne became a martyr for his ideas, despite his personal reluctance to bear such a title. His antiwar opinions caused him a certain kind of personal suffering. The split with Dewey prevented him from obtaining any academic position, and magazines for which he wrote banned his publications or went out of business. To a friend in France, Bourne wrote:

I feel very much secluded from the world, very much out of touch with my time. . . . The magazines which I wrote for die violent deaths, and all my thoughts seem unprintable. If I start to write on public matters I discover that my ideas are seditious, and if I start to write a novel, I discover that my outlook is immoral if not obscene.[86]

Nevertheless, Randolph Bourne started to work on his autobiography. A month later he died of pneumonia, just a few days before the official end of the First World War. Such a coincidence provided the background for the Bourne legend created by intellectuals of the twenties.

Since he had died before the end of the war, Bourne could be depicted as its victim. Moreover, his few literary friends viewed him as a martyr for the whole innocent generation of Progressive reformers who believed that they could change their world. "He was our bannerman of values in the general collapse," stated his friend Paul Rosenfeld.[87] "A tiny twisted unscared ghost in a black cloak . . . crying out in a shrill soundless giggle 'war is the hell of the state,' " wrote John Dos Passos in his book *1919*.[88] James Oppenheim, the editor of *Seven Arts*, dedicated a poem to Bourne's memory in which he portrayed him as a universal martyr for the whole age:

Bitter-sweet and Northwest wind
To sing his requiem
Who was
Our age
And who becomes
An imperishable symbol of our ongoing
For himself
He rose above his body
And came among us
Prophetic of the race
The great hater
Of the dark human deformity
Which is our dying world
Of the spirit of youth
Which is our future's seed . . .
Glimpse of awaited spring.[89]

To Van Wyck Brooks

he was the new America incarnate with that stamp of a sort of permanent youthfulness on his queer, twisted, appealing face. . . . He was a wanderer, the child of some nation yet unborn, smitten with an inappeasable nostalgia for Beloved Community. . . . It was the dream he had brought back from the bright future in which he lived, the dream he summoned us to realize.[90]

To the intellectuals of the lost generation Randolph Bourne became both a martyr for unachieved Progressive reforms, which had died in the war much as Bourne had, and the herald of a new culture free from the democratic mythology and its deceptive crusades. In that sense it was a very odd martyrdom—a sacrifice for something that was never realized. But for the intellectuals of the twenties, who viewed themselves as free from democratic and progressive illusions, such sacrifice for a negative purpose merited deep appreciation.

Over time Bourne's image accumulated some mythical elements. The story that he had died lonely and poor, hounded by the Justice Department, which had seized his manuscripts, was repeated in dozens of memoirs, several poems, and at least two novels. Most of these stories had little basis in fact and later biographies even denied his poverty and destitution, stressing his plan to marry the woman who loved him. As Carl Resek noted in the introduction to Bourne's war essays, the Bourne legend was a necessary part of the intellectual history of the twenties. "It has to do with the habit of seeing a creative artist as an outcast, a victim, at the best a martyr.

Bourne, with his bent back and twisted face, his death at the age of 32, seems to express it. Bourne himself rarely allowed himself this martyr image."[91]

There is no doubt that World War I provided a new context in which Progressive individuals could embrace martyrdom. To antiwar figures such as Jane Addams and Randolph Bourne, the war period created ample opportunity for suffering that might be interpreted as a sacrifice for an ultimate ideal. Progressive supporters of the war, like George Herron and Josiah Royce, used sacrificial rhetoric as an ideological weapon: Herron regarded Germany as the incarnation of Satanic forces and embraced sacrifice and martyrdom in the last battle, which would bring about the universal kingdom of God on earth.[92] Josiah Royce looked upon the war as a purging experience and extolled the nobility and purity that came from sacrifice for the cause on the battlefield.[93] All these individuals, whether they opposed or supported the war effort, were part of the Progressive reform tradition, which ended with the Great War, but none of them became a national martyr for a Progressive reform. Ironically, the only figure who might have approached national martyrdom was the man who initiated the intervention in the First World War—the Progressive president of the United States, Woodrow Wilson.

Woodrow Wilson reached the summit of his political career as president of the United States when he decided to enter World War I or in order to build a new world order based upon peaceful and democratic foundations. But in spite of the military victory Wilson did not achieve his purpose. The European allies, as well as American politicians refused to endorse his plan for peace and security. In 1918 and 1919 Wilson devoted most of his time and energy to making the world safe for democracy, but the world refused to cooperate, and even his compatriots rejected his peace initiative and stayed out of the League of Nations. The battle for ratification of the League and its tragic end turned Woodrow Wilson into the most well-known martyred figure of the time. In 1920, when the Republicans gained the presidential office, Woodrow Wilson was a defeated and broken idealist. Physically he died in 1924. Politically as well as psychologically, he was "killed" by the events of 1919. When he collapsed of exhaustion in his last unsuccessful effort to convince his nation to ratify the peace treaty, the whole Progressive and reform movement was already dead. His tragedy, however, was portrayed as the ultimate fate of an idealist who devoted his life to reform and many people believed that progressivism as a reform movement died with his failure.

Woodrow Wilson was born in Staunton, Virginia, on December 28, 1856. He grew up under the influence of stern Presbyterian religion. His father, Joseph, a minister of indomitable character and theological distinction, left a strong impression upon the character of the future president. Wilson's Christian ethics were shared by many Progressives who dealt with national affairs in religious and moralistic terms. In that sense he followed those reformers who continued to affirm the idealistic worldview of the genteel tradition.

Wilson's high idealism, together with a practical commitment to reform issues, characterized his activities as president of Princeton University and as governor of New Jersey. In both cases he firmly initiated reform, which he considered as both morally right and practically correct and efficient. He always had a magnetic influence on his devout supporters as well as uncompromising contempt for his many opponents. A Democratic candidate for the presidency, he was elected in 1912. His administration achieved many legislative reforms that went far toward creating a new social and economic order. During the First World War he first tried personal mediation to end the war and opposed American military intervention. He was elected to his second term in 1916 on a program of neutrality and peace. It was then that he decided to intervene on behalf of the Allies in order "to make the world safe for democracy." Wilson personally drafted the fourteen points for peace, and in 1919 he spent his time in Europe working to create a new world order. On June 28, 1919, the Versailles treaty with Germany was signed and the following day Wilson sailed back to the United States.

The strain of the peace conference affected the president's physical and mental strength. He was not well equipped to overcome his Republican opponents who, under the leadership of Henry Cabot Lodge, demanded some amendments as a condition for ratifying the treaty. Wilson refused to make any concessions and instead decided to embark upon a crusade on behalf of his original proposal. He set out on his western tour intending to meet with the people and to show the politicians that he had popular support for his uncompromising position. After thirty-four major addresses and scores of interviews, parades, and platform talks, his physical strength was drained. He was compelled to give up his tour in Pueblo, Colorado, on

September 25, 1919, and returned to Washington in a state of complete collapse. On October 2, he suffered a stroke that impaired the control of his brain over the left side of his body.

From that moment until the end of his administration Wilson was kept isolated from men and affairs by his wife and his physician. From his sickroom he denounced the Senate resolution to approve the treaty with reservations and refused to arrange any further compromise. He hoped to bring the issue to popular referendum in the election of 1920. Meanwhile, he twice urged his followers to vote against the ratification of the proposal incorporating reservations, and in March 1920 the Congress failed to provide the two-thirds vote necessary to ratify the resolution. The United States stayed out of the League of Nations. Wilson's hope for popular support proved false when the American people elected a Republican candidate in 1920 who ran under the slogan Back to Normalcy. Disappointed, sick, and embittered, he returned to private life. The legal and literary activities he had anticipated lay beyond his physical powers. On February 3, 1924, he died.

The period between his decision to go on his western tour and his death provided the arena for his martyrdom. Immediately after his death, close friends, popular biographers, political supporters, and literary admirers, embarked upon the task of portraying Wilson as a new martyred president. "World War I . . . sacrificed twenty-five years of his life upon the altar of his country and he went to his grave in all the pathos of martyrdom," declared Lucian Lamer Knight, a state historian of Georgia, in an address in Atlanta on February 10, 1924. "Men who were his friends yesterday became his enemies today. Some who hailed him 'Liberator' afterward asked 'Crucify him!' . . . and . . . as the ghost of Caesar marshalled the fields of Philippi, so the spirit of Woodrow Wilson will yet lead the world's democracy into a peace."[94] Many of Wilson's admirers claimed that precisely because he was so aloof, and could hardly cooperate with other human beings, he had probably experienced some superhuman relationship with divinity. In verse as well as in prose he was portrayed as a typical martyr bearing witness to a divine truth.[95] "He had worked tirelessly in solitude, had held himself inflexibly to his task," noted Bliss Perry, Wilson's colleague from Princeton. "It is the ancient story of heroes—and of martyrs."[96]

Even in a modern period that played down the necessity of suffering as part of the world order, Wilson's mythmakers heavily emphasized his quest for sacrifice.[97] Dr. Edwin Anderson Alderman, the president of the University of Virginia, who delivered a memorial address before the United States Congress, on December 25, 1924, stated that Wilson himself used to glorify sacrificial death. " 'We die but once, and we die without distinction if we are not willing to die the death of sacrifice' . . . and now he could of right claim the supreme distinction as his very own."[98] In a biography on Wilson Harold Garnett Black extolled the virtue of such suffering and sacrifice.

To be ready to suffer and die for duty and country and humanity—that is the supreme lesson that the race, as well as the individual must learn; for after all, the finest and noblest thing in our fragile mortal life is to sacrifice it, to throw it away for an ideal. . . . Just as the figure of Lincoln has grown greater, more luminous, and more revered with the flight of years, so will that of Woodrow Wilson.[99]

Wilson's admirers depicted him as a martyr neither for a specific group nor for the American nation, but rather as one who suffered vicariously for an unregenerated humanity.[100] "Wilson's fate was the familiar fate of the visionary," stated Bliss Perry in a commemorative tribute before the American Academy of Arts and Letters. "The old order of Europe, and America of 1919, were not ready for his gospel."[101] "History was to repeat itself," wrote Josephus Daniels, Wilson's secretary of the navy. "Always mankind has crucified its saviors."[102] Poetry was the best medium to express these tragic ties between an idealistic martyr and an undeserving humanity. Indeed, many people wrote poems in which they blamed themselves for having failed to see Wilson's great vision.[103] Elizabeth Barrett Browning described this failure in the following lines:

A great man (who was crowned one day)
Imagined a great deed. . . .
He fed it with large thoughts humane
to help the people's need. . . .
O generous deed, heroic deed
Come forth, be perfect, succeed
Deliver by God's grace.
Then sovereign statesmen, North and South
Rose up in wrath and fear
"A great deed at this hour of day?
A great just deed and not for pay
Absurd—or insincere. . . .
But he stood sad before the sun
(The people felt their fate)
"The World is many—I am one

My great deed was too great.
God's fruit of justice ripens slow:
Men's souls are narrow; let them grow.
My brothers, we must wait."[104]

Although the poem described an undeserving humanity, it implied that more concrete figures were responsible for humanity's failure—the politicians. Indeed, one of the favorite themes among Wilson's supporters and admirers was his fight against the politicians.[105] He emerged from the various addresses and biographies as a president who sacrifices his life for the people while combating the selfish, greedy, and office-seeking politicians. Ironically, no one mentioned that Woodrow Wilson himself had been a politician. Like Lincoln he became a kind of popular tribune who derived his authority directly from the people without reliance upon political machines.[106]

Wilson's western tour provided his mythmakers with a specific scene for a martyr's battle. "He was forewarned that his life might be the forfeit of his enterprise," declared Dr. Alderman in his congressional address. "He replied 'I would forfeit my life to attend the end I seek' and he meant it. . . . Woodrow Wilson fell stricken as if in battle at Pueblo, Co. on Sept. 25, 1919."[107] Biographer Edith Reid depicted Wilson as one who had planned his martyrdom when he refused to give up the western tour. Yet the people themselves had betrayed him by joining the politicians against the idealist president.[108] The attitude of the people, according to some discourses, was ambivalent. On the one hand, they were on the martyr's side, but on the other hand they were depicted as an ignorant and simpleminded mass who admired the president but did not fully comprehend his vision and consequently did not provide him with the necessary support.[109]

Although he fought the politicians of his country, Wilson was depicted as a martyr for American democracy. Professional politicians especially glorified the president who had died in order to perpetuate American values of liberty, democracy, and peace and to fight the reactionary forces of the status quo. Al Smith, the governor of New York; Franklin D. Roosevelt, former assistant secretary of the navy; Judge Otto A. Rasalsky, all eulogized him as another martyred president, second to Lincoln, who had lived and died for his country and its democratic tradition. Whether the foe was the old Princeton academic establishment, the New Jersey political machine, corrupt businessmen, the monarchies of Europe, or the Republican politicians in the Congress, Wilson's friends stressed his battle for the realization of American democratic and Progressive ideals.[110] "Like most prophets and seers he was destroyed by those who opposed change," declared Senator Caraway of Arkansas.[111] Joseph P. Tumulty, Wilson's personal secretary, composed a fictional statement which the dead president would have made to the mourning people:

We have begun a fight against special privilege but you know that . . . men are put into this world to go the path of pain and struggle. . . . men have sacrificed everything in this struggle. America has undertaken to lead the way. America has undertaken to be the heaven of hope, the opportunity for all men. . . . Don't you see the light starting and don't you see the light illuminating all nations. . . . What difference does it make if we ourselves do not reach the uplands? We have given our lives to the enterprise. The world is made happier and humankind better because we have lived.[112]

From this perspective, an American martyr for reform at home had expanded the scope of his activities in order to reform the world, and even if he had failed in this last effort, he had immortalized the universal mission of American democracy.[113]

World War I offered the dramatic context for Wilson's martyrdom. His contemporaries pictured him as both a fallen soldier and martyr for peace, as both an American patriot and a universal leader aiming to end war forever. The image of Wilson, presented by these various addresses differed significantly from his real activities in the war period. The identification with the fallen soldiers linked the martyred president with the society for which he had supposedly died. Just as in the cases of John Brown and Lincoln, this identification provided the sacrificial ties between the famous political martyr and the many anonymous individuals who had sacrificed their lives in the war. Just as Wilson himself always had compared his battle for the treaty with the soldier's battle in the trenches of Europe, so many of his supporters stated that he was the last and most precious casualty of the whole war effort.[114] "The Unknown Soldier lies in Arlington with the heroic dead of all wars in which America has taken part," wrote Josephus Daniels. "Sharing with him the national gratitude is the Known Soldier, the President who called him to arms and gave his life as truly for the cause as if he had fallen on the battlefield."[115]

Wilson's contemporaries awarded him the title *martyr for peace*. It had a specific national meaning to many Americans who identified war with the Old World of monarchy and political intrigue, and peace with their blessed conditions of democracy and freedom. Woodrow Wilson had embodied this

American spirit of peace and freedom and committed himself to bringing it to the belligerent Old World. His failure to achieve this goal would consecrate forever the American people to complete his work.[116] Josephus Daniels thus wrote, "We have accepted the truth and we are going to be led by it, and it is going to lead us and through us the world out into pastures of quietness and peace such as the world never dreamed before."[117] Yet instead of pastures of quietness and peace, the world entered the hell of fire and blood in the Second World War. This did not prevent some prominent politicians from arguing for the ultimate triumph of Wilson's peace ideas. World War II proved the prophetic quality of the martyred president, while the second and more successful attempt to establish the United Nations manifested his ultimate triumph.[118] Referring to the war effort of the Allies in 1942, the *New York Times* wrote: "The League is dead—and it lives. Though fifty nations failed to make it operative by discussion, twenty-six are now engaged in making it operative by all their armored strength and all their spiritual devotion. Woodrow Wilson's body, like John Brown's, lies moldering in the grave, but his soul is marching on."[119]

The title *martyr for peace* had more then a national significance. Especially in poems it implied a certain cosmic vision by turning Wilson into a messianic redeemer.[120] An example of such a message was the poem "The Man of Peace" written in Washington, D.C., by Grace Guille Purse:

Behold how down the centuries
There shines a gleaming sword
Red with the martyred blood of those
The Prince of Peace adorned!
For right must conquer in the end
And Peace shall have her day
Ev'n though these mighty, peaceful men
Fall on the soldier's way
Then rise, ye unthinking bare your heads
A man of peace goes by
Who for your country's sake has bled
And for the world did die
And hush, ye throbbing drums; be still
War banners, he ye furled!
There goes a man of peace who fought
To purify the World.[121]

Like all martyred figures Wilson was compared to Jesus Christ.[122] The fact that he failed in his efforts on behalf of a universal peace program rather than a specific American enterprise made the analogy even more valid. "Christ did not die for one country, a remote . . . province of the Mediterranean," declared Lucian L. Knight. "He died to redeem a world from bondage and he died not alone for his friend but for his enemy."[123] Wilson's avowed idealism reinforced the comparison to Christ. He himself had resorted to such an analogy in his last essay when he wrote, "Our Civilization cannot survive materially unless it be saved spiritually by becoming permeated with the spirit of Christ."[124]

Despite the many analogies with Christ's fate, Wilson's image remained apart from the Christian eschatology. His supporters and admirers avoided religious visions of millennium and apocalypse. They described a more secular future which would vindicate Wilson's sacrifice. Resorting to the rhetoric of binary contrasts they claimed that Wilson's failure was only a temporary stage on the way to success and his personal martyrdom would pave the way for the ultimate triumph of his ideals.[125] Bliss Perry explained how the working of binary contrasts manifested the ideals for which the martyred president had stood:

His body broke but not his will. . . . In the case of a true visionary, those trumpets of the sad fifth act and the fall of the tragic curtain are impertinences. Upon idealists such as he, the curtain does not fall. . . . The illogical impertinent bullet that pierced Lincoln's brain has now become a portion of his glory. "I met him at every turn" said Thoreau of John Brown after he was hanged, "he is more alive than ever he was." . . . [Wilson's] ultimate fame will depend upon the triumph of the political ideals which he clothed with fitting words. We make our guesses even now, but fifty years hence, we shall begin to know something of the verdict of mankind.[126]

Wilson's supporters hoped that this verdict would turn their fallen martyr into a triumphant hero.

But while Lincoln's mythmakers or John Brown's admirers had no doubt about the inevitable triumph of martyrdom, Wilson's supporters were more skeptical. Perhaps because they belonged to a different period, they consciously contemplated, discussed, and even sometimes doubted the effectiveness of martyrdom in the political career of Woodrow Wilson. Writing with a certain perspective of time, Thomas Bailey stated that when most Progressive reformers had opposed Wilson's position toward the peace, he had begun to develop something of a martyr complex. "Like the early Christian martyrs he gloried in sacrificing himself for his principles," wrote Baily, But unlike Lincoln's or Brown's biographers, Bailey was uncertain about the benefits of such an attitude. "It is well enough, when the occasion demands it, for men to die for their convictions. It is often better—as it would have been in this case—to live and work for them. . . . The president was willing to give his life for his principles, and in a sense he did. He killed himself and in killing himself killed the Treaty."[127]

Former ambassador John W. Davis and Dr. Edwin A. Alderman both explained Wilson's fate as analogous to Greek tragedy. They asserted that fate had called him to play a greater role than had been set for any other American and that he had failed as any human being would have failed in such a position. But his failure had provided the world with its required catharsis. "Tragedy . . . reaches its tragic end when the individual perishes; but, through his ruin the disturbed order of the world is restored and the moral forces reassert their sway," declared Dr. Alderman.[128] Wilson sacrificed his life when he tried to achieve an impossible human task, but his personal tragedy made this task an inspirational ideal for the whole society, and in that sense his martyrdom was worthy.

Some of Wilson's biographers called his fate a "living martyrdom."[129] "Probably no man has ever lived in the flesh, helpless and all but physically dead, to see his own immortality," wrote William Allen White in his early biography in 1924. Later biographers viewed this "living martyrdom" as a harmful event rather than beneficial. Thus A. L. Rowse noted in 1948 that when Wilson's objective was nothing less than achievement of an ideal world order, there was no way to escape failure but through a glorious death. "This was denied to him for the stroke which cut him down in the midst of his last campaign was not mortal."[130] Thomas Bailey confirmed the former senator Albert J. Beveridge's remark that if the president had died that night on the platform at Pueblo, he could have eclipsed Lincoln as the American national martyr. But "the fates were unkind to Wilson: Having set the stage for a great martyrdom they suddenly changed their minds. If he had died the U.S.A. probably would have entered the League."[131] Such statements concerning the effectiveness of Wilson's martyrdom were uttered by firm supporters of the president. They generally extolled the martyr tradition but they saw Wilson as a martyr manqué.

The different cultural milieu of the twentieth century prevented Wilson's later sympathizers from depicting him as a legendary martyr whose sacrifice would redeem a sinful mankind. They described his fate as a glorious human tragedy rather than a mythical story. "Wilson was . . . the greatest peace maker, the greatest tragedy," wrote Thomas Bailey. "Reaching for the stars he crashed to the earth. . . . But his was a magnificent failure, and in some ways a successful failure."[132] Similarly his opponents did not portray him as Satan or a demonic villain. Instead they stressed Wilson's unrealistic and uncompromising approach, his ridiculous self-righteousness, and his lack of tolerance, which caused him "to love humanity but to hate people."

Among the various reformers who used the concept of martyrdom and experienced a certain degree of personal suffering, Woodrow Wilson had the best chance of becoming a national martyr. He was identified with reform issues prior to his presidency, at Princeton and in New Jersey. As the president of the United States he initiated tariff reform, established the Federal Reserve Board, advocated and endorsed three Constitutional amendments, and accomplished the passage of some of the most prominent reform acts that Progressive reformers had advocated. His tragic failure followed by political defeat was the central event of the postwar years. The Great War, in which Wilson hoped to end all wars, became a personal tragedy to the man who failed in his last peace effort. This dramatic context of the president's sacrifice enlarged his potential for martyrdom. Wilson's idealism and Christian ethics draped his political activities in a crusading and prophetic ideology. Thus when he fell at the end he, more than any other Progressive figure, was worthy of the crown of martyrdom.

But other elements undermined these prospects for a lasting martyrdom: Wilson suffered for an undeserving humanity rather than declared sinners. His sacrifice was tragic more than redemptive. No specific movement used his tragedy as an ideological device in the way that the Republican party used the assassination of Abraham Lincoln or the abolitionists used the execution of John Brown, and Wilson's image as a martyr-reformer for universal peace was shared only by close friends and admirers. The fact that most Progressive politicians refused to endorse the president's peace program added an ironic dimension to the whole tragedy of Wilson, who was closely identified with the Progressive reform movement.

Thus Progressive reformers did not produce a national martyr for the cause, and Woodrow Wilson became neither another Lincoln nor even another John Brown. Without a tragic death, Wilson lacked the ritualistic context that might have turned him into a celebrated martyr. The Great War, which ended for many Americans in disillusion, turned its main crusader into a tragic, if not a grotesque, figure rather than a victorious martyred hero. Yet in addition to these specific circumstances more general reasons accounted for the absence of a well-known martyr for Progressive reform.

As noted earlier in this chapter, the general climate of opinion at the turn of the century differed from that of the midnineteenth century. The Calvinistic Christian cosmology of sin, fall, sacrifice, and redemption, was less appealing to generations who had started to cast doubt upon the whole genteel tradition and even interpreted religious eschatology in social terms. Such an interpretation affirmed social commitment in order to promote a better future, but undermined its cosmic significance and denied any catastrophic apocalypse as a necessary stage on the path of reform. The martyred figure who by definition appeared precisely in the period of apocalypse, had less effectiveness when many Americans had ceased to believe in the real existence of such a period. When more and more people viewed their history as something apart from the biblical order rather than a reflection of it, they diminished the role of biblical figures and images in their lives.

The pluralistic nature of the Progressive movement prevented its members from focusing on one particular individual who suffered for the cause of reform. In fact many Progressive individuals such as Jesse Jones, George Herron, Frank Parsons, Benjamin Flower, Jane Addams, Randolph Bourne, and Woodrow Wilson fought and occasionally suffered for various reform issues. But they never belonged to a coherent reform group with a specific ideology. Politicians, businessmen, workers, women, intellectuals, journalists, ministers, social workers, professionals, and many others engaged in various reform activities but did not belong to a central reform movement such as the Anti-Slavery Society. Lacking the institutional agencies that could articulate the reform ideology, the Progressive reformers had no central system of symbols and myths to give an inspirational form to such an ideology.

Moreover, the reform ideal encompassed a vast array of sometimes contradictory reform goals, and Progressive reformers attacked various economic, political, and social shortcomings of modern industrial America. They defined their opponents as the plutocracy but the term had a vague meaning. Essentially, they opposed the new corporate business order, the landlords, the immoral bankers, the corrupt politicians, the municipal bosses, the fundamentalist ministers, the radical anarchists, and many more. Without a central organization, without a focus on one reform ideal and without a concrete foe, Progressive reformers had very little likelihood of producing a well-known martyr.

Yet famous Progressive individuals resorted to the martyr concept either to explain their own suffering or to inspire their society to further commitment to still-unachieved reform goals. In that sense Woodrow Wilson became a well-known martyr for peace and democracy when the world refused to be reformed according to his idealistic program. In his book *Ministers of Reform,* Robert Crunden argued that Wilson's tragedy embodied the fate of the whole Progressive movement, which died with his failure, unable to regenerate and reform human society.[133]

Indeed, the general mood of reform was dead in the 1920s. Nevertheless, many concrete reform issues advocated by Progressive reformers were incorporated into the American political system. Perhaps the very success of concrete reform measures such as women's suffrage, antitrust legislation, progressive income tax, or labor regulations, undermined in the long run a serious attempt to create an inspirational martyr for the dying age of reform. A happy middle class reluctant to engage in more reform crusades benefited from the concrete achievements of the Progressive movement. It regarded the Great War as an insignificant, if not unnecessary, enterprise and consequently refused to lament the failure of Wilson's idealistic peace program. Many who did not reach the status of the middle class experienced little relief as a result of the new achievements of the Progressive movement. Some of them created their own organizations, aimed not at reforming the system but at destroying it and creating a new one. Obviously these "un-American" radicals glorified their own suffering and sacrifices and produced a specific image of their martyred heroes.

6

On Revolution's Altar

In *Jane Addams and the Liberal Tradition*, Daniel Levine defined radicalism in relative terms: "People who want to change a lot of important things rapidly are more radical than people who want to change less important things, or fewer of them, less rapidly."[1] He rejected the identification of radical tradition with revolutionary Marxism and asserted that if historians would cease defining radicalism as a total opposition to the capitalistic system, they would find a vigorous and living radical tradition in America. But such a definition makes it difficult to differentiate between reformers and radicals. Both shared a sense of discontent about the existing order. Both aimed to change it and to create a better future. Both had a certain utopian vision of the good society and tried to ameliorate their own society according to this vision. Who can determine when the changes are either important enough or fast enough to turn a reformer into a radical? In order to distinguish between a reform movement and a radical movement in the context of American history, the definition of *radicalism* must be made more specific.

Radicals differed significantly from reformers in their attitude toward the existing order. Most reformers criticized many institutions of their present society and worked to replace them with new and more enlightened ones. Nevertheless, they intended to use the present institutions as foundations for further amelioration and change. Radicals, on the other hand, argued that the structure of their present society had to be destroyed before any new institutions could be built. Only upon the ruins of an older order could they fashion a new future. Some radicals defined this act of destruction as a revolution that would be the first step toward a better society.

Thus, while reformers announced their dissatisfaction with the existing order, radicals declared open war on it. In an introduction to the autobiography of the convicted anarchists and labor leaders of the Haymarket Affair, William P. Black, who defended them in the trial, articulated this radical vision. "The vision suggests," he wrote, "the overthrow by force of the old order to make room for the new. Destruction to clear the way to construction — revolution against the old, preceding the evolution of the new — this is the lesson of history."[2]

This commitment to the destruction of the existing order led many radicals to advocate the use of violence. Yet violence in itself cannot be used as the dividing line between reformers and radicals in the United States where violence accompanied many social struggles. Furthermore, such a famous radical as the avowed anarchist Emma Goldman, who advocated the overthrow of capitalism, never resorted to violence in her battle against the system. John Brown, on the other hand, fought a specific institution and used outright violence in this fight, but never planned to overthrow the entire political system in America.

Both John Brown and Emma Goldman conceived of themselves as radicals. They both generated hostility by challenging the existing order. In the eyes of their contemporaries, however, John Brown became a revered martyr reformer and Emma Goldman remained a dangerous radical. This difference in image seems to be determined by the extent to which a majority of Americans could identify with the goals of a particular reformer. Thus, when a large segment of the American public shared many of the values of the advocates of change, it tended to regard them as reformers, and conversely, when the public viewed the opposition groups as dangerous creatures and feared the consequences of their agitation, it often defined them as radicals. Whereas Americans in general were open to the idea of reform as a vehicle to improve the democratic system, they feared radicals who overtly stated that their aim was to overthrow this system.

The social status and values of an opposition group also determined whether its members would be perceived as reformers or radicals. A social dissident belonging to an upper-middle-class family with deep roots in the American tradition was more acceptable to his contemporaries than one who was a new immigrant and spoke little English. Similarly, a person who shared general American religious convictions was less likely to be defined as radical by his contemporaries than an avowed atheist. A self-made career also won sympathy for a social critic since it made him part of the American dream. Without such a career his criticism could be interpreted as opposition to basic American values and he could be labeled an "un-American" radical. The less an opposition group shared certain common cultural characteristics, the more susceptible it was to the stigma of radicalism. Thus abolitionists, despite their radicalism, were seen as reformers, while anarchists or socialists, many of whom opposed violent destruction, were stigmatized as radicals.

Historical developments also contributed to drawing the line between reformers and radicals. A radical figure such as John Brown was transformed into a celebrated martyr shortly after his execution because of the Civil War and its outcome. The institution he had sought to overthrow was destroyed and he became a martyred hero of the victorious North and the emancipated blacks. Similarly, when the course of events affirmed the stand taken earlier by a social critic, he might be depicted by later generations as a reformer who could see beyond the limits of his contemporaries. Thus radical opponents of World War I, such as Randolph Bourne and Jane Addams, became heralds of the future in the eyes of many disillusioned Americans in the twenties. When, however, the course of events contradicted the vision of a social critic, he might eventually be perceived as a radical. Thus, in America, all those who advocated the destruction of capitalism and dreamed of a new order free from the domination of property, were defined as un-American radicals, and this definition will last just as long as capitalism remains the economic foundation of American society.

This chapter focuses on those figures who, according to this definition, can be described as radicals. Because they advocated destruction of the social, political, and economic system, the public in general feared them and aided the agents of the existing order in suppressing and persecuting them. Judicial institutions all over the country convicted them and sentenced them to jail or to the gallows. Sometimes mobs tortured and lynched them. Obviously, they shared few of the values of their society and were depicted as un-American both by their contemporaries and by later generations.

Anarchists, as well as labor leaders who opposed any compromise with the "capitalistic ruling class," provided the core of radicalism during the Gilded Age and the Progressive Era. Some of them acted as individuals, others belonged to syndicalist unions such as the Industrial Workers of the World, and still others affiliated themselves with political organizations such as the Socialist party. These opponents of the system produced their own martyrs for the cause. Despite their opposition to the political system, radicals addressed their speeches to other Americans and therefore had to describe their martyred heroes within the context of American political culture. The main purpose, however, for analyzing the radical version of martyrdom is to see in what ways this version deviated from cultural conventions: to what extent radicals added a specific meaning to their martyred heroes that was alien to the American political culture and even sometimes contradicted its basic ideological premises. An examination of these new elements of radical martyrdom can provide a more precise definition of the ideological limits of the American political tradition. The "un-American" martyrs revealed those elements of martyrdom that most Americans considered beyond the confines of their political culture. Thus the image of the radical martyr stands outside the accepted values, beliefs, and mores of American culture and thereby demarcates its boundaries more clearly.

After the Civil War, the United States entered a period of unstable industrial growth that resulted both in enormous technological advancement and extreme hardship on the part of the workers. Violent struggles between laborers and employers characterized the period from 1870 through the 1920s. Many struggles involved judicial executions, mob lynchings, and random shooting by police forces into crowds of striking workers. The victims of this violence adopted an uncompromising attitude toward the institutions of industrial capitalism, which estranged them from the mainstream of American society. In the eyes of the committed members of the radical labor movement, however, they became celebrated martyrs for the cause.

The first executed labor leaders were eleven coal miners from Pennsylvania known as the "Molly Maguires." Under enormous pressure from the mine owners, a jury found them guilty of terrorizing and killing other workers who had refused to submit to their revolutionary orders and sentenced them to death in June 1877. At the time, the execution did not generate intense public reaction. Thirty years later, however, writing in the socialist paper *Appeal to Reason,* Eugene Victor Debs, the leader of the American Socialist party, called them the first martyrs of the labor struggle against American capitalism:

On that day, history turned her lot and the fair face of truth was covered with the hideous mask of falsehood. . . . But the truth will out at last and the time is near when the history of the Pennsylvania tragedy . . . will be radically revised. . . . Marvelous have been changes in public sentiments since that day. They would not now be executed under the same circumstances. The workers today are too far advanced, too well organized and too conscious of their class interests and duties to submit to such monstrous outrage.[3]

Here Debs was using binary contrast to invest the tragedy with meaning. He depicted a topsy-turvy world that permitted such a travesty and appealed to history as the final judge that would demonstrate the triumph of the executed martyrs. History, according to many radicals, rather than a future eschatology, worked on behalf of their cause. The most well known radicals to view themselves as agents of history were the executed anarchists of the Haymarket Affair. Many of their radical followers shared this view.

On the night of May 4, 1886, a bomb was thrown into a group of policemen who had just begun to disperse a small group of workers in the Haymarket on Chicago's West Side. The police reacted by opening fire into the crowd. By the end of the incident several policemen and several workers were dead. The demonstration that ended so tragically had started as a peaceful gathering of working men who joined the strike of the eight-hour movement, which had been in progress since February 16 of that year at the McCormick Harvester Machine Company. Following the bloodshed, a number of anarchists were indicted. Although there was no sound evidence to prove that they had any connection with the actual bomb throwing, the judicial authorities found them guilty. Albert R. Parsons, August Spies, Samuel J. Fielden, Michael Schwab, Adolph Fischer, Louis Lingg, and George Engel were condemned to death. Oscar Neebe underwent fifteen years' imprisonment. Before the announcement of the verdict Judge Joseph E. Gary called upon the convicted men to speak. In these speeches they presented a certain version of radical martyrdom that several anarchist and socialist groups later used as an ideological device.

August Spies, who addressed the court first, declared that anarchistic ideas could not be crushed by the death penalty. "If death is the penalty for proclaiming the truth," he declared, "then I will proudly and defiantly pay the costly price!"[4] Louis Lingg, who committed suicide the day before the execution, declared, "I die happy on the gallows, so confident am I that the hundreds of thousands to whom I have spoken will remember my words: and when you shall have hanged us, then, mark my words, they will do the bomb throwing![5] Similarly, Adolph Fischer stated that no death could eliminate anarchistic ideals and principles. "If the ruling class thinks that by executing us . . . they can crush anarchy, they will be badly mistaken because the anarchist loves his principles better than his life. An anarchist is always ready to die for his principles. . . . The more the believers in just causes are persecuted, the quicker will their ideas be realized."[6]

Albert Parsons, who had voluntarily handed himself over to the authorities so that he could stand trial with his friends, delivered the longest address before the court. Like Adolph Fischer he expressed his confidence in the coming victory of anarchism, which would be the next stage of human history.[7] He elaborated the new vision of freedom that anarchists would fight for and proclaimed that the existing forces of tyranny, in their desperate attempt to avoid the coming of the new era of liberty, would resort to any crime and travesty in order to persecute anarchists. "All that I have to say in regard to my conviction is, that I was not surprised; for it has ever been that the men who have endeavored to enlighten their fellow men have been thrown into prison or put to death, as was the case with John Brown."[8]

But the martyred figures that emerged from these statements were different from John Brown. First, they completely ignored the divine context in which John Brown had so proudly placed himself. None of the convicted anarchists viewed themselves as messengers of God, and God was conspicuously absent from their statements. Second, none of the Haymarket anarchists depicted themselves as unique individuals who had witnessed some ultimate truth and had therefore been selected to die for this truth. Instead, they portrayed themselves as representatives of a deprived class who had been selected at random to die for it. They simply embodied the group for which they died—a vague group composed of all the sufferers and the poor, all the victims of the tyranny of the ruling class.

Indifferent to the very value of human life, all the Haymarket anarchists expressed their willingness to die. In the case of true believers like anarchists, this was more than a psychological device to cope with a tragic fate. It demonstrated a certain state of mind common among the ranks of committed revolutionaries, mainly that individual life was worthless and that everything was subordinate to the ideals of the revolution. Hence, there was no tragedy in losing life. Furthermore, inasmuch as death for an ideal would convert more people to this ideal, it was welcomed by the radical anarchists. Their sacrifice had no redemptive meaning; they died in a battle against the existing order, not to redeem this order from its sins, but to hasten its collapse. Thus they called upon their followers to continue the battle and even to avenge their deaths.

The state and federal supreme courts affirmed the death penalty and on November 11, 1887, Parsons, Spies, Engel, and Fischer were hanged. From that day the various radical movements in America, whether anarchists, socialists, or syndicalists, had their own martyrs for the cause. Famous figures such as Emma Goldman, Eugene Debs, or William D. Haywood repeated, refined, and articulated the radical concept of martyrdom that the Haymarket anarchists had enunicated in their court addresses. The fate of the Haymarket martyrs provided radicals with an opportunity to express their specific version of sacrifice for a radical cause. This rhetoric, when compared to discourses that commemorated national martyrs like Abraham Lincoln, revealed the extent to which the image of the radical martyr differed from the traditional image of the American martyred figure.

The glorification of death for the cause was the most distinct theme in the radical eulogies. Such indifference toward the value of human life contradicted a basic premise of American culture that viewed life as an inalienable right in and of itself. Radical martyrs not only welcomed their deaths, but intentionally planned to sacrifice their lives as part of their duty. Captain William P. Black, the defense attorney of the Haymarket anarchists, said in a speech at the funeral of Parsons, "To such men death had . . . no terrors, and their execution, which was self-immolation, could have no touch of shame."[9] Lizzie M. Holmes, a personal friend of Albert Parsons's, used the fact that he had voluntarily handed himself over to the court as proof of his willing self-sacrifice. "Voluntarily he gave up liberty for the cause he loved better than his life. That night the prison doors closed upon him never to open for him alive; the stone walls shut out the fair free earth forever and man repaid an act of unprecedented devotion with death."[10]

Since anarchists believed in something higher than life itself they did not view death as tragic. To them, martyrdom neither gave meaning to tragedy nor rationalized suffering as it did in the case of all other American martyred heroes. Martyrs became merely the means for increasing the movement's membership and reinforcing social devotion to the cause. Moreover, a martyr's death was necessary not only to those individuals who devoted themselves to the ideal of anarchism but also to the multitude that needed the martyr's blood to open its eyes and hearts and to destroy its illusions. "Every advance that the world has thus far known . . . has been an advance achieved by the few against the many," wrote William P. Black. "It is ordered that our hearts, the hearts of the multitudes, reject the truth until we see it written with the warm heart's blood of some man who stands a courier of the advancing dawn."[11] The martyr's blood cemented those select few who dedicated their lives to an ideal and created sacrificial ties among all the living members of a movement committed to a radical cause. The glorification of death served as a ritual for the devoted radicals, a device that helped them to give up their personal identity. Thus Lucy Parsons wrote that in his last minutes her husband "seemed to completely lose his identity and to feel that his spirit was no longer a part of his body. He stood like one transfigured."[12] He served as an example to his devoted followers.

An unswerving belief that history was on their side also enabled radicals to embrace death and to ignore its tragic dimension. This view, again, contradicted the general democratic culture, which emphasized the ultimate value of human life. The most prominent figure to articulate the various elements of radical martyrdom and their relationship to the American political culture was the famous agitator and anarchist Emma Goldman. In her long battle for anarchism she suffered from the existing order and occasionally resorted to the martyr tradition to explain her suffering. Although Emma Goldman died a natural death, in the eyes of many radicals her tragic struggle against capitalistic institutions turned her into a martyred hero for the cause.

Born in Kovno, Lithuania, in June 1867 into an Orthodox middle-class Jewish family, Emma Goldman spent her childhood and adolescence in St. Petersburg and Köningsberg. In 1885 she emigrated to the United States and affiliated herself with German socialists in Rochester, New York. She became associated with the Russian anarchist Alexander Berkman, who was sentenced to twenty-two years in jail in 1889 for attempting to assassinate the industrialist Henry Frick during the Homestead steel strike in Pittsburgh. Goldman declared her overt opposition to any form of government and authority and carried this message through innumerable lectures all over the country. She never had a family of her own and devoted her career entirely to the ideal of anarchism. In 1893 she was arrested and spent a year in prison for inciting a riot in New York and assaulting a police officer. She founded an anarchistic paper, *Mother Earth,* and resumed her association with Alexander Berkman after his release in 1906. They carried on anarchistic activities until 1917 when they were arrested for obstructing the military draft and served two years in prison. In 1919 the American authorities deported Berkman and Goldman to Russia. Emma Goldman, who had previously praised the Russian Revolution, was disappointed with the course of events in Russia and escaped back to the West. She went to England, France, and, later, Spain. In Europe she wrote her autobiography, which provided both a fascinating account of her stormy life and an elaboration of her ideas. Her request to reenter the United States was denied and she died in Toronto, Canada, on May 14, 1940.

To many Americans Emma Goldman embodied the prototype of "un-American" radicalism. Explicitly opposed to the existing order, she was also alienated from mainstream American culture as an immigrant, a feminist, an atheist, and an advocate of free love. Her few followers admired her but the public in general viewed her as a most dangerous rebel, one who threatened the existence of such sacred institutions as the family, church, and government. It was hardly surprising, then, that she was arrested after the assassination of President McKinley and that hysterical police officers demanded her indictment despite the fact that she had no connection whatsoever with the murder. From a historical perspective she continued to be depicted as a radical, especially since her ideas never materialized. Her image, however, became a source of inspiration to many individuals who later associated themselves with various countercultural movements in America and in other Western countries.

Troubled by her own suffering and her friends' tribulations, Goldman nevertheless explicitly rejected what Max Weber called the "theosophy of suffering." She never accepted the manner in which religion invested suffering with meaning and converted what would otherwise have been a source of social upheaval, into an instrument of human redemption. She suffered terribly but regarded it as a price to be paid for her struggle against the establishment. As an atheist she never believed in the cycle of sin, fall, sacrifice, and redemption and refused to use biblical eschatology as an explanation for suffering.[13] She substituted a human ideal for God, and tried to remove the political martyr from any superhuman sphere. "Has not some American ancestor said many years ago that resistance to tyranny is obedience to God? . . . I would say that resistance to tyranny is man's highest ideal," she wrote.[14]

Goldman believed that the United States was, like any other country in the world, a tyranny of the few who enslaved the many. Not born to freedom, but still in bondage—this was the real situation of most people in America according to Emma Goldman. Therefore, freedom for her was a future ideal that would require its heroes and martyrs. A well-known anarchist, Hippolyte Havel, explained that anarchists viewed themselves as freedom fighters. They fought the power of tyranny and suffered for their adherence to liberty. Voltairine de Cleyre, a famous anarchist and a close friend of Emma Goldman, interpreted Goldman's imprisonment in 1893 as a result of her commitment to freedom. "The spirit that animated Emma Goldman is the only one which will emancipate the slave from his slavery, the tyrant from his tyranny—the spirit which is willing to dare and suffer."[15] The freedom that anarchists advocated was defined by some scholars as positive liberty. It called for the unrestricted expression of human energy —unlimited by any form of authority. Emma Goldman explained this libertarian notion in her essay "Anarchism":

Religion the dominion of human mind, property the dominion of human needs, and government the dominion of human conduct, represent the stronghold of man's enslavement. . . . Anarchism stands for the liberation of human mind from the dominion of religion; liberation of human body from the dominion of property; and liberation from the shackles and restraints of government. . . . Anarchism stands for direct action . . . and resistance to all laws and restriction. . . . Therein lies the salvation of man.[16]

Such an open attack on law and order in the name of unrestricted freedom would claim the lives of many individuals and turn them into martyrs for freedom according to Emma Goldman. She advocated the use of martyrdom as a tactical device and argued that by being executed, exiled, tortured, and killed, the radical martyrs demonstrated to the public that freedom was a mockery in a country that claimed to be free. Like the abolitionists of an earlier era, Emma Goldman and her friends used every opportunity in their belligerent careers to refute the myth of American freedom. In their last letter written on American soil from their deportation station on Ellis Island, Alexander Berkman and Emma Goldman wrote to their friends:

Do not be sad about our forced departure. Rather rejoice with us that our common enemies, prompted by fear and stupidity, have resorted to this mad act of driving political refugees out of the land. . . . For now the American people will see more clearly than our ardent work of thirty years could prove to them, that liberty in America has been sold into bondage, that justice had been outraged and life made cheap and ugly.[17]

As an opponent of the institutions of law and order, Emma Goldman admitted that she sometimes had to overcome her human desires for affection and happiness in order to carry out the battle against the existing order. Yet she expressed an ambiguous and sometimes vague attitude toward the deliberate indifference to the value of human life. She disagreed with those anarchists who advocated total self-abnegation. In her autobiography she wrote that early in her career a young Russian anarchist had seen her dancing and whispered to her that it did not behoove an agitator to dance and that her frivolity would only hurt the cause.

I grew furious. . . . I did not believe that a cause which stood for a beautiful ideal of anarchism for release and freedom from conventional prejudice should demand the denial of life and joy. I insist that our cause could not expect me to become a nun and that the movement should not be turned into a cloister. . . . There was applause, mingling with protest that I was wrong, that one must consider the cause above everything. All the Russian revolutionaries had done that, they have never been conscious of self.[18]

When Alexander Berkman revealed to her his plan to kill Frick and then to commit suicide, she recalled that she had not been so sure that the cause of anarchism required such an action. "What if anything should go wrong?" she asked. But then she affirmed martyrdom and self-abnegation. "Our end was the sacred cause of the oppressed and exploited people. It was for them that we were going to give our lives. What if a few should have to perish? —the many would be made free and could live in beauty and comfort."[19]

When Emma Goldman saw the heavy price her friend Berkman had paid for his direct action she wrote an article in *Mother Earth* called "The Psychology of Political Violence." Referring to Bjornstjerne Bjornson's *Beyond Human Power,* she argued that "it is among anarchists that we must look for the modern martyrs who pay for their faith with their blood and who welcome death with a smile because they believe . . . that their martyrdom will redeem humanity." She asserted in the article that "the man who flings his own life into the attempt, at the cost of his own life, to protest against the wrongs of his fellow man, is a saint compared to the . . . upholders of injustice, even if his protest destroy other lives beside his own." But in the same essay she stated that "Anarchism more than any other theory values human life above things. All anarchists agree with Tolstoy in this fundamental truth: If the production of any commodity necessitates the sacrifice of human life, society should do without this commodity, but it cannot do without that life." [20]

Perhaps these inconsistencies developed out of Emma Goldman's acculturation to the American environment. Having emigrated to the New World when she was relatively young and spent most of her life in a democratic environment, she did not share the self-abnegation of her older Russian friends who had grown up in an autocratic environment that did not stress the value of individual human life. While ideologically she embraced total sacrifice for the cause, psychologically she continued to view any death as a tragedy. Nonetheless, whenever anarchists carried out a violent attack and paid dearly for it, Emma Goldman always defended them, sharing the agony of their suffering and even contributing to their image as martyred heroes. She supported Alexander Berkman and refused to condemn Czolgosz when he assassinated President William McKinley. Above all, she admired the Haymarket anarchists who died upon the gallows in Chicago. Goldman admitted that the Haymarket martyrs had converted her to the idea of anarchism, thus illustrating the power of martyrdom to create "sacrificial ties" among radicals. Hippolyte Havel noted that the authorities who executed the Chicago anarchists had failed to understand that "from the blood of a martyr grows new seed, and that the frightful injustice will win new converts to the cause." [21] He correctly wrote that both Emma Goldman and Voltairine de Cleyre were converted by the judicial murder of the Haymarket prisoners. But Emma Goldman herself wrote that the Chicago martyrs were more than a source of inspiration for her anarchism. She often identified with them and considered herself as the living embodiment of their ideals. She looked at their graves as a sacred shrine and expressed her desire to be buried next to them, a wish that was granted when she died. [22]

Goldman occasionally even looked forward to a similar fate. Describing her arrest after McKinley's assassination, she wrote:

Here I was, the spiritual child of those men, imprisoned in the city that had taken their lives, in the same jail. . . . Tomorrow I should be taken to Cook County jail, within whose walls, Parsons, Spies, Engel, and Fischer had been hanged. Strange indeed, the complex forces that had bound me to those martyrs through all my social conscious years! And now events were bringing me nearer and nearer—perhaps to a similar end? [23]

In a memorial address Goldman declared that

the spirit of Parsons, Spies, Lingg and their co-workers seems to hover over me and give deeper meaning to the events that had inspired my special birth and growth. . . . In time of ascent to heights, in days of faint-heartedness and doubt, in hours of prison isolation . . . in failure of love, in friendships broken and betrayed—always their cause was mine, their sacrifice my support.[24]

Thus, in her private and public life Emma Goldman elevated the Chicago martyrs to the sphere of spiritual leaders—regarding them almost as a devout Christian regarded Christ.

Emma Goldman deeply regretted that martyrdom did not influence the masses as it affected the few committed radicals.[25] Unlike many radicals who stoically accepted the fact that the path of the propagandist of social justice is "strewn with thorns," Emma Goldman refused to see this as a source of consolation. Reacting to a mob's demand to lynch her, she wrote that the people "forge their own chains and do the bidding of their master to crucify their Christs."[26] To her friend Emily Scott she wrote from her exile in St. Tropez: "I tried . . . to present to the world an ideal which to me contains all the beauty and wonder there is in life—the only raison d'être for my existence and the world less than ever wants to know anything about it."[27]

Indeed, radical martyrs did not provide the loose-knit and heterogeneous American working class with any sacrificial ties. Their deaths reinforced the coherence of the small and already dedicated group of radicals, but never penetrated the consciousness of most people who lived in a society that was built upon a functional relationship among its members. Only when a society undergoes a process of radicalism in face of a real or an imaginary foe, does it start to replace functional ties with sacrificial ties and to idolize some of its members as martyrs, as heroes whose blood cements the people together. Such a process of radicalism can occur in a situation of crisis, defeat, or war. America at the turn of the century, however, did not experience such a radicalization. The "people" whom anarchists sought to redeem were in reality a heterogeneous mass, part of the industrial society, with a large number of immigrants and fewer coherent communities. Without the consciousness of being "the people" the mass of Americans could not identify with a radical martyr who claimed to sacrifice his life for them.

For the close band of committed radicals, past martyrs became models for imitation, and potential martyrdom was viewed as a desirable fate.[28] It created sacrificial ties among radicals, which in turn provided the individuals who suffered for the cause with the comfort and consolation of friends. "If we have been among the most hated, reviled, and persecuted, we have also been the most beloved," wrote Emma Goldman and Alexander Berkman to their friends in their last letter before the deportation. "Wherever we shall be, our work will go on until our last breath. . . . May each of you give the best that is in him to the great struggle, the last struggle between liberty and bondage, between well-being and poverty, between beauty and ugliness."[29] History, according to Emma Goldman, worked in mysterious ways, which she interpreted by means of binary contrasts. The present victories of the existing order were only a deceit, while the real triumph in the future would belong to those radicals who suffered defeat in the present. Every act of persecution and each martyr added fire to the inevitable revolution. Every apparent failure only accelerated the process leading to final success. Emma Goldman noted that difficulties helped to rekindle her fighting spirit, asserting that "those in power never learn to what extent persecution is the leaven of revolutionary zeal."[30] "I have always believed that the deepest failures have very often been the greatest successes," Goldman wrote to a friend from exile. "You can imagine that I would despair utterly if I did not believe in the ultimate triumph of my ideal."[31]

Thus the importance of Emma Goldman lay in her ability to articulate the basic elements and dilemmas of radical martyrdom. She used the martyr image without an overt religious context and avoided the religious symbolism with which Americans imbued martyrs such as Lincoln, Wilson, and John Brown. She did, however, portray certain visions of the future in implied religious terms. Goldman showed how important the concept of martyrdom was to radicals who opposed the existing order and faced the hatred of the ignorant people they hoped to redeem. She expressed the difficulties an American radical had in embracing total self-abnegation but, nevertheless, regarded it as a necessary component of radicalism. She never welcomed death but praised individual sacrifice for the cause and viewed it as a step toward the ultimate triumph. Above all, Emma Goldman explained the relationship between a radical martyred figure and the radical group that used his martyrdom as a mean to strengthen sacrificial ties among its members, and also as a source of comfort and consolation.

The most famous of such dedicated radicals were the Industrial Workers of the World. They tried to create one big union of all the despised, downtrodden, and wretched workers who suffered under the capitalistic wage system. Operating in the same period as Emma Goldman, the IWW expressed their version of radical martyrdom and offered their own martyrs for the cause.

On June 27, 1905, William D. Haywood, then the secretary of the Western Federation of Miners, addressed an audience of two hundred delegates at Brand's Hall in Chicago. "Fellow workers," he said "this is the Continental Congress of the Working Class. We are here to confederate the workers of this country into a working-class movement in possession of the economic powers, the means of life, in control of the machinery of production and distribution without regard to capitalist masters."[32] Among the delegates were anarchists, socialists, radical miners, and revolutionary industrial unionists. On the speakers' platform beside William D. Haywood, were Eugene V. Debs, the leader of the American Socialist party, and Mother Jones, a famous labor agitator who had been active for almost half a century. Other well-known delegates were Daniel De Leon, the leader of the Socialist Labor party, A. M. Simons, editor of the *International Socialist Review*, Charles O. Sherman, general secretary of the United Metal Workers, Father Thomas J. Hagerty, editor of the *Voice of Labor*, and Lucy Parsons, the widow of Albert Parsons. After ten days of debate and voting, the convention framed the manifesto of the Industrial Workers of the World (whose members came to be known as Wobblies) in which it stated that "the working class and the employing class have nothing in common." The delegates formed a radical union to revolutionize the world and to eradicate capitalism wherever it existed. From that date until 1924, the IWW appeared to be the most radical organization in the United States, declaring open war upon the existing industrial system.

Appealing to the forgotten, unskilled, seasonal, and marginal laborers, the IWW never attracted more than 5 percent of all trade unionists, and their membership probably never exceeded 150,000 at the peak of their strength. But they had a significant impact on many Americans by challenging the structure and values of American society. The IWW provoked hostility, fear, and controversy. They failed in their battle against capitalism and attracted vigilante attacks and federal persecution and harassment. After the end of the First World War the organization was suppressed by the government, which, in fact, put an end to its existence in 1924. Yet in spite of this political failure, the IWW created a legacy of an American counter-culture, carried on in song, legend, and romance. The union also produced its own martyrs—individuals whom the existing order persecuted by legal action, troop fire, or mob violence.

The IWW stressed the anonymity of their martyrs. They eulogized specific individuals but hardly praised their personal characters. The value of a martyr's sacrifice was social not individual. He added his name to the silent and anonymous army of martyrs, thus playing his part in the revolutionary struggle. The assassinated individual represented the "workers' blood." His sacrifice was meaningful because it symbolized the workers' collective fate under a capitalistic wage system.[33] The more an individual was stripped of his own personality, the better his martyrdom served the workers. IWW martyrs had neither individual characteristics nor cosmic significance. They were social martyrs serving the collective group of deprived workers. According to IWW discourses, unknown martyrs for the working class created sacrificial ties with other laborers and increased the solidarity of those who dedicated themselves to avenge these deaths by overthrowing the wage system. Thus the *Industrial Workers* of Seattle wrote in memory of workers who had been killed on the steamer *Verona* at Everett, Washington, as a result of a class struggle in the lumber industry of the Northwest: "We shall never forget. . . . Against the wage system we have vowed our vengeance, against capitalism we are making our fight. . . . Again to you who died on November 5th 1916 we say: we never forget!"[34]

Laura Payne Emerson, in a eulogy to an old radical member of the IWW killed by a mob in San Diego on April 1912, expressed the main elements that made up the image of the unknown radical martyr for the cause.

He was a soldier of industrial freedom. When told by a friend he was too old to enlist in such a fight . . . he replied: "I have nothing to give but myself and life is not worth living when all liberty is gone." . . . From his ashes will spring ten thousand soldiers of freedom more powerful than he. . . . And today, standing beside the bier of this fellow worker martyr in the world's greatest revolution, we solemnly swear to carry on the battle with renewed energy and never stop until we avenge his death and achieve victory in the cause for which he died.

Emerson concluded by describing the dead martyr as an archetype of the downtrodden laborer:

Your weary body . . . often driven from place to place with no shelter, nowhere to lay your head, now finds a place of abode where hunger shall not overtake you, and where no policeman's club will bruise you, nor gruff voice bid you "move on." . . .

Although a private in the ranks you wear a laurel wreath upon your brow. . . . An injury to one is an injury to all. We shall not forget.[35]

Despite the emphasis on anonymous martyrs, three "known" individuals were depicted as a kind of trinity of IWW martyrs. Joseph Hilstrom, a thirty-three—year—old Wobbly poet better known as Joe Hill, was executed by Utah authorities on November 19, 1915, for allegedly killing a Salt Lake City grocer on January 10, 1914. Frank Little, a member of the IWW General Executive board, was lynched and hanged by six masked and armed men on the night of July 31, 1917, after speaking to miners in Butte, Montana. On November 11, 1919, Wesley Everest, a member of the IWW, fought a vigilante group in Centralia, Washington, and was tortured and lynched by unknown men who hanged him on a bridge over the Chehalis River.

Official spokesmen of the radical labor movement described these atrocities against members of the IWW in great detail. Reacting to the lynching of Frank Little, *Solidarity,* the official organ of the IWW, published poems calling for revenge. Little's fate demonstrated the Satanic nature of the capitalistic system and consequently spurred on the coming revolution that was to put an end to the existing order and bring about the final day of judgment.[36] The IWW publication about the Centralia tragedy started with R. W. Emerson's poem "A Tongue of Flame," which praised martyrs who fought an evil tyranny.[37] John Dos Passos compared Wesley Everest to Paul Bunyan, a mythical hero of American frontier lumber camps, in his novel *1919.*[38] The *Industrial Worker* of October 23, 1920, urged its readers to remember the known and unknown martyrs who sacrificed their lives in the battle for the coming revolution:

Let's not forget Centralia
Butte and Everett too.
Let's not forget the martyred dead
Who gave their last, their all.
On principles for which they died
We'll boldy stand or fall. . . .
Let's carry on the freedom fight
Right onward to the goal
To overthrow the tyrant's might
And free the human soul.
Worker, you who've not betrayed us
Join the Union of your class

And we'll not forget Centralia
Nor the lesson of the past.[39]

Among the known martyrs of the IWW, only Joe Hill turned into a legendary figure. Numerous articles, monographs, plays, and poems have been written about him and his tragic end. The phrase "pie in the sky" which he supposedly invented became an international slogan of the unemployed.[40] Historian Patrick Renshaw noted in *The Wobblies* that Joe Hill had become more than a labor-movement martyr. He had turned into a kind of King Arthur of the proletariat, who would return from the grave to help working men beat the boss everywhere in the world.[41] Unlike Frank Little and Wesley Everest, Hill was not an active member of the union but rather a fellow traveler who wrote many labor songs. Precisely this fact lent him a romantic aura, while his unknown background made it easy to turn him into a legendary folk hero. Joe Hill also spent nearly two years in jail before his execution, which was ample time for a martyr legend to be created around his image.

Joe Hill depicted himself as a revolutionary martyr—an embodiment of a collective group of workers. He stressed his obscure background and called himself "a citizen of the world" born on "the planet earth."[42] During the long struggle to mitigate the death verdict Joe Hill remained indifferent to his personal fate. He always claimed to welcome death and expressed his assurance that in spite of his innocence, the ruling class would execute him because of his affiliation with the working class. He declared his willingness to die to show to the world this travesty of justice. He urged members of the union not to spend additional money on his case.[43] One month before his execution when all requests to change the death penalty had been denied, he wrote to Ben Williams, the editor of *Solidarity:* "I have nothing to say only that I have always tried to make this earth a little better for the great producing class."[44] He wrote in his last telegram to IWW headquarters: "Goodbye, forget me, don't mourn, organize."[45] It seemed that another anonymous soldier had sacrificed himself in the battle against the system in order to promote the inevitable revolution.

But Joe Hill was a very well known poet among radicals. His songs "Pie in the Sky," "Casey Jones—The Union Scab," "Sing on Song," "There Is Power in the Union," "Nearer My Job to Thee," "The Rebel Girl," and many others became an essential part of the workers' culture. Various workers on strike sang these songs in their rallies even prior to Hill's execution. Others became famous after his death. Wobblies, Socialists, Communists, and—later—AFL-CIO members, transcended sectarian differences to sing Joe Hill's songs and to share his lore. Joe Hill knew the power of his songs, so he wrote his will in the form of a poem, "My Last Will," which was published in the *International Socialist Review* on December 15, 1915, and later in the official IWW songbook:

> My will is easy to decide
> For there is nothing to divide.
> My kin don't need a fuss and moan—
> "Moss does not cling to rolling stone,"
> My body—Oh!—If I could choose,
> I would to ashes it reduce,
> And let the merry breezes blow
> My dust to where some flowers grow.
> Perhaps some fading flower then
> Would come to life and bloom again.
> This is my last and final will.
> Good luck to all of you, Joe Hill.[46]

Thus, Joe Hill laid the foundation for the ritual that would turn him into a mythical martyred hero. Thirty thousand people attended his funeral in Chicago and marched through the streets singing his songs. O. N. Hilton, who delivered the funeral address, declared that "our beloved dead do not ever wholly die." Hill's ashes were distributed in small envelopes and scattered to the winds in every state except Utah and in any country where the IWW had its locals. Bill Haywood attached Hill's last song to all the envelopes he sent to IWW locals, instructing them to scatter Hill's ashes to the winds on the following May 1.[47]

The IWW as a group was most responsible for creating the martyr image of Hill within the pages of the "Little Red Song Book." Radical writers like Ralph Chaplin, Cash Stevens, Henry George Weiss and many others also contributed to Hill's legacy in their works. Later, with the weakening of the IWW, his legend was perpetuated mainly by individual writers. John Dos Passos told Hill's life story in *1919,* and Earl Robinson wrote the famous ballad "I Dreamed I Saw Joe Hill Last Night." These works helped to spread the myth of Joe Hill. According to literary critic Wallace Stegner, people made him a martyr because he had imagination. "He died for a cause, for a principle, . . . for things that fire the imagination."[48]

As in the case of other radicals, Joe Hill was turned into a freedom fighter who died while fighting the tyranny of capitalism. "Joseph Hilstrom, murdered by the hired assassins of the capitalist class who for a few dirty pieces of silver shot him to death," wrote Jim Larkin in the *International Socialist Review*. "He was shot because he belonged to an organization who declared revolt upon the system. . . . They shot him to death because . . . he was the voice of the inarticulate downtrodden; they crucified him on their cross of gold, spilled his blood on the altar of their God—profit."[49] Larkin compared the tyranny of capitalism to ancient tyrants who had crucified Christ because he pronounced the truth that would make man free.

As the archetype of a radical martyr, Joe Hill provided the necessary sacrificial ties to cement the ranks of the radical movement with blood. "The death orgy . . . has done more to cement together the forces that are about to overthrow the ghoulish capitalist system than anything that has happened in decades," wrote Ralph Chaplin in the *International Socialist Review*.[50] "Let his blood cement the many divided sections of our movement," declared Jim Larkin, "and our slogan for the future be: 'Joe Hill's body lies mouldering in the grave, but the cause goes marching on.' "[51]

Joe Hill's sympathizers portrayed him as an agent of history who brought the message of the new era to the world. Consequently, in the future, when history would prove the triumph of his ideals, the great jury of free human beings would reverse the final verdict in the case of Joe Hill. The Bolshevik Revolution, which occurred three years after Joe Hill's execution, signified the beginning of the historical triumph of the working class for many radicals. Thus, The *New Solidarity* wrote that "Joe Hill was symbolic of the coming man who worked for and died to help bring forth that new Era of labor in which the working class shall triumph over all the earth."[52] The same paper depicted a vision of the future in which the World Congress of Workers would decide to build a memorial to honor Joe Hill.[53] Such a vision of redemption within history gave meaning to the sacrifice of a radical martyr.

This vision was not realized, but the idea of martyrdom culminating in inevitable victory in history remained essential to radical opponents of the existing system. A martyred hero embodied the present fate of the radical movement and also strengthened the dedication of other radicals to continue their fight against the ruling class. Individual sacrifice was not perceived as a tragedy in the eyes of radicals since it only hastened the coming victory of those who believed history was with them. However, since such a martyred hero appealed only to a small group of dedicated radicals, when they tried to recruit more supporters to the movement, they modified this image. Thus, when Eugene Victor Debs, the most famous radical figure in industrial America, attempted to win converts to socialism, he depicted a more moderate and generally accepted martyr image in his speeches and writings. Similarly, Debs's supporters tried to place their leader within American political culture by portraying him as both a radical and a typical American martyr—a combination of Joe Hill and Abraham Lincoln.

Eugene Victor Debs was born in Terre Haute, Indiana, on November 5, 1855. His family immigrated to America from Colmar, Alsace, in 1849, and unlike most European immigrants at that time, neither parent was motivated by poverty to emigrate. Terre Haute experienced evangelical revivals during Debs's childhood, which were common in many other midwestern towns as a response to the strains of industrialization. This small-town and middle-class background moulded a significant part of Debs's character and, although he became a radical opponent of the American industrial system, he nonetheless remained firmly rooted in American tradition and culture. His deep commitment to the spirit of American democracy and his religious faith affected his radical rhetoric and his socialistic positions. It was only natural, then, that among all the radical figures, he was the most popular for large segments of American-born workers and also won the deep sympathy and esteem of many middle-class liberals and Progressive reformers.

Debs's public career spanned the years from after the Civil War to World War I, an era characterized by the development of American industrial capitalism. He started his political career as the founder and leader of the American Railway Union which was very active in labor struggles and strikes in the late nineteenth century. In 1894 Debs was sentenced to jail for violating a federal injunction during the Pullman strike. According to most records Debs became a socialist only after he was released from Woodstock jail in 1895.[54] John Spargo, one of the top leaders of the Socialist party, drew a general conclusion from Debs's conversion to socialism. In his article "Eugene V. Debs, Incarnate Spirit of Revolt," he wrote that any leader of revolution must first experience personal suffering. "To voice the cry of labor he must first endure its agony; to speak the protest of the doomed he must first endure the doom. . . . In the prison cell the Angel of

Freedom touched his [Debs's] lips with fire from the altar and set him free to proclaim the Revolution."[55]

Debs left jail a confirmed but nondoctrinaire Socialist and worked in the Socialists' ranks basically as a moral agitator and popular speaker. When it came to formulating a workable collectivist strategy, Debs vacillated between supporting left-wing unionism and endorsing moderate parliamentarianism. As an able conciliator between the various wings of the American Socialist party, Debs became the permanent Socialist candidate for the presidency, personifying basically the ethical force of the socialist critique. Four times he was the party's candidate for the presidency, and in 1912 and 1920 he won nearly a million votes in the elections. Opposing the Great War, Debs embodied the radical opposition to the Wilson administration and was perceived by various members of it as the most extreme enemy of the American war effort. On April 13, 1919, he was sentenced to ten years in prison after a jury found him guilty of violating the espionage and sedition acts. He started his term when the Great War had already ended but Woodrow Wilson refused to pardon him despite the enormous public pressure from many liberal and progressive Americans. Ironically, it was Warren G. Harding, a conservative Republican president, who released Debs in 1921 after he had spent almost two years in a federal penitentiary in Atlanta, Georgia. He came out of jail physically sick and exhausted, but morally undamaged. Until his death in 1926 he concentrated on literary works, which enhanced his image as a legendary hero of the working class.

Although Debs was neither executed nor murdered, his prison terms enabled friends and supporters to portray him as a suffering leader who personally shared the tribulations of the despised and the poor. Especially during his second prison term, Debs's friends depicted him as a martyr to convince the public and the president that he should be released. But beyond this concrete purpose they used his suffering as an example of the fate of radicals in America. Essentially, however, Debs's martyr image contained both "American" and "un-American" elements: as an individual he was deeply rooted in American tradition and culture, while he embodied a party that radically opposed the American socioeconomic system.

Toward the end of his public career, reflecting on his own sacrifice and suffering, Debs wrote:

> The trial and privations, the defeats and
> Discouragements, the pains, punishments and

> Persecutions were all good for me; they were all
> Needed in my life and I thank whatever gods
> There be for them all.[56]

Likewise Debs praised the martyrdom of John Brown, the "Mollie Ma-guires," and the Haymarket anarchists, noting that their executions had only promoted the cause and that history would prove them right.[57] Yet Debs never denied the human tragedy of the person who suffered or died for a radical cause. He valued the sanctity of human life and thus refrained from advocating total self-denial. Occasionally, he even interpreted martyr-dom within the context of the "theosophy of suffering," which Emma Goldman explicitly rejected and other radicals such as Albert Parsons or Joe Hill had simply ignored. Debs believed in historical progress, but he inte-grated this belief into the Christian view of a cosmic order with its cycle of sin, fall, suffering, and redemption. Consequently, he regarded sacrifice for a radical cause as a redemptive act within the context of a divine order. "I followed the inner light that God put there to guide me through dark places and it never led me astray and never will," he wrote from jail.[58]

Debs used the image of Jesus Christ to support the socialist cause and perceived Christ's martyrdom as relevant to the contemporary struggle against capitalism. In his article, "Jesus the Supreme Leader," which Debs later expanded into a book, he wrote that Christ was the martyr of the working class, "the inspired evangel of the downtrodden masses, . . . whose love for the poor. . . hallowed all the days of his consecrated life, of his death, and gave to the ages his divine inspiration and his deathless name."[59] To a minister who visited him in jail he said: "He [Jesus] denounced the profiteers, and it was for this that they nailed his quivering body to the cross and spiked it to the gate of Jerusalem, not because he told men to love one another."[60] In jail Debs used Jesus Christ almost as an alter ego. In his cell he hung not a portrait of Karl Marx, but a crucifix. The other inmates began to call him "little Jesus."[61] Debs developed paternalistic relationships with other prisoners whom he viewed as poor souls suffering under a wicked system and therefore in need of his support and consolation.[62] "It seems to me," he wrote to his brother in Christlike language, "that my heart is the very heart and center of all the sadness and sorrow, all the pain and misery and all the suffering and agony in the world."[63] It was not surprising then, that in public forums the analogy with Christ became a dominant theme. A minister from Ohio admitted that he viewed Debs as a "social savior . . . the vicarious victim of society's sins and his life is a continual crucifixion."[64] Many poems also compared him to Jesus Christ and thus imbued his martyrdom with Christian symbolism.[65]

In the play *Debs Has Visitors,* Charles Erskine Scott Wood described Christ's spirit's visiting the jail and addressing Debs: "If the world hates you, you know it hated me before it hated you. If they persecuted me they will also persecute you—but all these things they will do unto you for my name's sake because they know not Him that sent me." When Debs asked the figure if he was Christ who had been crucified in Jerusalem, the spirit answered that it had been crucified many times by priests and patriots, hypocrites and other sinners.

> In Jerusalem they crucified my body
> But today they crucify my soul. . . .
> And to testify—Out of discontent cometh redemption. . . .
> "Gene" you are of the prophets
> And you shall be stoned for my sake.
> But peace I leave with you
> My peace I give unto you
> Not as the world giveth, give I unto you
> Let not your heart be troubled
> Neither let it be afraid.[66]

It was this religious dimension, which he and his supporters gave to his martyrdom, that distinguished Debs from other radical martyrs. Those who described him as a radical martyr did not totally abandon the religious millennial vision. While some followers remained in the pure radical tradition and viewed Debs as an agent of future history who would reach his ultimate triumph in the next stage of historical development—the stage of the socialist revolution[67]—others described him in religious terms and interpreted his martyrdom in the light of biblical cosmology. He was elevated to the sphere of Christian saints and biblical prophets, a realm that was irrelevant to other radical figures who suffered for the cause.

Many radicals perceived Debs as another representative of a universal class of the oppressed, fighting the tyranny of capitalism wherever it existed. For example, the devoted radical Ruth Le Prade, who edited the book *Debs and the Poets,* praised Debs's willingness to become a martyr for the labor movement, comparing him to other figures who had changed the course of history while suffering from the authorities of law and order.[68] "We are not fit to kneel beside thy feet. . . . We . . . would claim thee still—yet we dare not. For at thy side stand Socrates and Christ, Savanarola and John Brown—the martyrs and the heroes of the world."[69] An anonymous writer even thanked these authorities for producing radical martyrs:

> I drink the blood ye have spilled
> I drink and I give you thanks!
> For every heretic burned
> For every key ye have turned
> A million lamps have ye lit![70]

Other supporters portrayed him as a "suffering servant"[71] for unfortunate humanity and repeatedly printed his statement: "While there is a lower class I am in it. While there is a criminal class I am of it. While there is a soul in prison I am not free."[72] In spite of his release in 1921, Debs was still deprived of his American citizenship, a fact that permitted Henry Schnittkind to write that "from now on he became a man without country . . . by doing this they [his tormentors] made him a citizen of the world."[73]

Such statements however, did not always fit the image Debs himself projected when he interpreted his struggle for the labor movement both as universal and as specifically American. Thus, he often lamented in his speeches that industrial America had distorted the nation's glorious heritage but, unlike other radicals, he never denied the value of his heritage. In his view, America had initially been the land of freedom, but somehow businessmen had destroyed this liberty, which now could only be restored through socialism. After his release from his first prison term on November 22, 1895, he expressed his appreciation for basic American institutions and ideals in a speech in Chicago: "I challenge the world to assign a reason why a judge under the solemn obligation of an oath to obey the constitution should in the temple dedicated to justice, stab the Magna Carta of American liberty to death in the interest of corporations."[74] Debs often referred to American national heroes such as Abraham Lincoln and John Brown in his various discourses. One paragraph of his plea to the jury was closely and perhaps unconsciously modeled on John Brown's final address to the court of Virginia in 1859.[75] In his address before the Supreme Court when his conviction was confirmed he declared: "Sixty years ago the Supreme Court affirmed the validity of the Fugitive Slave Law to save chattel slavery. Five years later that infamous institution was swept from the land in a torrent of blood. I despise the Espionage Law with every drop of blood in my veins, and I defy the Supreme Court and all its powers of capitalism to do their worst."[76] Ray Ginger wrote in his biography of Debs that he used

Lincoln as an inspirational example and sometimes regarded himself as the potential second emancipator of the workers of America.[77]

Indeed, many other supporters of Debs, who considered themselves radical opponents of the American capitalist system, depicted him precisely as a national martyr, despite his lack of citizenship. They looked upon him as another individual in the glorious chain of heroes who suffered to redeem the American people and through it the whole of mankind.[78] They compared him to other American martyrs, and most frequently he emerged as a combination of Abraham Lincoln and John Brown: both as champion of the coming emancipation of the new slaves of industrial America and as a rebel who defied unjust laws. He resembled Lincoln in his method of nonviolence and suffered like Brown from the violence inflicted upon him in the name of law and order by the foes of freedom and democracy.[79] William Leonard, author and professor of English at the University of Wisconsin, noted that Eugene V. Debs reincarnated for him the spirit of John Brown, Whittier, Garrison, Lovejoy, Phillips, Lincoln, and Walt Whitman, "the great lovers of their fellow man who struggled for human emancipation and thus vitalized the meaning of heroic Americanism."[80]

In the play *Debs Has Visitors,* the spirits of Walt Whitman and Abraham Lincoln also visited Eugene V. Debs in the Atlanta jail. They both represented the American idealism for which Debs suffered. Whitman's spirit declared that Debs's imprisonment proved his own error at the time when he had thought that America was a democratic nation.[81] Lincoln's spirit in the play revealed the main elements of American political martyrdom and ascribed the title of *American martyr* to the jailed socialist leader:

> So you are in jail because you spoke for freedom. . . .
> I'm sorry I was never jailed.
> There is something there I guess I missed. . . .
> There were plenty who would have liked to have seen me in jail.
> Or hung, but we rebels then had grown too strong. . . .
> They fought for property we fought for men—
> The same fight you are making now.
> John Brown was jailed.
> The rope that strangled him was the same power that put you here. . . .
> We fought to strike the chains from poor black men
> But there are chains eyes cannot see. . .
> You fight to strike those shackles off. . . .
> They call me "The Emancipator"
> "Gene," I pass the title on to you.[82]

In this play, as in other writings, Debs was depicted as an American martyr for reform. His imprisonment demonstrated how far capitalistic America had deviated from its original ideals and goals. In that sense Debs suffered to restore America to its initial democratic purpose rather than for a future revolution. Upton Sinclair, for example, declared that the campaign for Debs's release was conducted by those Americans who wished their country to return to its old traditions of freedom of speech.[83] Thus Debs took his place among other American martyrs. Those who would benefit from his sacrifice were not only the humble toilers of universal mankind but also the American people in particular.

In sum, Debs and his supporters combined an unflinching willingness for self-sacrifice with deep reverence for the value of individual human life, which turned each necessary sacrifice into a human tragedy. In his suffering the martyr redeemed both the poor masses of mankind and the American people. Debs was depicted not only as an unknown soldier who suffered for his class but also as an American citizen who suffered to restore his country to the democratic ideal by fighting capitalism. The secular context of the inevitable revolution within history was juxtaposed with religious eschatology, in which Debs's apparent defeat and sacrifice would turn into victory and redemption. In that sense Eugene V. Debs bridged the gap between radical martyrs and more "acceptable" martyrs for reform; between "un-American" martyrs such as the Haymarket anarchists and IWW victims and American martyred heroes such as Abraham Lincoln. Nonetheless, despite these "American" characteristics of his martyrdom, Debs never became another Lincoln in the eyes of the American public in general since he remained the leader of an "un-American" party that radically opposed the basic structure of American capitalism.

7

Contemporary America: Decline and Resurrection of the Martyr

The martyr embodies symbolically a rich biblical tradition of sin, fall, suffering, sacrifice, and redemption. This tradition, which has given meaning to the American experience, is not only a religious manifestation but also a cultural phenomenon, an essential part of what can be called the American civil religion. Yet, like all cultural phenomena, this tradition is dynamic, contextual, and variable. Many factors determine the degree of its significance in any given period and among specific groups in society. As we have seen in previous chapters, in the context of American history at least three general factors are crucial for developing the martyr tradition: (1) the belief of a majority of the society in biblical religion and its applicability to historical circumstances; (2) its compatibility with other cultural traditions that give meaning to human experience, such as the sanctity of human life, the ideal of freedom, the belief in progress, or the commitment to reform; (3) specific tragedies that require certain explanation in order to become meaningful.

In the second third of the nineteenth century all three of these factors were dominant in the United States: most Americans still interpreted their experience in biblical terms and used religious terminology to explain historical events. In particular, a basic belief in the morality of the universe, in man's ability to free himself from sin and tyranny, and in salvation as the ultimate purpose of life, created fertile ground for the whole tradition of martyrdom. An ideology of commitment to collective salvation through the perfection of the democratic process emerges from the various discourses of the period. This ideology was more receptive to concepts like suffering, sacrifice, and martyrdom than the later individualistic ethos. It even bridged, for the most part, the gap between the affirmation of suffering and the pursuit of happiness, between the glorification of sacrifice and the veneration of human life.

Starting with the reform movements of the 1830s, the culture of sin, sacrifice, and redemption was incorporated into politics by abolitionists and reached the peak of its influence in the Civil War. The war and Lincoln's assassination provided an excellent historical context for incorporating the tradition of martyrdom into the American national consciousness. "For us and our country," wrote the poet Robert Lowell, analyzing the meaning of the Gettysburg Address, "he [Lincoln] left Jefferson's ideals of freedom and equality joined to the Christian sacrificial act of death and rebirth. I believe this is a meaning that goes beyond sects of religion and beyond peace or war, and is now part of our lives as a challenge, obstacle and hope." [1]

Indeed, as we have seen, martyrdom as a sublime concept remained potent in America throughout the nineteenth century and well into the twentieth. Authors, poets, artists, journalists, orators, preachers, educators, and politicians all used the idea of martyrdom in order to explain tragedies and to invest meaning in the suffering, death, and persecution of public figures of their time. During the Gilded Age and the Progressive Era, however, certain cultural developments undermined the effectiveness and the centrality of concepts such as suffering, sacrifice, and martyrdom. These concepts still gave meaning to the American experience between 1870s and the 1920s, especially among the reform and radical movements. Nonetheless, as was shown in previous chapters, the ideological significance of sacrifice and martyrdom was challenged by new worldviews, such as a more liberal version of Christianity, the individualistic success ethos, the spirit of pragmatism, and a whole attack on the foundation of the genteel culture.

These cultural developments accelerated after World War I and many authors and writers indeed considered the period of the 1920s as the beginning of our own modern time. [2] Although the martyr image did not disappear from the American consciousness, its significance declined in the modern culture of the twentieth century. Even the image of such an enduring martyr as Abraham Lincoln underwent certain changes. From the 1920s the number of addresses and sermons on Lincoln greatly diminished, and the tendency of de-mystification, so common in our modern culture, also undermined the martyr image of the Civil War president. Certainly Lincoln, together with George Washington, is still the outstanding American national hero, but those who fostered the Lincoln legacy basically stressed his achievements and character rather than his suffering and sacrifice.

One explanation for the decline of the martyr tradition in the modern United States derives from basic changes in American religious perceptions. Despite being the most religious people in the Western world, Americans no longer use religious symbols or biblical images to interpret their entire historical experience. Liberal Christianity undermined doctrine and diminished the value of suffering and sacrifice. Happiness and self-fulfillment replaced martyrdom and sacrifice as a desirable purpose and the final goal of many congregations in the twentieth century. "There is even a tendency visible in many evangelical circles," wrote Robert N. Bellah in *Habits of the Heart,* "to thin this biblical language of sin and redemption to an idea of Jesus as the friend who helps us find happiness and self-fulfillment."[3] It certainly influenced the political culture of the twentieth century which suffered from a certain "symbolic poverty" and decline in its civil religion. Even those who use religious language in their political discourses tend to select concepts such as love, forgiveness, brotherhood, liberation, and responsibility, rather than sin, sacrifice, and redemption. In fact, many public figures avoid religious language altogether, some out of choice, others simply as a result of ignorance. In a society that stresses instrumentalism, functionalism, utilitarian individualism, and efficiency, moral language saturated with religious symbols sounds like empty phraseology and seems politically counterproductive. But even those who struggled against this utilitarian culture and strove to fight human alienation with language that stressed commitment and social responsibility, avoided sacrificial terminology and refrained from glorifying suffering and martyrdom.

The disappointment with the Progressive crusade and its fiasco in the 1920s weakened the whole reform tradition in America at least until the 1960s. Indeed, American society absorbed many of the concrete reform measures that the Progressive reformers had advocated, and, especially on the municipal and state level of politics, as well as among big corporations, certain reform goals became part of the established system. On the whole, however, the crusading spirit of the reformer, the culture of commitment that certain Progressive figures had celebrated, disinterested altruism as a middle-class norm, all died with the end of the First World War.[4]

During the 1920s most sections of the American middle class were busy achieving their specific interests rather than engaging in reform crusades to regenerate America, This different attitude was reinforced by the new psychoanalytic approach, which emphasized personal fulfillment, individual happiness, and self-expression, rather than collective salvation, group effort, and social responsibility. This new therapeutic tradition denied the whole significance of martyrdom. Moreover, the modern business ethos, which stressed efficiency, productivity, and wordly success on the one hand, and on the other hand, the new bohemian counterculture, which emphasized hedonism and nihilism, also combined to undermine the value of martyrdom. Both searched for a meaningful and happy present and refused to endorse suffering in the present for a better future.

Despite all these new cultural developments the American public had an opportunity to hear the phrase *our martyred president* during the 1920s. It was applied to President Warren G. Harding, who died of a stroke on August 2, 1923, in San Francisco. His death in office inspired his friends to describe him almost as a second Lincoln, as one who "gave his life to the service of our country as truly as any one in our history."[5] However, the revelation, shortly after his death, of the many scandals of the Harding administration made his presidency synonymous with corruption and inadequacy. To the extent that he is remembered at all, Harding is viewed as an incompetent president rather than as a martyred hero. Perhaps the true martyred heroes of this period were the two executed anarchists Niccola Sacco and Bartolomeo Vanzetti, but their martyrdom was meaningful only to a few alienated intellectuals and radicals who incorporated their names into the legacy of "un-American" martyrs.

It is interesting to note that while the depression years of the 1930s were the worst collective trauma Americans had experienced since the Civil War, the general public rarely used the concepts of sacrifice and martyrdom to explain the suffering. Some radical intellectuals who affiliated themselves with the Communist party resorted to the martyr spirit in their effort to mobilize the people to fight capitalism and sacrifice everything for the triumph of the working-class revolution.[6] But deep agony, a sense of despair, helplessness, and apathy characterized the public reaction to the depression, more than a fighting spirit rationalized and rekindled through the rhetoric of sacrifice and martyrdom. Moreover, when President Franklin D. Roosevelt embarked upon the radical plan of the New Deal he approached it not as a crusade to regenerate the country, but rather as a concrete experiment aimed at reducing the general suffering. His whole attitude to reform was practical rather than idealistic. In that sense he was diametrically opposed not only to radicals who vowed to sacrifice their lives for a better future, but also to those progressive reformers who strove to redeem America and to build the kingdom of God through commitment to altruistic reform.[7] Likewise, when President Roosevelt entered the Second World War he explained it not as a crusade "to make the world safe for democracy" but as a military reaction to the Japanese attack.

When Roosevelt died in the middle of his fourth term some public spokesmen tried to portray him as another martyred president. Yet the term *martyr* in the case of FDR was soon abandoned: nothing in his death resembled a martyr's death, and the whole spirit of the time was not receptive to such an image. FDR is remembered as a national hero because of the domestic and international achievements during his twelve years of office, and not because he died in office or sacrificed himself for the cause.[8] Despite the war, Americans did not celebrate a famous martyr hero during the 1940s and the 1950s. Modern times seem to be indifferent to this whole tradition, and no central figure in American politics experienced a tragic death that transformed him into a modern martyr and revived the tradition. Nonetheless, during the 1960s no fewer than four famous political leaders were assassinated within a period of five years. Hence, no discussion of the significance of martyrdom in American political culture can ignore the events of these years and their potential for creating new American martyred heroes.

The short historical perspective makes a serious discussion of the martyrs of the 1960s almost impossible. The generation that experienced the assassinations of President John F. Kennedy, Malcolm X, Martin Luther King, Jr., and Robert F. Kennedy, is still alive and will continue to live for many years to come. It is therefore difficult to determine whether one of these assassinated public figures will eventually be perceived as an enduring martyred hero and will provide inspiration for future generations. Nevertheless, it is possible to trace how these public figures have already become part of the American political heritage and to speculate about their future as national martyred figures.

On November 22, 1963, while riding in an open car in Dallas, Texas,

President John F. Kennedy was shot by an assassin and died a few minutes later. This was the fourth assassination of an American president. On February 21, 1965, Malcolm X, a radical and militant black leader who preached violence and the secession of blacks from the United States, was assassinated in upper Manhattan. Three years later, on April 4, 1968, Martin Luther King, Jr., the famous black leader of the civil rights movement, was assassinated in Memphis, Tennessee. Although King was an apostle of nonviolence and a winner of the Nobel Peace Prize, his assassination set off a wave of rioting across the country. Three months later, on June 5, Robert F. Kennedy, a presidential candidate on the Democratic ticket, was shot to death in Los Angeles, on the night of his victory in the California primary. These four assassinations all shocked the nation profoundly. It is safe to assume that, from among these four different victims, Malcolm X, who radically opposed the American establishment, will not become a nationally acknowledged American martyr hero. In this respect he can be compared to other radical figures such as the Haymarket anarchists or Joe Hill: while the Black Moslems will use his image as an ideological weapon and source of inspiration for their ongoing battle against white America, and while some black leaders will admire his romantic figure, the public in general will continue to view him as a dangerous radical and will remain indifferent to his assassination. The other political murders of the 1960s, however, had an enormous impact on the American public in general and each victim, in his own way, seems to have the potential for becoming a modern American national martyr.

President Kennedy's assassination had the most shattering effect on contemporaries. The unprecedented coverage that the media gave to the assassination and subsequent events turned almost everyone into an active participant in the ritual of grief, agony, and mourning. For four whole days Americans virtually ceased their usual activities and immersed themselves in the event that entered their living rooms through massive television coverage. Never before, and never since, has the American public been so saturated with the details of a single event. Indeed, research that examined public reaction to the assassination revealed that many Americans personalized the event and experienced symptoms similar to those following the loss of a close friend or relative. Some people cried for the entire four days, others felt shame and outrage as if they had personally killed their chief executive. Physical symptoms such as fatigue, loss of appetite, tears, and tension were very common.[9] Between November 22 and November 27 Americans again seemed to participate in a collective baptism of blood that transformed them into a single family of mourners. "Through the medium of television the nation had communally experienced, and vicariously participated in a magnificently staged rite of passage from life to death, to myth and legend."[10]

"A blast from the trumpet of the Angel Gabriel announcing the end of time could hardly have affected us Americans more than did the news of the assassination of President John F. Kennedy," wrote the Catholic monthly, *Christian Century*. "Everything stood still. . . . In offices, on the streets, in homes, men and women who had never seen President Kennedy in the flesh wept. Games were cancelled, business and schools closed, theaters locked up. The mood of apocalypse was on us all. . . . All over America people flocked to their churches."[11] Religious magazines were not alone in expressing the apocalyptical mood that followed the assassination. Even a popular journal such as the *Saturday Evening Post* wrote: "The unbelievable had happened. It was a moment that changed every life in the nation. It changed the color of the sky, left a dark cloud over the country, left every American feeling not only stricken but somehow dishonored. . . . The vivid, confident, high-spirited figure of John F. Kennedy is gone. . . . The new frontier is behind us."[12]

Indeed, the personality of the assassinated president, as well as the image he and his administration had projected, intensified the sense of agony and grief. A young, charismatic, attractive, and vital president who had conveyed new hope and exercised new dimensions of power, had been slain without apparent reason at the peak of his success. Portrayed by his supporters as one committed to fighting poverty, to eliminating racial injustice, and to bringing peace to the world, John F. Kennedy embodied a new style of politics and idealism to millions of Americans. His exuberance, promise and idealism especially appealed to a new generation of young liberals. Yet he had only begun his career and had not yet fulfilled his vision. "But the bright promise of his administration, as of his life, was cut short in Dallas," wrote the historian Arthur M. Schlesinger, Jr., who personally participated in the Kennedy administration.

John Kennedy's death has greater pathos [than Lincoln's], because he had barely begun—because he had so much to do, so much to give to his family, his nation, his world. . . . He saw America not as an old nation, self-righteous, conservative, satisfied in its grossness and materialism, but as a young nation, questing, self-critical, dissatisfied, caring for the qualities of mind, sensibility, and spirit, which sustain culture, produce art, and elevate society.[13]

Many obituaries and eulogies following the assassination drew on the traditional element of the martyr figure, describing the slain president as a new type of politician, committed to reforming both the nation and the world, and creating an image that was closer to Lincoln's than to that of Garfield and McKinley. Indeed many addresses drew direct analogies with Lincoln's fate and some even predicted a similar glorious future for Kennedy—as the modern martyred hero who had died in order to regenerate the American people and to rededicate the United States to its destiny as the world's redeemer.[14]

The erratic flow of history has given this nation a role we did not ask for, may not want and, surely, have not yet fully accepted . . . international responsibility. We must now prove under a different leadership that the image he [Kennedy] projected was in fact the signal of this people's willingness to accept the burdens and the dangers as well as the prestige of its unique role in world affairs.[15]

John William McCormack, the Speaker of the House, delivered a eulogy on November 24, to Congress, in which he portrayed the slain president as a leader sent by God to the Chosen People in order to save the country from peril.[16] The editor of the *Christian Century* only echoed many sermons and tributes when he portrayed the event as God's punishment and urged Americans to repent their sins.

We saw in the flash of an assassin's rifle the lightning of God's judgment on us and on our society. . . . The lifting of the burden of guilt requires that we confront our lack of sympathy with the poor, with persons of racial minority status, with the mentally disturbed, with the outsiders and the lost . . . that we abjure our resistance to change.[17]

Other tributes drew a more optimistic lesson from the tragedy, asserting that Kennedy's death could provide inspiration for a new and vibrant America.[18] Chief Justice Earl Warren urged Americans to live up to Kennedy's ideals and to work to fulfill his goals of justice and peace. "If the wound we sustained is also a blessing, a true sacrifice which makes new things possible, it lies in the opportunity it gives us to reach beyond ourselves in protectiveness and care," wrote the journalist Richard Gilman in the *Commonweal*.[19]

When more political assassinations occurred in the 1960s, however, this hopeful message of sacrifice for a new beginning seemed ironic, if not cynical. What followed the president's death was not love and peace but strife, chaos, and more violence. Until the end of the decade the nation experienced racial hatred and violence, riots on campuses and in urban ghettos, increasing poverty, the trauma of Vietnam, and a general collapse of JFK's dream. The tragic and meaningless murders of Martin Luther King, Jr., and Robert F. Kennedy in 1968 epitomized for many Americans the end of idealism and underscored the very shaky foundations of their nation. More and more people viewed these events not as a necessary warning for the redeemer nation to reform its behavior and rededicate itself to its mission, but rather as manifestations of a doomed and sick nation that killed its saviors in order to hasten its damnation. For many Americans these two assassinations reinforced the tragic denial of their great future.[20] "We are the first generation that learned from experience, in our innocent twenties, that things were *not* really getting better, that we shall not overcome," wrote Jack Newfield, one of Robert Kennedy's admirers. "We felt by the time we reached thirty, that we had already glimpsed the most compassionate leaders our nation could produce, and they had all been assassinated. And from this time forward, things would get worse; our best political leaders were part of memory now, not hope."[21] He expressed here the sentiments of many disillusioned young Americans at the end of the decade.

This mood typified the attitude of modern culture toward the whole tradition of martyrdom. Without the belief in a redemptive future martyrs cannot exist. Martyrs are agents of hope, of a better tomorrow, closer both to the utopian stage of the future and to the perfect initial stage of the past. A martyr's sacrifice will promote the redemption of civilization. Thus, if Americans in the late 1960s conceived of their society as a doomed and sick one, they could not transform any of these assassinated leaders into an enduring national martyr.

Indeed, John F. Kennedy did not become such a martyr. For various reasons the enchantment of Camelot embodied by the charismatic Kennedys faded rapidly and JFK's image in particular weakened even before the end of the decade. Such a phenomenon, though inconclusive because of the short perspective, has been noted by many journalists, biographers, and historians. The *New York Times Magazine* wrote early in November 1965 that Europeans had started to consider the man, not his death. "If he really possessed 'vision' and idealism, it was without moral purpose. . . . He was fortunate in his season because he could capture its mood without any deep intellectual or imaginative insights. Other seasons cannot find what he had to say."[22] "Not only on college campuses and in the underground press, but also in liberal journals JFK's ringing inaugural address now seems hollow, even dangerous to some of those who once admired it," wrote the editor of *Time* in February 1970. "The most damaging evidence against Kennedy is the distance the nation has moved since his inauguration."[23] The *New York Times* noted that Kennedy's promise to " 'pay any price, bear any burden . . . to assure the survival and success of liberty' appears, in retrospect, to have been the summons to Vietnam."[24] Other factors than Vietnam undermined the Kennedy image. Something in the aristocratic life-style of all the Kennedys, which had appealed to their followers and admirers at the time, seemed corrupt and arrogant to later critics. It contradicted basic "democratic" values of American political culture. "Kennedyism is the assertion of the right of those property-endowed—by education, upbringing, leisured high purpose, and yes, by birth if need be—to rule," wrote Midge Decter, the executive editor of *Harper's Magazine,* in the *Commentary* of January 1970. "The demand to be ruled in an attractive way is a reactionary demand—regardless of the radical rhetoric."[25]

One could dismiss this critique and argue that in general the positive image of Kennedy has prevailed over time despite the revisionists intention to debunk any national heroic figure. But even the favorable accounts admitted that JFK had became a controversial hero and had certainly not turned into an enduring martyr.[26] "He was not a martyr who died for the cause," wrote Ralph G. Marlyn in *A Hero For Our Time.* James Reston, one of Kennedy's close friends, wrote that the tragedy of JFK was greater than the accomplishment, "but in the end the tragedy enhances the accomplishment and revives the hope.[27]

While it is still not clear whether the tragedy made John F. Kennedy a popular hero, his martyr image has certainly suffered. "The 'New Frontier' was a limited exercise in civilizing the status quo," wrote Henry Fairlie somewhat cynically in 1965.[28] This explains why Kennedy's fate resembles more the fate of Garfield and McKinley than that of Lincoln. He simply was not a reformer. He neither envisioned nor fulfilled some new mode of existence despite the rhetoric of the "New Frontier" and the image of Camelot. It seems almost impossible to portray this attractive, young, vital, and somehow chauvinistic president as a "suffering servant" who sacrificed his life for redemptive purposes. Certainly the cultural atmosphere of the midtwentieth century was less receptive to the idea of the martyred hero than that of the nineteenth century, while biblical symbols had far less appeal than in previous generations.

Thus, by looking at the images of both John and Robert Kennedy from a current perspective, one is compelled to acknowledge the decline of the martyr tradition in modern America. They are not revered today as inspirational martyrs because American society seems reluctant to praise sacrifice, suffering, and martyrdom as part of its ideology of commitment. A revival of this tradition could happen only when a well-known figure who had constantly used the language of commitment and devoted his life to far-reaching reforms suffered a tragic death. These historical circumstances characterized the life of Martin Luther King, Jr., who invigorated the whole ideology of sin, suffering, sacrifice, and redemption in his political career. It is interesting, therefore, to examine whether his assassination also resurrected a new martyr image, and gave new life to the concept of martyrdom in American political culture.

Garry Wills, in *The Kennedy Imprisonment*, counterposed the fate of the Kennedys to that of Martin Luther King, Jr., and implied why King, and not Kennedy, had become an American martyred hero.

King, though more revolutionary in some people's eyes, was not "charismatic" in the sense of replacing traditional and legal power with his personal will. . . . His death, as tragic as Kennedy's, did not leave so large an absence. His work has outlasted him; more than any single person he changed the way Americans lived with each other in the sixties. His power was real, because it was not mere assertion—it was a persuasive *yielding* of private will through nonviolent advocacy. . . . His power was the power to suffer, and his killer only increased that power. . . . The changes King wrought are so large as to be almost invisible. . . . While Washington's "best and brightest" worked us into Vietnam, an obscure army of virtue arose in the South and took the longer spiritual trip. . . . King rallied the strength of broken men, transmuting an imposed squalor into the beauty of chosen suffering. The "Kennedy era" was really the age of Dr. King. The famous antitheses and alliterations of John Kennedy's rhetoric sound tinny now. But King's eloquence endures, drawn as it was from ancient sources—the Bible, the spirituals, the hymns and folk songs. He was young at his death, younger than either Kennedy; but he had traveled farther. . . . He has no eternal flame—and no wonder. He is not dead.[29]

It is time to explain, in the light of this whole study, why Martin Luther King, Jr., "is not dead."

Martin Luther King, Jr., embodied the whole reform experience of the 1960s known as the civil rights movement. Dedicated to transforming American society, the movement succeeded in abolishing the system of legal discrimination in the South. King advocated and practiced nonviolent means of struggle, such as mass rallies, civil disobedience, marches, boycotts, and defiance of evil laws that put him in jail more than twenty times. He was, however, much more than a leader of a particular reform movement; he became a moral agent for a better America committed to its ideals and purposes as a redeemer nation. He also symbolized an alternative to the individualistic, competitive, and egocentric culture of the "me" generation of contemporary America.

By showing the gap between American ideals and reality, and through his active commitment to change the reality and bring it closer to the ideals, King led a movement for total transformation that aimed far beyond the mere correction of the evil legal system in the South. The editor of the *Nation* defined him as "the senior voice of moral integrity and humane determination in the United States."[30] King frequently justified his activities in a moral language based on traditional American values and called for complete regeneration of his country. "America you've strayed away," King said in one of his eloquent sermons for social justice. "You've trampled over 19 million of your brethren. All men are created equal. Not some men. Not white men. All men. America, rise up and come home."[31] His assassination in Memphis in the midst of his struggle to reform American society increased his potential for becoming a new tragic hero.

Although our closeness to the events makes it hard to assess whether King will become an enduring national figure, there are, nonetheless, clear signs that point to this tendency. Indeed, small children today in many preschools all over the country are familiar with King even before they learn about Washington and Lincoln. Moreover, the fact that in January 1986 his birthday became a national holiday ensures that his image will be remembered in the future. By this act, the American government institutionalized King's career and created an opportunity for a recurring collective ritual in which King would be remembered at least once a year. Thus it seems probable that King will transcend the specific time period of the 1960s and become, like Abraham Lincoln, a meaningful popular hero for generations to come.

The question that concerns us here is whether or not King also has the potential for becoming an enduring *martyred* hero, despite the cultural climate of modern times, which has devalued the significance of suffering, sacrifice, and martyrdom. Part of the answer lies in his personality: a son of a minister and himself a minister who received his Ph.D in theological studies, King naturally used biblical symbolism and viewed Christ as his main source of inspiration. He was influenced by the personality of Gandhi and regarded him as the first person in history to have used the love ethic of Jesus as a powerful, effective social force. He also accepted Hegel's analysis of the dialectical process that convinced him that growth and progress come through suffering, pain, and struggle.[32] Throughout his career King perceived himself as a potential martyr for the cause and resorted to the concept of martyrdom as an ideological device. He consciously used it as a political weapon, arguing that suffering and sacrifice were essential to the nonviolent resistance to Evil, as well as to the triumph of any reform measure. In that sense he resembled abolitionists such as William L. Garrison, Wendell Phillips, and John Brown rather than the "modern" Progressive reformers who rejected the "theosophy of suffering." In Montgomery, during the bus boycott, King stated: "I want young men and young women . . . who will come into this world with new privileges and new opportunities, . . . to know and see that these new privileges and opportunities did not come without somebody suffering and sacrificing for them." In Montgomery jail he quoted Gandhi declaring that "the real road to happiness lies in going to jail and undergoing suffering and privations there in the interest of one's country and religion."[33]

Indeed King's foes resorted to physical violence, causing injuries, suffering, and even death to many members of the civil rights movement. When racist whites bombed black churches in Montgomery King's reaction was one of personal involvement: "I hope none will have to die as a result of our struggle for freedom in Montgomery. . . . But if anyone has to die, let it be me." When somebody found an unexploded bomb on King's own porch, he addressed a gathering crowd the next morning with the following phrases: "Tell Montgomery that they can keep shooting and I'm going to stand up to them; tell Montgomery they can keep bombing and I'm going to stand up to them. If I had to die tomorrow morning I would die happy because I've been to the Mountaintop and I've seen the Promised Land, and it's going to be here in Montgomery."[34] This sacrificial language had a powerful impact on many people, black and white, who heard and read this speech. King also expressed his conviction in the power of suffering when he addressed the court in Montgomery, or when a mentally disturbed woman made the first assassination attempt on him. After the victory in Montgomery, when King realized that his role in the city was over, he handed in his resignation as Dexter's pastor. In his final address in January 1960, he said that freedom was "always purchased with the high price of sacrifice and suffering," thus reminding his supporters that the struggle was not over.[35]

From the pulpit of Shiloh Baptist Church in Albany, Georgia, King preached to his supporters: "Go to jail without hating the white folks. . . . They can put you in a dungeon and transform you to glory; if they try to kill you, develop a willingness to die."[36] He used jail as a tactical device in his struggles by defying segregation laws, refusing to pay bail, and preferring jail to a fine. "In order to serve as a redemptive agency for the nation," he told a *Life* reporter, "you go to jail and you stay. . . . You have broken a law which is out of line with the moral law and you are willing to suffer the consequences by serving the time.[37] King's thirteenth and most famous imprisonment, in Birmingham, Alabama, ended with his influential *Letter from a Brimingham Jail*. Millions of copies of this pamphlet circulated in churches and many periodicals published this moral call to the religious leaders of the country.

In this letter King fully expressed the three elements necessary for developing a meaningful tradition of suffering, sacrifice, and martyrdom. First, he used biblical analogy, identifying his fate with that of biblical prophets and martyrs. "Just as the . . . prophets left their little villages and . . . just as the Apostle Paul left his little village of Tarsus and carried the gospel of Jesus Christ . . . I too am compelled to carry the gospel of freedom beyond my particular home town."[38] He compared the tactics of civil disobedience to the famous stories of the early Christians, and portrayed the scene of the crucifixion on the hill of Calvary. "It was during that period when the early Christians rejoiced when they were deemed worthy to suffer for what they believed," wrote King when he criticized the religious establishment of his time. "If the Church of today does not recapture the sacrificial spirit of the early Church, it will lose its authentic ring, forfeit the loyalty of millions, and be dismissed as an irrelevant social club with no meaning for the twentieth century."[39]

Secondly, throughout the letter King was able to show how his sacrifice and suffering coalesced with other American ideals and values. Stressing the meaning of freedom to the American people, King noted: "We know through painful experience that freedom is never voluntarily given by the oppressor; it must be demanded by the oppressed."[40] But "we will reach the goal of freedom in Birmingham and all over the nation, because the goal of America is freedom."[41] He praised the American tradition of social progress but asserted that "human progress never rolls in on wheels of inevitability. It comes through the tireless efforts and without this hard work time itself becomes an ally of the forces of social stagnation. . . . Now is the time to make real the promise of democracy, and transform our pending national elegy into a creative psalm of brotherhood."[42] King emphasized that disinterested devotion and constant sacrifice for the cherished ideals of American democracy would regenerate the American society, thus creating a better future. Yet without such a commitment these ideals remained only clichés to justify the status quo. Toward the end of the letter he expressed his hope that the struggle of blacks in America, despite the sacrifice and suffering, would be worthwhile because it was compatible with the whole tradition of American democracy. "If the inexpressible cruelties of slavery could not stop us, the opposition we now face will surely fail. We will win our freedom because the sacred heritage of our nation and the eternal will of God are embodied in our echoing demands."[43]

Finally, throughout the letter King described the tribulations, humiliation, and persecution of blacks and portrayed eloquently the suffering of the black people in the South.[44] He referred to some of the martyred heroes of the civil rights movement, such as James Meredith and others who had challenged the segregation rules in the universities, buses, restaurants, and churches of the South. He incorporated these figures into the American national heritage and envisaged a glorious future for their memory.[45] In the last paragraph of the letter King portrayed his own hard conditions in jail, thus depicting himself as martyr for the cause. The Birmingham jail provided the last element in the sacrificial ties between the black people, the activists who challenged the segregation acts, and Martin Luther King, Jr.—a concrete example necessary to revive the whole tradition of martyrdom. Thus the *Letter from a Birmingham Jail*, which later became the credo of the civil rights movement, characterized King's ability to invigorate this tradition despite the cultural climate of modern times.

On the streets of Birmingham Martin Luther King announced: "We must say to our white brothers all over the South who try to keep us down: We will match your capacity to inflict suffering with our capacity to endure suffering." When a bomb exploded in Birmingham's Sixteenth Street Baptist Church on September 15, 1963, killing four black girls, King delivered the eulogy and stated: "They did not die in vain. . . . The innocent blood of these little girls may well serve as the redemptive force that will bring new light to this dark city."[46] In this tribute, as well as in many other addresses, King demonstrated that suffering for a cause had more than personal significance for him. Unlike reformers such as John Brown, Wendell Phillips, George Herron and Woodrow Wilson, who viewed only themselves as martyrs for the cause, King portrayed martyrdom as a collective phenomenon and fused himself with the members of the movement he represented. "When the years have rolled past," he declared in Oslo upon receiving the Nobel Peace Prize, ". . . men and women will know and children will be taught that we have a finer land, a better people, a more noble civilization— because these humble children of God were willing to suffer for righteousness' sake."[47] The many victims of the civil rights movement who died in the struggle for racial equality provided a real context for such rhetoric.

As in the case of the radical martyrs, King believed that martyrs for the cause created necessary sacrificial ties among the members of the civil rights movement. But unlike the anarchists and IWW martyrs, who viewed these ties as a way to separate their movements from the rest of the society, King emphasized martyrdom for the cause as a way to attach the rest of society to the reform movement. For him, the rest of society would regard the martyrs of the movement as examples of ultimate altruism. Thus he declared in Ebenezer Baptist Church in Atlanta on February 4, 1968: "Every now and than I think about my own death. . . . If any of you are around when I have to meet my day, I don't want a long funeral. . . . I'd like somebody to mention that day that Martin Luther King, Jr. tried to give his life serving others."[48]

King did serve others. After the victory in the battle against legal segregation in the South he engaged in a struggle for racial equality all over the country. He participated in the battle against poverty and committed himself to the growing peace movement against the Vietnam War. As a minister and scholar King continued to apply biblical terminology to the American national experience and thus gave fresh meaning to biblical symbols that were at the heart of the American civil religion. He interpreted his commitment to non-violence as an adherence to Christ's love. Freedom for him was more than freedom from Jim Crow regulations or freedom from jail. It constituted also freedom to express one's energy without hatred, without discrimination, without prejudice, without exploitation. He redefined the

American dream in his famous speech, "I Have a Dream," showing how the dream was still unfulfilled. The pharaohs were for him the racist Southern establishment, which would never voluntarily renounce oppression. He defined the black struggle as an Exodus and regarded the Chosen People as people free from the bondage of fear, black and white alike, who had a special responsibility to deliver the oppressed from the Egypt of oppression, by "the sword of peace, love, and forgiveness." The Promised Land was for him a worldwide vision "in which justice would run like water."[49] He considered blacks as "creative dissenters who will call our beloved nation to a higher destiny . . . to more noble expression of humaneness."[50]

In the context of this vision King depicted himself as the martyr, whose sacrificial death was required before a new birth could come. The daily death threats that he received strengthened this conviction and anchored them in a concrete context. "If there is any one fear I have conquered, it is the fear of death," he told his close friends. And he would quote, "If a man has not found something worth giving his life for, he is not fit to live."[51] To the members of the Southern Christian Leadership Conference (SCLC) he noted in 1965, "It's a time for martyrs now. And if I'm to be one, it will be in the cause of brotherhood. That's the only thing that can save this country."[52]

King's yearning for martyrdom increased during the late 1960s when he tried to help blacks in the North fight racism and poverty in the large cities. In this battle King felt a deep agony and failure, which also can explain his wish for martyrdom as a sort of psychological remedy. His many white friends deserted the movement after the victory over legal discrimination in the South, arguing that further struggles in the country at large were unnecessary and counterproductive. On the other hand, many of King's black followers criticized his nonviolent tactics and explained the failure in the North as a result of them. Consequently they were attracted by more radical and militant black leaders who advocated a violent alternative and rejected King's moderate approach.

After members of the Black Power movement in Chicago booed him and interrupted his speeches, King resorted to a somewhat personal martyr complex: "Selfishly I thought of my suffering and sacrifices over the last twelve years. Why would they boo one so close to them?" But then he expressed patience and understanding for those young people and noted that "they were now booing because they felt that we were unable to deliver on our promises."[53] When liberal citizens of Chicago, white and black, vilified King for being too radical and urged him to stop the marches in the city, he again depicted himself as a suffering servant compelled by a divine mission: "I have no martyr complex. I want to live as long as anybody in this building. . . . So I'll tell anybody, I'm willing to stop marching. I don't march because I like it. I march because I must, and because I'm a man, and because I'm a child of God."[54]

Arriving in Memphis to help sanitation workers, King delivered a speech at Mason Temple on April 3, 1968, in which he reacted to the threat on his life.

I don't know what will happen now. We've got some difficult days ahead. But it really doesn't matter with me now. Because I've been to the mountaintop. . . . I just want to do God's will. And he has allowed me to go up the mountain and I've looked over. And I've seen the Promised Land. And I may not get there with you. But I want you to know tonight that we as a people will get to the Promised Land. So I'm happy tonight. I'm not worried about anything. I'm not fearing any man. Mine eyes have seen the glory of the coming of the Lord. I have a dream this afternoon that the brotherhood of man will become a reality. With this faith, I will go out and carve a tunnel of hope from a mountain of despair. . . . With this faith, we will be able to achieve this new day, when all of God's children—black men and white men, Jews and Gentiles, Protestants and Catholics—will be able to join hands and sing with the Negroes. . . . "Free at last! Free at last! Thank God almighty we are free at last."[55]

The next day Martin Luther King, Jr., was shot to death.

There is no doubt that King's personality contributed to his image as a martyr. All over the country speakers and writers noted the fact that he had planned his martyrdom and had viewed himself as a sacrifice for the cause. "He was prepared," wrote *Crisis,* the official organ of the National Association for the Advancement of Colored People, "and was called upon to make the supreme sacrifice. He did so unflinchingly and with foreknowledge of his probable fate."[56] But the transformation of Martin Luther King, Jr., into an enduring national martyr derived from factors that transcend his personality. As this study has shown, an avowed reformer had the potential for becoming a martyr figure in America if he was subjected to suffering and a tragic death. But this potential could be fully realized only if other social and cultural factors reinforced this martyr image over time. It seems that in the case of Martin Luther King, Jr., these factors were plentiful.

First, there were the nonviolent techniques that King used that saved him from the fate of John Brown. Trials, prisons, police harassments, all helped to portray King as a courageous warrior, thus increasing the dramatic element in his whole quest for reform. However, he was aware that total repudiation of the legal system was counterproductive in the context of the American democratic system. Unlike John Brown in the nineteenth century and Malcolm X in his own time, King ideologically rejected violence and never initiated violence. Therefore he could not be depicted by his many foes as a dangerous criminal. He challenged certain laws nonviolently and was willing to bear the consequences because of his commitment to a "higher moral law," and therefore his suffering was accepted by those American citizens who were aware of the injustice of the laws King had defied.

The assassin was a Southern white, and so the violence could be attributed to King's enemies. Following the assassination black militants who had always opposed King's tactics provoked unprecedented riots and looting in the urban ghettoes all over the country, but here, again, the violence could be attributed to his adversaries. "The death of a non-violent man . . . could have a bite for a moment stronger than that of the violence which killed him," wrote the *Commonweal*.[57] It asserted that from a Christian perspective the whole tragedy resembled the crucifixion, "which is not a repudiation of Jesus's message, but history's judgment upon the character of our provisional present."[58]

A second factor was that Martin Luther King, Jr., the Nobel Peace laureate, though not an official office holder of the civil rights movement, was viewed as its most famous and charismatic leader. The individual's place in a reform movement affects his potential for martyrdom. Thus, a famous leader has greater potential for becoming a known martyr than a member of the rank and file. In the civil rights movement King's martyrdom, together with the sacrifice of many other members, contributed to his Christlike image. Like Lincoln and the fallen soldiers of the Civil War, Wilson and the victims of the First World War, so King's martyrdom had special appeal because it followed the sacrifice of other, less-known martyrs for the cause of civil rights. "Martin Luther King Jr. has now joined a long list of other martyrs in the struggle against racism—men and women, black and white, who died that others might enjoy the fruits of their labors," wrote the *Crisis,* mentioning a long list of civil rights victims.[59]

The nature and the place of a reform movement in society in general determines its ability to create a national martyr. In that sense a third factor was that the whole civil rights reform experience created a perfect context for King's martyrdom. Though it originated in the South and mainly among blacks, the movement grew in the sixties to include many segments of American society. It appealed to many Northern liberals, many young people, many clergymen and educators all over the country, many community workers in the cities, many intellectuals, and even to politicians. The civil rights movement, unlike the movements of radical reformers such as abolitionists, anarchists, or Black Panthers, was directed toward the rest of American society and not against America. Thus Martin Luther King, Jr., could become a national martyr-reformer rather than a sectional martyr appealing only to blacks.

Fourth, churches and the schools—two grass-roots institutions that have a key role in conveying and inculcating values in the context of American culture—delivered King's message to many Americans who had never participated in the reform movement. Such permanent and widespread institutions propagated King's legacy and promoted his martyr image much better than had the annual dinners of the Republican party in the case of Lincoln, the conservative clubs in the case of McKinley, ex-abolitionists in the case of John Brown, radical labor unions in the case of Joe Hill, or UN diplomats in the case of Woodrow Wilson. Public schools and churches reached everybody in the country and indeed transformed Martin Luther King, Jr., into a martyr of the entire people.[60] This point is seen even more clearly if we consider the ways in which Kennedy and King have been commemorated: both certainly have been honored with artefacts such as medals, stamps, and coins; their names appear on highways, schools, libraries, and cultural centers all over the country and abroad. However, while it was the media and political institutions that brought Kennedy's image to Americans, it was the churches and schools that took on this task in the case of King. While the media and political institutions tend to focus upon the visible cases, sensational and well-published events, and the somehow one-dimensional images of "stars," the schools and churches, by contrast, stress morals, values, lessons for the future, normative behavior, and meaningful models. Thus, by their very nature the media and political institutions presented a short-lived image of a popular martyred hero, while the schools and churches succeeded in creating an enduring image of a national martyred figure.

Fifth, Martin Luther King, Jr., was not a conventional politician but rather a reformer who dissociated himself from political office. Thus he could be depicted as an idealist and consequently as a martyr for an ideal. Politics as a profession has somewhat negative connotations in American society. The greed for office, the self-interested ambition, the quest for power, the endless manipulation—all these features undermine the pure devotion of a reformer to an ideal. Even Lincoln's image as a martyr was marred by the fact that he was a politician, and his later mythmakers deliberately ignored his background as a Whig, a congressman, and a compromise candidate for the presidency. Likewise, when Wilson's followers wanted to make a martyr of him, they depicted him as an uncompromising idealist who had fought the politicians in the name of the people. After all, the very mechanism of compromise, so essential to the American political system, damaged the image of a martyr as a pure idealist. King, however, unlike Lincoln, Wilson, or Kennedy, was not a professional politician. He could be depicted as a Southern Baptist minister who suffered and even sacrificed his life because he refused to give up his idealism for any political expediency. He devoted his life to a principle without any practical interest. In a more mythical way, he was like Socrates, not the statesmen of Athens, he was the prophet, not the king, the Christ, not the caesar. "For the first time in American history a President of the United States ordered flags to be flown at half-mast to honor a simple Baptist preacher," wrote the *Interpretation*.[61] As years passed it seemed that the very fact of his being a simple Baptist preacher increased King's chances of becoming an enduring national martyr.

Finally—and perhaps this is the most decisive factor—Martin Luther King, Jr., only partly accomplished his task. He succeeded in the struggle against legal discrimination in the South and witnessed the crumbling of Jim Crow regulations; but he failed in his goal to eliminate racial prejudices, to abolish poverty, and to force the nation to undertake certain responsibilities toward the underprivileged. The civil rights movement achieved significant success in its struggle to enforce court decisions on desegregation and in its lobbying for active government involvement on racial issues that resulted in civil rights legislation. However, the movement's attempt to enlarge the commitment of the community to its poor and its pretensions to find a democratic and moral alternative to corporate capitalism, ended in fiasco. Paradoxically, these partly fulfilled accomplishments increased King's potential for becoming a national martyr and coalesced with both the traditional image of the religious martyr and with the specific American political culture.[62]

As a mythical and religious figure, the martyr was neither a triumphant winner nor a complete loser. In the biblical tradition he became meaningful as one who pointed out the way to redemption, not as one who had already achieved it. He appeared and died so that later generations would continue to march his way. Had he achieved all his goals, the martyred figure would have ceased to be a source for further inspiration. Had he failed completely, no one would have remembered him at all. Triumph through failure, redemption though sacrifice, glorious future through agonizing present, everlasting existence through apparent demise, these are the binary contrasts that make a "suffering servant" so meaningful and sublime. The slender thread between failure and success is the meaningful sphere of the martyred hero in the biblical religious tradition.

This sphere could easily be applied to the fate of Martin Luther King, Jr., by many Americans. He had stood against the status quo, but also against violent overthrow of the system. He had started an enormous reform enterprise aimed both at creating a better future for all Americans and at dedicating the country to its original normative ideals. But he never fulfilled his dream. The Saturday Review wrote in reaction to the assassination that King had led the battle for racial justice, given American blacks their own voice, created a popular movement, worked on the pride of blacks and the conscience of whites to revolutionize the American spirit. "The march interrupted in Memphis—has indeed, barely begun. . . . King's agenda will remain unfulfilled . . . a commitment forever in a stage of revision and development."[63]

Hence, King's image as a martyr fitted into the tradition that viewed the American democratic experience as a never-ending process of never-ending progress.[64] An essential part of the American political culture is a dream that will never come to full realization and thus will always serve as a normative ideal.[65] Martin Luther King, Jr., articulated this dream and later generations identified him with the meaning of such a dream. He emerged as a hero who had struggled to bring America closer to its dream and even sacrificed his life for it. The speech "I Have a Dream" has become part of the American heritage. It has its place among other "sacred" documents such as the Declaration of Independence, the Constitution and the Gettysburg Address. Calling for events to commemorate King to be included in the bicentennial celebrations, the *Christian Century* wrote that "rightly understood, the bicentennial should illuminate the unfinished revolution that began in 1776 and supply the impetus for its successful completion within the framework of our democratic institutions. Affirming the aims of Martin Luther King, Jr.'s struggles would be a good start in that direction."[66]

Yet history moves in an ironic way. Conservatives who stigmatized King in the 1960s as troublemaker and extremist, later in the 1980s incorporated his image into the American historical heritage. They stressed his achievements and ignored his tragic failure. They portrayed him as one who had fulfilled the American dream by abolishing the last residue of legal inequality in America, thus making any quest for further reform redundant. In the first celebration of Martin Luther King, Jr., Day on January 20, 1986, the *New York Times* dedicated a whole page to King, citing the following two sentences: "By wisely choosing its heroes, a country shapes its destiny. Thank you Dr. Martin Luther King, Jr. for making an impossible dream come true."[67]

Such a slogan, so typical of memorial addresses delivered by various politicians of the Reagan administration, angered many veterans of the civil rights movement. "It seems to focus almost entirely on the dreamer and not on . . . the antiwar activist, not on . . . the challenger of the economic order, not on . . . the opponent of apartheid, not on the complete Martin Luther King," said Julian Bond, a Georgia state senator and long-time civil rights activist.[68] The Reverend Wyatt Tee Walder who had helped Dr. King plan the 1963 demonstrations in Birmingham, told the audience that celebrations of the King holiday were empty without activism against racism, poverty, and war. King's close friends still remembered the hostile attitude of conservative politicians to the aims and means of the civil rights movement. The Reverend Jesse Jackson even led a memorial protest march on the Justice Department, accusing President Reagan of hypocrisy. Nonetheless, the very fact that conservative politicians delivered memorial addresses in honor of Martin Luther King, Jr., demonstrated that he had indeed transcended his particular historical and social context to become an enduring national martyred hero. "No one can claim Dr. King. He transcends all of us," argued Newt Gingrich, a conservative Representative from Georgia.[69]

Liberals, civil rights veterans, war opponents, black leaders, and reform-oriented politicians conveyed, however, a different message. They asserted that King was a national martyr precisely because of his unfulfilled goals. They stressed that King's significance lay in the fact that he had shown an alternative way to American democracy, one that replaced self-interest with altruistic commitment and utilitarian individualism with social and communal responsibility. Thus King's image as a martyr hero would inspire the nation to renewed commitment and provide American society with a viable alternative to achieve its dream. Because he had just started a process of regeneration, and not because he had fulfilled his dream, King's image would increase in significance with the coming years, argued many of his initial supporters.[70] Until the 1960s only Lincoln had embodied this unfulfilled revolution as a committed reformer who had given the nation a new birth of freedom closer to its original ideals.[71] It seems today that the image of Martin Luther King, Jr., has absorbed similar elements. He has transcended his particular context to resurrect—at least once a year—the tradition of suffering and sacrifice through his image as a martyr, thereby explaining and giving meaning to human tragedy and death.

Beyond specific circumstances, the image of the martyr hero combined biblical symbolism with the American political culture. He emerged as a unique individual as well as a typical American, destined by God to suffer and to die in order to bring about the nation's rebirth and renew its commitment to its original mission. The martyr was described as a martyr for freedom, though the precise meaning of this freedom varied according to context. A martyr's death cemented the nation together, more by immortalization of the hero's perfect American nature and his idealistic activities in life, than by fascination with his sacrifice. The martyred figure had a cosmic meaning as Christ's follower whose suffering brought the American nation, and through it all mankind, closer to the kingdom of God. American martyred heroes were mostly perceived as heralds of redemption, yet concepts of sin, atonement, and apocalypse, which sometimes contradicted other elements in the American political culture, were only implicit in the portrayals of these martyrs.

This study aimed at finding concrete manifestations of the tradition of martyrdom in the context of American political culture. It analyzed the martyr image of political leaders who suffered tragedies and death. Most of them did not transcend their time to become enduring American heroes. Only Lincoln became a national martyred hero, portrayed as an American "suffering servant" who had ultimately sacrificed his life in order to reform American society and to rededicate the Chosen People to their mission as a redeemer nation. A radical reformer such as John Brown or a famous "suffering president" like Woodrow Wilson acquired national significance as martyr figures, but their image fell short of that of celebrated American heroes. Other reformers like Elijah Lovejoy, William L. Garrison, and Wendell Phillips who "suffered for the cause" resorted to the concept of martyrdom and were perceived as martyrs by certain reform movements. But they never became national heroes. Martyrs such as the assassinated presidents James A. Garfield and William McKinley, who died while defending the existing order, could not provide further inspiration in a political culture that praised constant change and progress. Radical martyrs such as Albert Parsons and Joe Hill, who sought to overthrow the American political system, never became heroic figures in the eyes of millions of Americans who feared revolutions and viewed their country as the best possible place on earth even if not yet perfect.

The study has demonstrated that the tradition of martyrdom declined in the twentieth century but did not disappear. Even in modern times, when a famous individual could be portrayed as one who had suffered and died for reform, he had the potential for becoming an enduring national martyred hero. It seems at present that contemporary Americans have found a new martyr in Martin Luther King, Jr. His personality, the context of his reform activities, his ability to articulate the tradition of suffering, sacrifice, and martyrdom in modern times, and his tragic death, contributed to creating an enduring national martyr image. The fact that King's birthday has been made a legal holiday—he is the only American hero apart from Washington to have been honored in this way—reinforces the basic thesis of this study that the culture of suffering, sacrifice, and martyrdom is still a part of American civil religion. It may decline in our time, but it certainly will not disappear. Glorification of death and fanaticism, which place sacrifice above life, seem alien to the American democratic culture, but precisely because suffering, tragedy, and death per se need explanation, a society resorts to the concept of martyrdom. Celebrated martyr figures invest suffering and tragic death with meaning. The exact message the martyr conveys varies from culture to culture and the very image of a martyr changes over time. Nonetheless, in the context of the American political culture, an avowed reformer, committed to transforming American society, who ends his life in a tragic way, has the potential even in our own times for transcending his particular period and place to become an enduring national martyr hero.

Notes

Introduction

1. For information about religious literature in early America see Schneider and Dornbusch, *Popular Religion.*
2. For a discussion of the American self-perception as God's Chosen People see Burns, *American Idea;* Hay, "Providence"; Bloomenfield, *Alarms and Diversions;* Nimmo and Combs, *Subliminal Politics,* 227–39; Tuveson, *Redeemer Nation;* Bercovitch, *Puritan Origins,* 136–63 and *American Jeremiad;* Moorehead, "Progress and Apocalypse."
3. Walt Whitman, "The Death of Abraham Lincoln," in Barton, *Lincoln and Whitman,* 228.
4. Ninde, *American Hymns,* 252.
5. Auden, *Poems,* 335.
6. Wolf, in *Freedom's Altar,* described the martyr complex in the abolitionist movement. Bercovitch, in *American Jeremiad,* offered a philosophy of American history in which Christianity and its secular impress are paramount. Within his analysis on the Puritan concept of errand he mentioned the idea of sacrifice and martyrdom. Michael Rogin, in his article "The King's Two Bodies," analyzed the martyr self-image of presidents Lincoln, Wilson, and Nixon. To the best of my knowledge these are the only works that analyze the concept of martyrdom and the image of a martyr from a historical perspective.

1. Suffering for the Sin of Slavery

1. Marineau, *Martyr Age,* 82, 84.
2. On the concept of American civil religion, see Bellah, *Broken Covenant.*
3. "All over the North men heard eulogies of abolition martyrs, sacrificed to the

inhumanity of the slave holder, and the conviction grew that there could be no peace in America until Southerners lived according to the Christian and democratic principles." Wolf, *Freedom's Altar*, xi.

4. Tanner, *Martyrdom of Lovejoy*, 90–91.
5. Thompson, *Prison Life*, 14–15.
6. Perry, *Radical Abolitionism*, 48.
7. Ibid., 90.
8. *Liberator*, Jan. 1, 1831.
9. Quoted in Merrill, *Wind and Tide*, 46.
10. Garrison and Garrison, *Words of Garrison*, 15.
11. Merrill, *Wind and Tide*, 48.
12. Ibid., 107.
13. Wendell Phillips, "Helen Eliza Garrison," in Phillips, *Speeches, Lectures, and Letters*, 455.
14. I gathered most of the information on abolitionist martyrs from historical monographs, relying especially upon Hume, *Abolitionists;* Wolf, *Freedom's Altar;* Sorin, *Abolitionism;* Duberman, *Antislavery Vanguard;* Stewart, *Holy Warriors*.
15. Stone, *Martyr of Freedom*. This address was delivered at East Machias, Nov. 30, 1837, and Machias, Dec. 7, 1837, by Thomas T. Stone, pastor of a church in East Machias, Maine.
16. *The Martyr*, a discourse delivered in Broadway Tabernacle, New York, and in Bleecker Street Church, Utica, by Beriah Green, president of the Oneida Institute; Root, *Memorial;* Tracy, *Sermon*.
17. *Liberator*, Oct. 19, 1833.
18. Tanner, *Martyrdom of Lovejoy*, 68.
19. Thompson, *Prison Life*, 14–15.
20. F. G. Villard, *Garrison on Non-Resistance*, 33–34.
21. *Liberator*, Nov. 4, 1837.
22. Ibid., Dec. 15, 1837.
23. Ibid., Dec. 16, 1837.
24. Quoted from Merrill, *Wind and Tide*, 109–10; also see Swift, *Garrison*, 387.
25. Garrison and Garrison, *Words of Garrison*, 13.
26. *Liberator*, Nov. 7, 1835.
27. Tanner, *Martyrdom of Lovejoy*, 8–9.
28. Ibid., 159–62.
29. Ibid., 159–60.
30. Ibid., 164–65.
31. "Does anyone ask how we feel in view of our sentence?" wrote George Thompson from jail, "we answer, happy, contented, cheerful, . . . being assured that our King will cause 'the wrath of man and praise Him' and extend the great cause for *Liberty* by our unworthy suffering." *Liberator*, Nov. 26, 1841.
32. Martyn, *Phillips*, 164–65.
33. Madison, *Critics and Crusaders*, 65.

34. Tanner, *Martyrdom of Lovejoy*, 68, 70.

35. Dimmock, *Lovejoy*, 14. This is an address he delivered at the Church of the Unity, St Louis, Mar. 14, 1888.

36. Crosby, *Garrison*, 131, 133.

37. Stearns, *Fugitive Slave Law*, 25–26.

38. A. H. Grimké, *Eulogy*, 23, 37–38. This eulogy was delivered in Tremont Temple, Boston, Apr. 9, 1884.

39. Dimmock, *Lovejoy*. In this address the speaker regretted that almost nobody knew the name Lovejoy, and with the passage of time all his martyrdom would sink into oblivion.

40. F. G. Villard, *Garrison on Non-Resistance*, 70.

41. Lucy Stone's tribute in *Tributes to Garrison*, 18; Wendell Phillips Stafford, associate justice of the Supreme Court of the District of Columbia, oration on Nov. 28, 1911, at Park Street Church, Boston, in Stafford, *Wendell Phillips*, 6–7, 30; Crosby, *Garrison*, 124.

42. Garrison and Garrison, *Words of Garrison*, 12.

43. Lovejoy compared himself to a prophet in his letters, see Tanner, *Martyrdom of Lovejoy*, 91; Crosby called Garrison a Hebrew prophet, *Garrison*, 55.

44. Chapman, *Garrison*, 134, 181–82.

45. John G. Whittier, Introduction to Johnson, *Garrison and His Times*, xx.

46. *Tributes to Garrison*, 11; Stafford, *Wendell Phillips*, 9.

47. Samuel Villard, in Tanner, *Martyrdom of Lovejoy*, 233.

2. *John Brown's Body — And Spirit*

1. Sanborn, *Life and Letters*, 582.

2. Ibid., 598.

3. Ibid., 604.

4. Ibid., 586, 590–91, 597.

5. Ibid., 609.

6. In a letter to Thomas B. Musgrave he stated, "Man cannot imprison or chain or hang the soul." Ibid., 593.

7. Ibid., 579.

8. Ibid., 599.

9. Ibid., 604.

10. Ibid., 620.

11. Ibid., 577–78.

12. Quoted in Warren, *John Brown*, 382, 392.

13. Quoted in Gold, *Life of John Brown*, 56.

14. Quoted in O. G. Villard, *John Brown*, 545.

15. Gold, *Life of John Brown*, 57.

16. *Liberator*, Dec. 31, 1859.

17. Ibid., Jan. 7, 1860.

18. Henry David Thoreau, "The Last Days of John Brown", in Boyer, *Legend of John Brown*, 24.
19. *Liberator*, Dec. 9, 1859.
20. Wolf, *Freedom's Altar*, 123–24.
21. Ralph Waldo Emerson, "John Brown", in *John Brown*, ed. Ruchames, 270.
22. Thoreau, *Writings*, x, 237–48.
23. "The Death of John Brown," editorial, *Liberator*, Dec. 30, 1859; "Death," poem, ibid., Feb. 10, 1860; speech by the Reverend J. Sella Martin, former slave, in Termont Temple, Boston, on Dec. 9, 1859, in *Blacks on John Brown*, ed. Quarles, 26–30; "The 2nd Day of December," editorial, *Radical* (a magazine for religious issues) 4 (Dec. 1868): 463.
24. Howells, "Old Brown." The poem was written in Dec. 1859.
25. Quoted in O. G. Villard, *John Brown*, 564.
26. Oates, *Purge This Country*, 355.
27. Quoted in Warren, *John Brown*, 395.
28. Henry C. Wright, in Perry, *Radical Abolitionism*, 258.
29. Quoted in ibid., 266.
30. Wendell Phillips, "John Brown and the Spirit of Fifty Nine," in *Best Orations*, ed. Brewer, 8:3183, 3186.
31. Wendell Phillips, "The Puritan Principle and John Brown," in Phillips, *Speeches, Lectures, and Letters*, 299.
32. Henry David Thoreau, "A Plea for Captain John Brown," read to the citizens of Concord, Massachusetts, Oct. 30, 1859, in Thoreau, *Yankee*, 166.
33. Theodore Parker, "A letter from Rome to Francis Jackson in Boston, Nov. 24, 1859," in *John Brown*, ed. Ruchames, 256.
34. Wendell Phillips's oration at the burial of John Brown delivered at the grave in North Elba, on Dec. 8, 1859, in ibid., 269.
35. The Reverend J. C. White in a memorial service in Cleveland, Ohio, quoted in Oates, *Purge This Country*, 354.
36. Ibid.
37. Many poems appeared in the *Liberator* depicting John Brown as a sacrifice upon the altar of humanity. Among them "Elba," "The Martyr of December 2nd," and "Death," *Liberator*, Feb. 2, 1860.
38. Whittier, "Freedom's Martyr," *Liberator*, Feb. 3, 1860.
39. "Now the first disinterested martyr . . . has freely delivered up his life for the liberation of our race in this country," declared black citizens who met in Detroit on the execution day. "We now loudly call upon to arouse . . . and to concentrate our efforts in keeping the Old Brown liberty bell in motion and thereby continue to kindle the fires of liberty upon the altar of every determined heart upon man." Quoted in *Blacks on John Brown*, ed. Quarles, 22. For various speeches delivered by blacks on John Brown immediately after the execution see also 25–31.
40. J. Sella Martin in *Blacks on John Brown*, ed. Quarles, 25; Theodore Parker in Warren, *John Brown*, 265.
41. The Reverend Frederick Forthingham, sermon in Park Street Church, Port-

land, Maine, Dec. 4, 1859, *Liberator*, Dec. 30, 1859; Charles C. Burleigh, speech at the annual meeting of Massachusetts Anti-Slavery Society, quoted in Wolf, *Freedom's Altar*, 122–23; Wendell Phillips compared John Brown to Wycliffe and Huss, martyrs of the Reformation "who died violent death for breaking the law of Rome," quoted in Boyer, *Legend of John Brown*, 21.

42. *Radical*, Sept. 2, 1859.

43. Quoted in Rhodes, *History of The United States*, 2: 412.

44. Quoted in O. G. Villard, *John Brown*, 569.

45. Ibid.

46. Wolf, *Freedom's Altar*, 129–30.

47. Kimball, "John Brown Song."

48. O. G. Villard, *John Brown*, 589.

49. Perry, *Radical Abolitionism*, 279–80.

50. Quoted in Stulter, "Lincoln and Brown," 299.

51. Rosenberg, *Custer and Defeat*, 217.

52. Quoted in Rhodes, *History of the United States*, 2: 403.

53. Quoted in Holst, *John Brown*, 198–99.

54. Greeley, *American Conflict*, 280–83; Avey, *Capture and Execution of Brown*, 75–77; Rhodes, *History of the United States*, 2: 384; Barton "Brown and Lincoln," speech delivered at Lake Placid Club, May 9, 1928, *Lake Placid News*, May 18, 1928.

55. Holst, *John Brown*, 75.

56. O. G. Villard, *John Brown*, 10.

57. Sanborn, *Life and Letters*, 578; Charles Sheldon, "God's Angry Man," *Independent* 69, no. 3216 (July 1910): 113; J. Max Barber, a black leader and one of the founders of the Niagara Movement, in *Blacks on John Brown*, ed. Quarles, 115.

58. Avey, *Capture and Execution of Brown*, 89–90: *New England Magazine* 30 (1904): 234; *McClure Magazine* 10, no. 2 (1897): 279.

59. Holst, *John Brown*, 80.

60. Rhodes, *History of the United States*, 2: 399–400.

61. *McClure Magazine* 10 no. 2, 278; Howe, *Reminiscences*, 256; Negro lullaby by Countee Cullen, a black poet, in *Blacks on John Brown*, ed. Quarles, 120; Benet, *John Brown's Body*, 69; Sanborn, *Life and Letters of John Brown*, 582; O. G. Villard, *John Brown*, 510, 545.

62. Frederick Douglass, "John Brown," an address at the 14th anniversary of Storer College, Harper's Ferry, West Virginia, May 31, 1881, in Ruchames, *John Brown*, 283.

63. Ibid., 298.

64. Quoted in Quarles, *Blacks on John Brown*, 71.

65. Francis Grimké, an address in Washington, D.C., Dec. 5, 1909, in F. J. Grimké, *Works*, 1: 124–27; W. E. B. Du Bois, at the celebration of John Brown Day, Aug. 17, 1906, before the 2d Niagara Convention, in Quarles, *Allies for Freedom*, 7; J. Max Barber, an address unveiling Brown's bronze statue in May 1935, at North Elba, New York, in *Blacks on John Brown*, ed.

Quarles, 109; centennial article in the *Chicago Defender*, by Langston Hughes, a black columnist, Oct. 17, 1959, reprinted in *Blacks on Brown*, ed. Quarles, 121–23; an editorial of the *Chicago Defender* for the centennial of John Brown's birth, in *Blacks on Brown*, ed. Quarles, 124–25.

66. Reverdy C. Ranson, an article on John Brown in the *Colored American Magazine* of Aug. 1906, reprinted in Quarles, *Allies for Freedom*, 8.

67. W. E. B. Du Bois, *John Brown*, 287, 289.

68. An ideological supporter like F. B. Sanborn wrote that "Brown had become . . . one of the immortal champions of liberty—historical and mythical—upon whom we reckon Leonidas, Maccabeus, Tell, Winkelried, Wallace, Hofer and Marco Bozzaric." *Century*, 4 (May–Oct. 1883): 414.

69. Boyer, *Legend of John Brown*, xx.

70. Reuben Shecler, address in Tallahassee, Florida, Oct. 16, 1959, in *Blacks on John Brown*, ed. Quarles, 133.

71. Bruce Rosenberg, in *Custer and Defeat*, 19, 265–74, argued that in order to turn a person into a mythical martyr an inspirational story of the last stand has to be created. The martyred hero is born in the last stand story that fictionalizes his death.

72. Quoted from "The Madness of John Brown," in *After the Fact*, ed. Davidson and Lytle, 144.

73. Quoted in Ruchames, *John Brown*, 266.

74. Apparently Brown did kiss the child of a white jailer. He also told the same jailer that "he should prefer to be surrounded in his last moments by a poor weeping slave mother with her children," *Davidson and Lytle, After the Fact*, 144.

75. Quoted in Quarles, *Blacks on John Brown*, 119–20.

76. Frank Paterson Stearns, "The Bust of John Brown," in Holst, *John Brown*, 187.

77. Quoted in Winkley, *John Brown*, 14–15.

78. H. P. Wilson, *John Brown*, 399.

79. McClellan, *A Hero's Grave*.

80. Greeley, *American Conflict*, 199; *Overland Monthly* 33 (Apr. 1884): 331; Holst, *John Brown*, 202.

81. *New England Magazine* 30 (1904): 241.

82. Quarles, *Allies for Freedom*, 7.

83. Ibid., p. 8

84. Horton, *History of the United States*, 61.

85. *Nation* 14 (Oct. 15, 1885): 324.

86. *Atlantic Monthly* 57 (1886): 272.

87. W. Wilson, *History of the American People*, 4: 185; Burgess, Civil War and The Constitution, 36.

88. Nicolay, *Campaigns of the Civil War*, 1: 158; *American Mercury* 268.

89. H. P. Wilson, *John Brown*, 400.

90. Burgess, *Civil War and the Constitution*, 39.

91. The Reverend Abner C. Hopkins, letter to the Honorable Thomas Hughes,

July 24, 1882, published in *Southern Historical Society Papers* 13 (1885–1886): 338–39.

92. Hassard, "Apology," 519, 526–27.

93. For a criticism of John Brown's activities from a legal perspective, see David N. Utter, "Sanborn's Life of John Brown," *Dial* 6 (1885–86): 139–40; "John Brown," Editorial, *New England and Yale Review* 45 (1886): 289–302; Leland H. Jenks, "The John Brown Myth," *American Mercury* (1924): 268.

94. Utter, "Sanborn's Life of John Brown."

95. Burgess, *The Civil War and the Constitution,* 42.

96. Bryant and Gay, *Popular History,* 431.

97. E. N. Vallandigham, "John Brown—Modern Hebrew Prophet," *Putnam's Monthly* 7, no. 3 (Dec. 1909): 296.

98. Utter, "Sanborn's Life of John Brown," 139.

99. *Atlantic Monthly* 57 (1886): 272.

100. *American Mercury* 1 (1924): 273.

101. Captain John Avis, the jailer and executioner of John Brown, letter to the editor, *Southern Historical Society Papers* 13 (1885): 341–42.

102. H. P. Wilson, *John Brown,* 231.

103. *American Mercury* 1 (1924): 268–271.

104. H. P. Wilson, *John Brown,* 406.

105. Burgess, *Civil War and the Constitution,* 44.

106. Realf, *Poems,* 162.

107. Ingalls, "John Brown's Place," 150.

108. F. P. Stearns, Epilogue to Holst, *John Brown,* 162.

109. H. P. Wilson *John Brown* 399–400.

110. Editorial, *Chicago Defender,* reprinted in *Blacks on John Brown,* ed. Quarles, 124.

111. Oates, "Brown and His Judges."

112. Winkley, *John Brown,* 124–25.

113. Quarles, *Blacks on John Brown,* 133, 137.

114. Rhodes, *History of the United States* 2: 414–15.

3. *Abraham Lincoln—The National Martyr*

1. Congressman Garfield on the occasion of the assassination of President Abraham Lincoln, in *World's Eulogies,* ed. McClure, 16.

2. *New York Times,* Apr. 20, 1865, 1.

3. Bishop Simpson's oration at Springfield burial, May 5, 1865, in *Our Martyred President,* 399.

4. *New York Times,* June 3, 1865, 2.

5. John Andrew, the governor of Massachusetts, in *Message,* 5; Rev. Albert Hunt, sermon, in *Our Martyred President,* 323; Rev. Samuel T. Sapear, sermon, in ibid. 299; Rev. Richard Edward, an address delivered at the Hall of Normal University, Normal, Illinois, Apr. 19, 1865, published in the *Magazine of*

History, extra no. 45 (1916): 6; the Reverend Dr. Boynton, chaplain of the House of Representatives at a memorial service in honor of the late president, Feb. 12, 1866, *New York Times,* Feb. 13, 1866, 1; Phillips Brooks, "Abraham Lincoln," an oration in Philadelphia Episcopal Church, Apr. 1865, in Brooks, *Perfect Freedom,* 174; Rabbi Samuel Adler, address in New York City, Apr. 19, 1865, in *Abraham Lincoln,* ed. Hertz, 179; the Reverend Dr. De-Witt of the North Dutch Church, New York, in *New York Times,* June 2, 1865, 3; Rev. J. C. Rockwell in *Our Martyred President,* 283.

6. *Our Martyred President,* 300, 347.

7. *Magazine of History,* extra no. 61 (1917): 10; ibid., extra no. 77 (1921): 15; *Our Martyred President,* 11, 125; *New York Times,* Apr. 21, 1865; *New York Tribune,* Apr. 16, 1865.

8. *Our Martyred President,* 171; Stewart, "Lincoln's Assassination," 188; Monaghan, "Lincoln Funeral Sermons," 43; Gurley, *Faith in God,* sermon at the funeral of Abraham Lincoln, 24; editorial, *Harper's Weekly,* Apr. 29, 1865, 258, quoted again in 1889 by William H. Herndon in Herndon, *Herndon's Lincoln;* Andrew, *Message,* 6; funeral oration by Ralph Waldo Emerson at Concord, 1865, in *Magazine of History,* extra no. 25 (1913): 558; eulogy by Dr. Elkan Cohn in Congregation Emanuel, San Francisco, Apr. 15, 1865, in *Western States Jewish Historical Quarterly* 2, no. 4 (1970): 195; the Reverend Dr. Vinton in *New York Times,* June 2, 1865; Brooks, *Perfect Freedom,* 175; a sermon by Rev. John H. Egar, *Martyr President,* 6.

9. *United States Memorial Address* 91.

10. Andrew S. Draper, address delivered at the celebration of the centennial of Lincoln's birth in the great hall of College in the City of New York, Feb. 12, 1909, in Draper, *What Makes Lincoln Great,* 63; memorial address by Rabbi Harrison in St. Louis, in *Chicago Tribune,* Feb. 13, 1909, 3; address by ex-Senator Davenport in the Methodist Episcopal Church of New York, Feb. 13, 1916, in *New York Times,* Feb. 14, 1916, 5; Hill, *Abraham Lincoln,* xviii; Richard Yates of Illinois, in a speech before the House of Representatives, Feb. 12, 1921, *Magazine of History,* extra no. 89 (1923): 20; Powler, *Patriotic Orations,* 91.

11. *South Atlantic Quarterly* 18 (1919): 21–23.

12. Draper, *What Makes Lincoln Great,* 35.

13. *New York Times,* Feb. 12, 1911, 2.

14. *New York Times,* June 1, 1865, 2.

15. *New York Times,* Apr. 30, 1865, 5; *Harper's Weekly,* Apr. 29, 1865, 258; poet Emeline Serman King described him as a democratic hero and not a king, in *Poetical Tributes,* 40–42.

16. *Martyr's Monument* 1.

17. *New York Times,* Feb. 12, 1909, 5; Ulysses Grant expressed this notion and was quoted in the Lincoln's birthday centennial edition of the *Chicago Tribune,* Feb. 7, 1909, pt. C, p. 10; see also A. Rothschild, the author of "Lincoln, Master of Men," in the *Chicago Tribune,* Feb. 7, 1909, pt. IX, p. 8;

Edward R. Sill in a poem dedicated to Lincoln's birthday centennial, *New York Evening Post*, Feb. 11, 1909; Dr. H. Agnew Johnson, eulogy, *New York Times*, Feb. 13, 1899, 10.

18. Hertz, *Abraham Lincoln*, 462.

19. *Chicago Tribune*, Feb. 13, 1909, 2.

20. Barton, *Abraham Lincoln*, 121.

21. W. H. Lampe, "Martyrdom and Inspiration," in *Suffering and Martyrdom*, ed. Horbury and McNeil, 121.

22. Ibid., 122

23. Ibid.

24. David Fluser, "Jewish Origins of Christian Martyrdom," in *Holy War*, ed. Historical Society of Israel, 135.

25. 2 Cor. 6:9; Heb. 12:6–11; 1 Pet. 1:6; Rev. 3:18.

26. Quoted from T. V. Smith, *Lincoln*, 74.

27. *Our Martyred President*, 171, 50.

28. *Magazine of History*, extra no. 25 (1913): 556. For further discussion of the idea of American innocence, see Lewis, *American Adam*.

29. *New York Times*, Apr. 20, 1865, 1; ibid., May 1, 1865, 1; Sumner, *Eulogy*, 56.

30. Mayo, *Martyr President*, 4; Thompson, *Lincoln's Grave*, 29; Cowgill, *Columbia Martyr*, 17.

31. *New York Times*, Feb. 23, 1909, 4.

32. Humanity is not strong enough to go on the road to progress without the help of men who shall form a chain from the average mass up through society, to the Savior and to God," declared the Reverend A. D. Mayo from Cincinnati in a sermon on the first anniversary of Lincoln's death. Mayo, *Martyr President*, 2.

33. William Kramer, "They Kill Our Man but Not Our Cause," editorial in the journal *Hebrew*, Apr. 21, 1865, reprinted in *Western States Jewish Historical Quarterly* 2 (4) 1970: 193–94.

34. *New York Evening Post*, quoted in *Magazine of History*, extra no. 129 (1927): 19

35. Sumner address in Boston, in *New York Times*, Feb. 13, 1866, 1; *New York Times*, May 6, 1865, 2; William Cullen Bryant, "Ode for the Funeral of Abraham Lincoln," had been read in New York, Apr. 25, 1865, published in Hertz *Abraham Lincoln*, 462; *Legislative Honors*, 27, 44; Webster, *Foe Unmasked*, 16.

36. *Harper's Weekly*, May 6, 1865, 274.

37. *Magazine of History*, extra no. 45 (1916): 23.

38. *Abraham Lincoln Quarterly* 1 (1940–1941): 55.

39. Thompson, *Lincoln's Grave*, 35.

40. Barton, *Lincoln and Whitman*, 229; an address by George Boutwell, a commissioner of internal revenue under Lincoln, a secretary of the treasury under Grant, and governor of Massachusetts, in *Reminiscences of Abraham Lin-*

coln, ed. Rice, 411; Drummond, *Abraham Lincoln* (an address delivered at the Pacific Branch of National Soldiers' Home, Sawtelle, California, Feb. 13, 1927), 4.

41. *New York Times,* Feb. 13, 1888, 2.

42. "The pardon of sin is with suffering brought," wrote Robert Henry Mewell of New York. See Mewell, *Martyr President,* 10.

43. *Chicago Tribune,* Apr. 26, 1865, 3.

44. In 1915 Colb Percival Bartlett published a fiction about Lincoln's return to America of 1915. In this book the fictional Lincoln advocated a powerful navy to keep America safe, but he was also bothered by America's lack of activity in the Great War. At the end of the book Bartlett has Lincoln say that the strongest nation must be the best, and the best the strongest. See Bartlett, *Martyr's Return,* 20–35, 40–50, 105.

45. In the First World War Lincoln's name served as an ideological symbol for the Allied leaders. Marshal Vivany, the French chief of staff, and Lloyd George, the British premier, emphasized Lincoln's role as liberator of the oppressed in their speeches on Lincoln Day of 1917, *New York Times,* May 8, 1917, 1; ibid., Feb. 11, 1917, 1. A year later Rabbi D. Lefkovits declared in Pittsburgh: "Is not this war of emancipation of all man, a universalization of democracy? . . . He will say that this war is the opportunity of the race to break every yoke and to let the oppressed go free." Hertz, *Abraham Lincoln,* 483.

46. Niccolls, *Assassination of Lincoln,* 16.

47. For a discussion of this concept of liberty, see Isaiah Berlin, "Two Concepts of Liberty," in Berlin, *Four Essays,* 122–31

48. *Western States Jewish Historical Quarterly* 2, no. 4 (1970): 193; *New York Times,* Apr. 21, 1865, 2; *Chicago Tribune,* Apr. 18, 1865, 2; *Magazine of History,* extra no. 73 (1921): 12; *Public Ledger,* Apr. 17, 1865, 2.

49. *Our Martyred President,* 171, 381, 461; *Poetical Tributes,* 16, 59–60, 114–115.

50. Charles M. Ellis, memorial address delivered in Boston, June 1, 1865, in *Magazine of History,* extra no. 65 (1920): 24; *Harper's Weekly,* 1865, 258, the Reverend Mr. Edward's address at Normal, Illinois, Apr. 19, 1865, *Magazine of History,* extra no. 45 (1916): 23.

51. Gurley, *Faith in God,* 23; *Daily Illinois State Journal,* Apr. 17, 1865, 2; *New York Times,* Apr. 27, 1965, 8.

52. Professor T. Dwight, president of Columbia Law School, in a memorial address, Feb. 12, 1881, *New York Times,* Feb. 12, 1881, 7; Senator Cullom's address before the Republican Club of New York City, Feb. 12, 1890, ibid., Feb. 13, 1890, 2; the Reverend H. C. Mayland, ibid., Feb. 12, 1891; *Putnam's Monthly,* Apr. 1907, 64; *Arena* 41 (1909): 483; *Chicago Tribune,* Feb. 7, 1909, pt. 2, p. 3; Hill, *Abraham Lincoln,* xix; *Columbia's Martyr,* 13; *New York Times,* Feb. 12, 1909, 5; *Magazine of History,* extra no. 77 (1921): 10, 16.

53. *World's Work* 17 (1908–9): 11420.

54. *Our Martyred President,* 272; *Magazine of History,* extra no. 25 (1913), 559;

Brakeman, *A Great Man*, 19; Bulkley, *Lincoln*, 7, 13; *Legislative Honors*, 23–25, 48–49.

55. *Our Martyred President*, 391–92.
56. *New York Times*, Apr. 21, 1865, p. 2.
57. Ibid.
58. Ibid., Feb. 23, 1866, 1.
59. *Chicago Tribune*, Apr. 13, 1866, 2; Memorial sermon at the White House delivered by Dr. Gurley, in Gurley, *Faith in God*, 24; *Public Ledger*, Apr. 17, 1865, 2; Hertz, *Abraham Lincoln*, 207; Webb, *Memorial Sermons*, 58; Eddy, *Martyr President* 20; Mewell, *Martyr President*, 22–23.
60. *Our Martyred President*, 252.
61. *New York Times*, Aug. 2, 1875; ibid., Feb. 12, 1888; ibid., Sept. 6, 1916; *Magazine of History*, extra no. 77 (1921): 17; ibid., extra no. 61 (1917): 56; *Putnam's Monthly*, Apr. 1907, 63; Wine, *Greatness of Lincoln* (an address delivered at the Lincoln Memorial, May 30, 1905), 25; tributes delivered by Mayor McCallen of New York and Governor Wilson of Kentucky Feb. 12, 1909, *New York Times*, Feb. 13, 1909, 2, 3.
62. *Chicago Tribune*, Feb. 13, 1909, 4.
63. Brown, *Meaning of Lincoln*, 8.
64. Niccolls, *Assassination of Lincoln*, 15.
65. Religious service in St. George Church, New York, *New York Times*, Apr. 21, 1865, 2; Hertz, *Abraham Lincoln*, 114; Henry Ward Beecher's address on Apr. 23, 1865, Herndon, *Herndon's Lincoln*, 580.
66. *Our Martyred President*, 108.
67. *Public Ledger*, Apr. 18, 1865, 2; *Harper's Weekly*, 1865, 258; *New York Times*, Apr. 19, 1865, 4; Sumner, *Eulogy*, 44; memorial address by Charles M. Ellis, Boston, June 1, 1865, *Magazine of History*, extra no. 65 (1920): 24; Oliver Wendell Holmes wrote in a poem:

> O let the blood by murder spilt
> Wash out Thy stricken children's guilt
> And sanctify our nation!

See *Poetical Tributes*, 74.
68. *New York Times*, Apr. 27, 1865, 8.
69. For further details concerning the funeral ceremonies see Monaghan, "Lincoln Funeral Sermons,"; and Lewis, *Myths after Lincoln*.
70. Whitman, *Death of Abraham Lincoln*, 48–49. Whitman delivered the same lecture in New York on Apr. 14, 1879, in Philadelphia in 1880, and in Boston in 1881.
71. Bulkley, *Lincoln*, 7.
72. *Atlantic Monthly* 16 (July–Dec. 1865): 491–503.
73. For the fallen-father/son theme see, "The Martyr" by Herman Melville, in Turner, *Be Aware*, 24; Walt Whitman, "O Captain my captain" in Barton, *Lincoln and Whitman*, 174–75; the Reverend Albert Hunt, in *Our Martyred President*, 237; Brooks, *Perfect Freedom* 172: Reverend R. Yard, *Magazine of*

History, extra no. 73 (1921): 29; *Chicago Tribune*, Apr. 18, 1865, 2; Mewell, *Martyr President*, 14; Webster, *Foe Unmasked*, 1–3.

74. *New York Times*, June 1, 1865, 2; *Our Martyred President*, 172.
75. *United States Memorial Address*, 64.
76. Barrett, *Mourning for Lincoln*, 72.
77. Ibid., 26–27.
78. Sumner, *Eulogy*, 10.
79. Ralph Waldo Emerson's funeral oration at Concord, *Magazine of History*, extra no. 25 (1913): 555.
80. *New York Times*, Apr. 17, 1865, 4; Brooks, *Perfect Freedom*, 157; Solomon Wolf, an address on Abraham Lincoln delivered in Washington, D.C., in February 1888, in *Abraham Lincoln*, ed. Hertz, 196. James Russell Lowell's poem to Lincoln, written in 1865 and published in many papers and magazines, had ended with "new birth of our new soil, the first American." *Magazine of History*, extra no. 61 (1917): 52; Mewell, *Martyr President*, 26; Webb, *Memorial Sermons*, 46–48; *Poetical Tributes*, 45; Bulkley, *Lincoln*, 8–9.
81. Rhodes, *History of the United States* 5: 143; Draper *What Makes Lincoln Great*, 47; *Putnam's Monthly*, Apr. 1907, 57; *New York Times*, Nov. 19, 1917, pt. 4, p. 476; Edmond Clearence Stedman, "The Hand of Lincoln" (1883), in M. A. D. Howe, *Memory of Lincoln*, 56–57.
82. *Chicago Tribune*, Feb. 7, 1909, pt. A, p. 1.
83. *New York Times*, Feb. 12, 1909, 10.
84. *Chicago Tribune*, Feb. 7, 1909, pt. ix, p. 12.
85. *Harper's Weekly*, 1865, 258; *New York Times*, June 2, 1865, 2; Brakeman, *A Great Man*, 6–7.
86. *New York Times*, Feb. 13, 1881, 7.
87. Examples of addresses that stressed the personal merit of Lincoln's poverty could be found in the *New York Times*, Feb. 13, 1888, 4; ibid., Feb. 12, 1912, 8; *Chicago Time Herald*, Sept. 13, 1895, 10; ex-President Harrison's eulogy in Chicago, *New York Times*, Feb. 13, 1898, 1; a speech by Richard Yates of Illinois in the House of Representatives, Feb. 12, 1921, *Magazine of History*, extra no. 89 (1923): 10; French, *Abraham Lincoln*, 365; Drummond, *Abraham Lincoln*, 3.
88. *Magazine of History*, extra no. 58 (1917): 125.
89. Rice, *Reminiscences of Abraham Lincoln*, 419.
90. *New York Times*, Feb. 13, 1911, 9.
91. Ibid., Sept. 12, 1896.
92. *Putnam's Magazine*, Apr. 1907, 64; *Chicago Tribune*, Feb. 7, 1909, pt. 2, p. 4; Hertz, *Abraham Lincoln*, 218, 222; *Magazine of History*, extra no. 140 (1928): 163, 165; Bartlett, *Martyr's Return*, 100; Powler, *Patriotic Operations*, 5–8.
93. *New York Times*, Apr. 27, 1909, 6.
94. *World of Today* 1909 16 (1909): 116.
95. *New York Times*, Apr. 19, 1865, 4.
96. *World of Today* 16 (1909): 116.

97. Anderson, *Abraham Lincoln;* Diggins, *Lost Soul,* 303–33.

98. A certain version of this idea can be found in the Old Testament through the figure of the Suffering Servant (Isa. 53). In the New Testament, the idea became more central and related to the whole existential situation of human beings from the time of Adam. Augustine summarized the idea in a short book of Christian faith entitled *Enchiridion:* "Since men were in this wrath through original sin . . . there was a need for a mediator . . . a reconciler who would propitiate this wrath by offering of that one and only sacrifice of which all the sacrifices of Law and Prophets were shadows cast beforehand." See Bowker, *Problems of Suffering,* 175.

99. *Our Martyred President,* 23, 50; *New York Times,* Apr. 17, 1865, p. 8; J. D. Strong, *Nation's Sorrow,* 13–14, a discourse on the death of Abraham Lincoln, Larkin Street Presbyterian Church, San Francisco, June 4, 1865; Hertz, *Abraham Lincoln,* 6.

100. The Reverend George D. Boardman of the First Baptist Church in New York, Apr. 16, 1885, and the Reverend William Sprague and C. Sutphen of the Second Presbyterian Church of Albany, April 16, 1865, in Stewart's "Lincoln's Assassination," 287; the Reverend Robert Lowry, in *Our Martyred President,* 311; the Reverend Dr. Dewitt of North Dutch Church, *New York Times,* June 2, 1865, 3; J. D. Strong, *Nation's Sorrow,* 11; *Magazine of History,* extra no. 129 (1927): 19; ibid., extra no. 34 (1914): 166.

101. "Abraham Lincoln," sermon delivered on Apr. 16, 1865, *Magazine of History,* extra no. 177 (1932): 54.

102. The Reverend S. C. Damon, Seamen's Chapel, "A Sermon on the Death of Abraham Lincoln," Honolulu, May 14, 1865, *Magazine of History,* extra no. 53 (1916): 11; the Reverend J. R. W. Sloan, *New York Times,* Apr. 21, 1865, 2; the Reverend Ives Budington, in *Our Martyred President,* 117–23; Egar, *Martyr President,* 5;

103. Monaghan, "Lincoln Funeral Sermons," 38.

104. Herndon, *Herndon's Lincoln,* 581.

105. Mewell, *Martyr President,* 10–12.

106. *Harper's Weekly,* quoted in *Magazine of History,* extra no. 165 (1919): 43.

107. *Atlantic Monthly* 64 (1899): 713–14.

108. Lewis, *Myths after Lincoln,* 95; *Our Martyred President,* 13, 125; *Liberator,* May 12, 1865, 76; *Harper's Weekly,* 1865, 258.

109. Lewis, *Myths after Lincoln,* 97, 102.

110. The Reverend Daniel C. Eddy stated in his sermon before the Baldwin Place Church on April 16, 1865, that Lincoln did not want to go to the theater on that evening. See Eddy, *Martyr President,* 6; *Our Martyred President,* 25–31, 47–48, 62–63; *Chicago Tribune,* Apr. 16, 1865, 2; ibid. Apr. 18, 1865, 3.

111. *New York Times,* Apr. 16, 1865, 3; *Magazine of History,* extra no. 53 (1916): 10 Monaghan, "Lincoln Funeral Sermons," 38; *Daily Illinois State Journal,* Apr. 17, 1865, 2.

112. The Reverend Albert Hunt, in *Our Martyred President,* 327; the Reverend W.

Bilows, in ibid., 63; Rev. Mr. De Witt, *New York Times,* June 2, 1865, 3; Reverend Mr. Maurry, *New York Tribune,* Apr. 17, 1865, 8; "Funeral Ode," anonymous poem in *Harper's Weekly,* 1865, 275.

113. *Atlantic Monthly* 16 (July–Dec. 1865): 503.

114. W. F. Flemington, "On the Interpretation of Colossians 1:24," in *Suffering and Martyrdom,* ed. Horbury and McNeil, 89.

115. J. C. O'Neill, "Does Jesus Teach That His Death Would Be Vicarious as Well as Typical?," in *Suffering and Martyrdom,* ed. Horbury and McNeil, 26–27.

116. E. B. Brian, *"Imitatio Christi* and the Lucan Passion Narrative," in *Suffering and Martyrdom,,* ed. Horbury and McNeil, 33.

117. Morna D. Hooker, "Interchange and Suffering," in *Suffering and Martyrdom,,* ed. Horbury and McNeil, 71.

118. Quoted from the tribute of the English satirical magazine, *Punch,* reprinted in *Chicago Tribune,* centennial edition, Feb. 7, 1909, pt. C, p. 10.

119. The Reverend D. Eaton, "Lincoln as a Christian," *New York Times* Feb. 12, 1899, 10; Rabbi J. Krauskopf, address in Philadelphia, Feb. 12, 1909, in *Abraham Lincoln,* ed. Hertz, 244; Colonel Hicks's essay, reprinted in *Magazine of History,* extra no. 61 (1917): 56; *New York Times,* Feb. 13, 1911, 9; ibid., Nov. 9, 1911, 6; "Lincoln's God," an essay by Carl Holliday (dean and English professor at the University of Toledo) in *South Atlantic Quarterly,* 18 (1919): 23; James M. Cox, the Democratic candidate for the presidency, in Springfield, 1920, *New York Times,* Oct. 11, 1920; "Lincoln's Religion," a poem by Frank B. Cowgill, in Cowgill, *Columbia Martyr,* 31; *Putnam's Monthly,* Apr. 1907, 63.

120. "Lincoln's Likeness to Christ," lecture delivered by Professor Kelly Miller in the American Missionary, February 1909, in *Magazine of History,* extra no. 117 (1926): 52; Dr. Hirsh tribute in Armory, Chicago, Feb. 12, 1909 in *Chicago Tribune,* Feb. 13, 1909, 2; Hill, *Abraham Lincoln,* 404.

121. Hill, *Abraham Lincoln,* 373–74.

122. William H. Herndon, "Lincoln's Religion," in "Illinois State Register Supplement 1879," facsimile in reprinted Holman Hamilton, *Lincoln and Herndon: Religion and Romance* (Kentucky, 1959).

123. Quoted in Wolf, *Almost Chosen People,* 192.

124. Arnold, *Abraham Lincoln,* 192, a paper read before The Royal Historical Society, London, June 16, 1881.

125. Noah Brooks's letter of Dec. 31, 1872, to J. A. Reed. Quoted from Reed's lecture in William E. Barton, *The Soul of Abraham Lincoln* (326.)

126. The historiography of Lincoln's religion appeared in Appendix 2 of Wolf, *Almost Chosen People,* 197–200.

127. *New York Times,* Feb. 12, 1899, 10.

128. *South Atlantic Quarterly:* 18 (1919): 17–20; *Magazine of History,* extra no. 85 (1922): 51; ibid., extra no. 89 (1923): 21; Reverend Mr. Lemmon of New York Methodist Church, in *New York Times,* Feb. 20, 1906, 16; Rev. Mr.

Cannon, in ibid., June 3, 1911, 10; Hill, *Abraham Lincoln*, 167, 261; Cowgill, *Columbia Martyr*, 31.

129. Niebuhr, *Irony of American History*, 172.
130. Flemington, "Interpretation of Colossians 1:24," 84.
131. Rogin, "King's Two Bodies," 561.
132. Tuveson, *Redeemer Nation*, 205; *Atlantic Monthly* 16 (July–Dec. 1865): 491–503; the Reverend S. C. Damon, in *Magazine of History*, extra no. 53 (1916): 11; the Reverend R. Yard, ibid., extra no. 73 (1921): 29; Rev. Dr. J. P. Thompson, in *New York Times*, May 5, 1865, 1.
133. Strong, *New Era*, 362–63.
134. Rauschenbusch, *Christianizing the Social Order*, 90.
135. William E. Barton, in the first broadcasted sermon on Feb. 11, 1928, stated, "The kingdom of God is really a republic of God." Barton, *Abraham Lincoln*, 7.
136. Aaron, *Unwritten War*, 238.
137. Whitman, *Death of Abraham Lincoln*, 51–53.
138. "Some who were near him," wrote Charles H. Powler, "think that he saw himself dying for the Republic." *Patriotic Orations*, 91.
139. Barrett, *Mourning for Lincoln*, 88.
140. Lasting Burrows, *Palliative and Prejudicial Judgments Condemned* (Richmond, 1865), 3–8, 11–12.
141. Richard Waston Gilder, "To The Spirit of Abraham Lincoln," in *Memory of Lincoln*, ed. M. D. W. Howe, Drummond, *Abraham Lincoln*, 4.
142. Barrett, *Mourning for Lincoln*, 20–21.
143. Wendell Phillips, "Lesson," 15.

4. Sacrifice for Law and Order

1. Charles Henry Parkhurst, "Sermon on Garfield, Sept. 25, 1881," in *Orations*, ed. Hazeltine 24: 10477.
2. Henry Ward Beecher in Plymouth Church, Brooklyn, Sept. 25, 1881, *New York Times*, Sept. 26, 1881, 6; President Hinsdale of Hiram College in an address delivered before the Soldiers' Regiment of Students of Hiram and William College in the First Presbyterian Church, Cleveland, Ohio, Sept. 25, 1881, in *World's Eulogies*, ed. McClure, 56; *Chicago Tribune*, Sept. 21, 1881, 4.
3. John Wanamaker's eulogy of President McKinley, in *Life of McKinley*, ed. McClure and Morris, 419.
4. *New York Times*, Sept. 24, 1881, 5; ibid., Sept. 26, 1881, 6; Everett, *Life of McKinley*, 107, 402; McClure and Morris, *Life of McKinley*, 404–5; Rufus Choate in a memorial meeting in Boston, in *Memorial Life*, ed. Townsend, 422.
5. *New York Times*, Sept. 20, 1881, 4; *New York Tribune*, Sept. 20, 1881, 7;

Professor Swing's address in Chicago, Sept. 25, 1881, in *World's Eulogies,* ed. McClure, 33: the Reverend David Magie in the First Presbyterian Church, Patterson, New Jersey, Sept. 25, 1881, in *New York Times,* Sept. 26, 1881, 6; *Atlantic Monthly* (November 1881): 707; Richard Oglesby, "Lincoln and Garfield," delivered in Leadville, Colorado, Sept. 26, 1881, in *World's Eulogies,* ed. McClure, 210; Charles F. Warwick, the mayor of Philadelphia, in an address unveiling the James A. Garfield memorial, *Pamphlets on Biographies* 13: 14; Henry E. Heighton, "Garfield," an oration at the laying of the cornerstone of Garfield Monument in Golden Gate Park, Aug. 24, 1883, in Highton, *Two Orations,* 10.

6. Thayer, *From Log-Cabin,* 4–7.

7. McClure and Morris, *Life of McKinley,* x; Townsend, *Memorial Life,* 103–4.

8. *New York Times,* Sept. 16, 1901, 5; Mrs. Florence Earl Coates, "Memorial Ode," in *Life of McKinley,* ed. McClure and Morris, 420; John D. Long (ex-secretary of the navy) in a tribute at statue unveiling in Adams, Massachusetts, Oct. 10, 1903, *New York Times,* Oct. 11, 1903; Nicholas Lloyd Ingraham, "Poem," in *William McKinley,* ed. Gordon, 151.

9. Pell, Buel, and Boyd, *McKinley and Men of Our Times,* 206.

10. *Memorial of Garfield,* 16; McCabe, *Our Martyred President; Chicago Tribune,* Sept. 16, 1901, *New York Times,* Sept. 15, 1901, 6.

11. *New York Times,* Sept. 26, 1881, 6; *New York Tribune,* Sept. 23, 1881, 8; *Harper's Weekly,* 1882, 50; Henry Ward Beecher's memorial address, *New York Times,* Sept. 23, 1881, 2; *Memorial Service at Fourth Street in Memory of James A. Garfield* (Honolulu, Hawaii, Oct. 6, 1881), 7; McClure and Morris, *Life of McKinley,* 405; *San Francisco Chronicle,* Sept. 16, 1901, 5; *Cleveland Gazette,* Sept. 21, 1901, 1.

12. *Chicago Tribune,* Sept. 20, 1881, 4; *New York Times,* Sept. 26, 1881, 6; Mary Garfield, "Garfield's home life," Sept. 21, 1893, in *Garfield of Hiram,* ed. Davis, 45; Hoar, *Garfield,* 42; funeral sermon for William McKinley, delivered in the Methodist Episcopal Church of Canton, Ohio, by the Reverend C. E. Manchester, in *Life of McKinley,* ed. Everett, 419; the Reverend Morgan Dix, a sermon, in ibid., 400; memorial tribute by Cardinal Gibbons of Maryland, in *Life of McKinley,* ed. McClure and Morris, 402; James Radkin Young, Introduction to *Memorial Life,* ed. Townsend, vii (Young was a member of the Congress and clerk of the United States Senate); *San Francisco Chronicle,* Sept. 20, 1901, 7; *Leslie's Weekly Illustrated,* Sept. 21, 1901, 254; *New York Times,* Sept. 16, 1901, 5; Oscar C. Carlstrom (former attorney general of Illinois) in a memorial address delivered in Chicago in February 1936, in *William McKinley,* ed. Gordon, 36; Ernest Lee Jahncke (former assistant secretary of the navy), in a memorial tribute in Louisiana on January 27, 1941, in ibid., 100.

13. McClure, *World's Eulogies,* 42.

14. Holzer, Boritt, and Neely, *Lincoln Image,* 170, 173, 175–86.

15. For an analysis of the domestic sphere as part of the millennial vision, see Douglas, "Consolation Literature."

16. Townsend, *Memorial Life,* 407.

17. *Memorial Service at Fourth Street,* 3.

18. Eversol, *Sir Knight,* 28.

19. Nathaniel P. Banks, eulogy to Garfield, in *Memorial of Garfield,* 74; Frederick O. Prince, mayor of Boston, in ibid., 16; poem by Joaquin Miller in the *Boston Globe,* reprinted in ibid., 376; the Reverend L. B. Bates, memorial sermon to McKinley, in the *Boston Evening Transcript,* Sept. 16, 1901, 2; poem by S. W. Small from the *Constitution,* Atlanta, Georgia, in *Life of McKinley,* ed. McClure and Morris, 420; Halstead, *Life of McKinley,* 268.

20. Hoar, *Garfield,* 43.

21. General William F. Draper's Address in Milford, Sept. 19, 1901, in the *Boston Evening Transcript,* Sept. 20, 1901, 3; Dr. C. E. Manchester, funeral sermon in Canton, Ohio, in *Life of McKinley,* ed. Everett, 421.

22. William McKinley, "American Patriotism," in *Orations,* ed. Hazeltine 24: 10491, 10493.

23. The Reverend James M. Pullman, Sept. 25, 1881, in *New York Times,* Sept. 26, 1881, 6; the Reverend J. A. M. Chapman, in ibid.; *Pamphlets on Biographies* 9: 1; memorial address by Andrew D. White, president of Cornell University, Ithaca, New York, Sept. 26, 1881, in ibid. 4: 1; *New York Times,* Sept. 20, 1881, 4.

24. The Reverend J. P. Bodfish, Sept. 25, 1881, in *World's Eulogies,* ed. McClure, Highton, *Two Orations,* 22; Samuel Gustine Thompson, *Pamphlets on Biographies* 13: 20; *New York Times,* Sept. 25, 1991, 6; Charles Henry Parkhurst, in *Orations,* ed. Hazeltine 24: 10483; the Reverend J. W. Hamilton, *Boston Evening Transcript,* Sept. 27, 1881, 6; Andrew White, *Pamphlets on Biographies* 4: 1.

25. Ex-Governor C. K. Davis, St. Paul, Minnesota, Sept. 26, 1881, "A Nation Mourns," in *World's Eulogies,* ed. McClure, 139–40.

26. *New York Times,* Sept. 7, 1931, 16; see also Robert D. Marcus, "James A. Garfield: Lifting the Mask," *Ohio History* 88 (1979): 78–83.

27. *San Francisco Chronicle,* Sept. 20, 1901, 9; *Boston Evening Transcript,* Sept. 20, 1901, 9; Everett, *Life of McKinley,* 430.

28. *San Francisco Chronicle,* Sept. 14, 1901, 6; ibid., Sept. 15, 190, 5; ibid., Sept. 16, 1901, 5; ibid., Sept. 19, 1901, 6; Senator Hoar's tribute, *Boston Evening Transcript,* Sept. 14, 1901, 6; Bishop Lawrence's sermon in Boston, ibid., Sept. 20, 1901, 6; the Reverend George T. Purves, a sermon in New York, Sept. 15, 1901, *New York Times,* Sept. 16, 1901, 5; a memorial tribute by ex-Secretary of State William R. Day, Canton, Ohio, Sept. 14, 1902, ibid., Sept. 15, 1902, 2; an address by James Jeffry Roch, in *Memorial Life,* ed. Townsend, 269; Townsend, *Memorial Life,* 397.

29. *Chicago Tribune,* Sept. 15, 1901, 1.

30. *Boston Evening Transcript,* Sept. 20, 1901, 6.

31. General Fitzhugh Lee, in *McKinley and Men of Our Times,* ed. Pell, Buel, and Boyd, 268.

32. *Boston Evening Transcript,* Sept. 19, 1901, 5.

33. An address by Democratic ex-Congressman Henry Watterson, Sept. 26, 1881, Jefferson, Kentucky, in Brown, *Life and Public Service,* 332; *San Francisco Chronicle,* Sept. 16, 1901, 5; Conwell, *Life of Garfield,* 13; Henry Ward Beecher's memorial service in New York, *New York Times,* Sept. 23, 1881, 2; *Atlantic Monthly* 48 (1881): 709; Dr. Comming in Chicago, *Chicago Tribune,* Sept. 26, 1881, 5; Rev. Dr. Rankin in Washington, D.C., Sept. 25, 1881, in *World's Eulogies,* ed. McClure, 220; Frederick O. Prince, mayor of Boston, in *Memorial of Garfield,* 12; *New York Tribune,* Sept. 20, 1881, 8; Keifer, oration at the unveiling of the statute of James A. Garfield in Washington, D.C., on May 12, 1887, in Keifer, *Oration,* 34; *New York Times,* Sept. 16, 1901, 5; McClure and Morris, *Life of McKinley,* 415; Everett, *Life of McKinley,* 430; *Chicago Tribune,* Sept. 15, 1901, 12.

34. Bundy, *Life of Garfield,* 271.

35. *Boston Evening Transcript,* Sept. 20, 1901, 3.

36. *New York Times,* Sept. 26, 1881, 4; McClure, *World's Eulogies,* 151–52, 245; *World,* Sept. 16, 1901, 6; *New York Times,* Sept. 14, 1901, 6; General Fitzhugh Lee, in *McKinley and Men of Our Times,* ed. Pell, Buel, and Boyd, 29–30; Townsend, *Memorial Life* 104; *San Francisco Chronicle,* Sept. 16, 1901, 5.

37. Robert P. Twiss, "The Nation's Prayer," a poem in *Life of McKinley,* ed. Halstead 377; Charles Henry Parkhurst, "Sermon on Garfield," Sept. 25, 1881, in *Orations,* ed. Hazeltine 24: 10474; the Reverend J. A. Gruzan, in *Memorial Service at Fourth Street,* 6; "Brotherhood," a poem in *Harper's Weekly,* Oct. 10, 1881, 670; John G. Whitier, a letter, in Conwell, *Life of Garfield,* 381; *Chicago Tribune,* Sept. 25, 1881, 10; Banks, eulogy, in *Memorial of Garfield,* 48.

38. Dr. T. DeWitt Talmage (clergyman, editor, and lecturer; edited the *Christian Herald*), oration in Brooklyn, Sept. 25, 1881, in *World's Eulogies,* ed. McClure, 42; Hoar, *Garfield,* 42; William H. Whitmory, in *Memorial of Garfield,* 22; address by Henry Watterson, in *Life and Public Service,* 331; Charles Henry Parkhurst, in *Orations,* ed. Hazeltine 24: 10479; the Reverend Emory Haynes in Washington Avenue Baptist Church, Brooklyn, Sept. 25, 1881, *New York Times,* Sept. 26, 1881, 6; ibid., Sept. 26, 1881, 4; "Our Dead President," an article by Dr. Talmage in the *Christian Herald, Life of McKinley,* ed. Halstead, 391; Townsend, *Memorial Life* 187–88.

39. Blaine, *Memorial Address,* 60, delivered on Feb. 27, 1882.

40. *Harper's Weekly,* Sept. 24, 1881, 642.

41. McClure, *World's Eulogies,* 126, 251; *Chicago Tribune,* Sept. 26, 1881, 9; Brown, *Life and Public Service,* 296; *New York Times,* Sept. 23, 1881, 2; memoir by William Balch, in *Garfield's Words,* ed. Balch, 27; the Reverend J. P. Bodfish, in *World's Eulogies,* ed. McClure, 245; Henry Higham's address in Golden Gate Park, San Francisco, Aug. 24, 1883, in Highton, *Two Orations,* 7; *Alger, From Canal Boy to President,* 333; Rev. Mr. Cruzan, *Memorial Service at Fourth Street,* 7; President Eliot of Harvard University in a memorial address, Sept. 26, 1881, *Boston Evening Transcript,* Sept. 27, 1881, 6; the

Reverend Henry Ward Beecher in Plymouth, New York, Sept. 25, 1881, *New York Times,* Sept. 26, 1881, 6; the Reverend James E. Clarke, Boston, Sept. 25, 1881, in *World's Eulogies,* ed. McClure, 178; *Harper's Weekly,* July 30, 1881, 522; the Reverend Emory J. Hay, sermon in New York, *New York Times,* Sept. 26, 1881, 2.

42. McClure, *World's Eulogies,* 44–45.

43. Charles Henry Parkhurst, in *Orations,* ed. Hazeltine 24: 10481–82.

44. Rev. Mr. Cumming's sermon, *Chicago Tribune,* Sept. 26, 1881, 5; Professor Swing's address, ibid., 9; a poem by M. F. Savage in the *Boston Globe,* in *Life and Public Service,* ed. Brown, 381.

45. Henry Watterson, in *World's Eulogies,* ed. McClure, 63–64; Brown, *Life and Public Service,* 11; *Atlantic Monthly* 48 (1881): 718; *San Francisco Chronicle,* Sept. 21, 1881, 2; *New York Tribune,* Sept. 23, 1881, 1; *Boston Evening Transcript,* Sept. 27, 1881, 6; Deihm, *Garfield Memorial Journal,* 3.

46. *Memorial of Garfield,* 20.

47. Conwell, *Life of Garfield,* 380.

48. Wayne McVeagh (attorney general in Garfield's cabinet), in *Memorial Life,* ed. Townsend 391; Rufus Choate at a memorial meeting in Boston, in ibid., 422; George Foss, congressman from Illinois in an address before the House of Representatives, Jan. 29, 1916, in *William McKinley,* ed. Gordon, 150.

49. *Boston Evening Transcript,* Sept. 14, 1901, 6.

50. McClure and Morris, *Life of McKinley,* 416.

51. Halstead, *Life of McKinley,* 395; *Evening Post,* Sept. 19, 1901, 10; *Leslie's Weekly Illustrated,* Sept. 28, 1901, 228; Townsend, *Memorial Life,* 228.

52. Halstead, *Life of McKinley,* 386.

53. Charles H. Parkhurst, in *Orations,* ed. Hazeltine 24: 10483; *Boston Evening Transcript,* Sept. 27, 1881, 6; ibid., Sept. 21, 1881, 4; *New York Tribune,* Sept. 23, 1881, 8; *New York Times,* Sept. 20, 1881, 4; ibid., Sept. 26, 1881, 6; *Chicago Tribune,* Sept. 26, 1881, 9; McClure, *World's Eulogies,* 251.

54. *Boston Evening Transcript,* Sept. 27, 1881, 6; *Harper's Weekly,* Oct. 1, 1881, 670; *New York Times,* Sept. 27, 1881, 2; *San Francisco Chronicle,* Sept. 21, 1881, 2.

55. Hoar, *Garfield,* 42; Alger, *From Canal Boy to President,* 320; McClure *World's Eulogies,* 70, 148.

56. *San Francisco Chronicle,* Sept. 24, 1901, 6; Olcott, *Life of McKinley* 2: 333, 390; Pell, Buel, and Boyd, *McKinley and Men of Our Times,* 199, 245; Gordon, *William McKinley,* 151; McClure and Morris, *Life of McKinley,* 387; Everett, *Life of McKinley,* 114; *Chicago Tribune,* Sept. 15, 1901, pt. 2, p. 1; *New York Times,* Sept. 16, 1901, 6; ibid., Oct. 11, 1903, 1; *Boston Evening Transcript,* Sept. 16, 1901, 8; *San Francisco Chronicle,* Sept. 20, 1901, ibid., Sept. 16, 1901, 5; Townsend, *Memorial Life,* 329.

57. *Chicago Tribune,* Sept. 14, 1901, 6.

58. Hon. John Whitehead (president of the New Jersey Society of Sons of the American Revolution), at New Haven, Connecticut, Apr. 30, 1903, Whitehead, *Memorial Sketch,* 6.

59. Conwell, *Life of Garfield*, 46–54; *Buffalo Express*, Sept. 20, 1901, in *Pamphlets on Biographies* 9: 1; McCabe, *Our Martyred President*, 3; the Reverend Isaac Erret's address at the burial of Garfield, in Conwell, *Life of Garfield*, 369; Banks, eulogy, in *Memorial of Garfield*, 47; Thayer, *From Log-Cabin*, 7; J. Oglesby, "Lincoln and Garfield," in *World's Eulogies*, ed. McClure, 310; *New York Times*, Sept. 23, 1881, 2; Vincent, *Story of Garfield*, 5–24.

60. Blaine, *Memorial Address*, 10.

61. Townsend, *Memorial Life*, iv.

62. Bishop Andrews's funeral oration to President McKinley, Washington, D.C., Sept. 17, 1901, in *Life of McKinley*, ed. Everett, 363; George E. Foss (a congressman from Illinois), an address before the House of Representatives, Jan. 29, 1916, in *William McKinley*, ed. Gordon, 148; Blaine, *Memorial Address*, 3–8; Balch, *Garfield's Words*, 7–8; Senator Hoar's eulogy in Worcester, Massachusetts, Dec. 13, 1881, in Hoar, *Garfield*, 15.

63. *Pamphlets on Biographies* 13: 13.

64. "A Memorial Sermon to Garfield," delivered in Oakland on Sept. 25, 1881, in *Pamphlets on Biographies* 9: 6.

65. *New York Times*, Sept. 23, 1881, 2; ibid., Sept. 266, 1881, 4, 6; *Chicago Tribune*, Sept. 26, 1881, 5; *Pamphlets on Biographies* 9: 1; Horace Davis's address in the Golden Gate Park, 4 July, 1885, in *Pamphlets on Biographies* 4: 10; memorial address by Andrew White, president of Cornell University, Ithaca, Sept. 26, 1881, in ibid., 2–6; Alger, *From Canal Boy to President*, 10; John H. Craig, address in San Francisco, Sept. 26, 1881, in *World's Eulogies*, ed. McClure, 148; Henry E. Highton, address at the laying of the cornerstone of the Garfield Monument in Golden Gate Park, Sept. 24, 1883, in Highton, *Two Orations*, 11.

66. McCabe, *Our Martyred President*, 3.

67. William Jennings Bryan, an address, in Halstead, *Life of McKinley*, 267; the Reverend Edward L. Clarke, a sermon, *Boston Evening Transcript*, Sept. 20, 1901, 7; Congressman Charles Dick of Ohio, ibid., Sept. 14, 1901, 6; General William F. Draper, address in Milford, Massachusetts, Sept. 19, 1901, ibid., Sept. 20, 1901, 3; Bishop Andrews's funeral sermon, in McKinley and Men of Our Times, ed. Pell, Buel, and Boyd, 206; George Foss, in *William McKinley*, ed. Gordon, 145.

68. Powler, *Patriotic Orations*, 192.

69. *United States Memorial Address*, 186.

70. *New York Times*, Sept. 15, 1901, 6; ibid., Sept. 17, 1901, 6; memorial tribute by ex-Secretary of State William R. Day at Canton, Ohio, Sept. 14, 1902, ibid., Sept. 15, 1902, 2; *San Francisco Chronicle*, Sept. 14, 1901, 6; McClure and Morris, *Life of McKinley*, 18; Powler, *Patriotic Orations*, 239–40.

71. *Memorial of Garfield*, 12; Dr. T. DeWitt Talmage, Brooklyn, Sept. 25, 1881, in *World's Eulogies*, ed. McClure, 48; the Reverend Dr. Rankin, Washington, D.C., Sept. 25, 1881, in ibid., 219; Governor C. K. Davis of Minnesota, St. Paul, Sept. 26, 1881, ibid., 139–40; Hon. R. Stockett Mathews, Baltimore,

Sept. 16, 1881, in ibid., 108–9; *New York Times*, Sept. 23, 1881, 8; *Chicago Tribune*, Sept. 26, 1881, 9.

72. The Reverend L. J. Withrow, *Boston Evening Transcript*, Sept. 27, 1881, 6; the Reverend J. A. M. Chapman, *New York Times*, Sept. 26, 1881, 6;

73. Haskell, *True Greatness*.

74. Charles Henry Parkhurst, in *Orations*, ed. Hazeltine 24: 10483–84.

75. *Chicago Tribune*, Sept. 26, 1881, 9.

76. The Reverend Robert M. Kemp, *World*, Sept. 16, 1901, 6; *New York Times*, Sept. 15, 1901; *Boston Evening Transcript*, Sept. 20, 1901; *San Francisco Chronicle*, Sept. 15, 1901, 5; ibid., Sept. 16, 1901, 5; the Reverend Morgan Dix," in *Life of McKinley*, ed. Everett, 464; *New York Times*, Sept. 16, 1901, 5; the Reverend Dr. C. E. Manchester, the funeral sermon in Canton, Ohio, in *Life of McKinley*, ed. Everett, 421; the funeral service in Washington, D.C., Sept. 17, 1901, prayer by the Reverend D. Naylo, in ibid., 360; the Reverend Dr. Frank Gunsaulus, Chicago, Sept. 17, 1901, in ibid., 397.

77. Charles Henry Parkhurst, in *Orations*, ed. Hazeltine 24: 10475; Bishop Clarkstone of Iowa, Sept. 26, 1881, in *World's Eulogies*, ed. McClure, 203; Ex-Governor Richard J. Oglesby of Illinois, Sept. 26, 1881, in ibid., 214; *Chicago Tribune*, Sept. 26, 1881, 9.

78. *Memorial of Garfield*, 60; Henry Ward Beecher's service in New York, *New York Times*, Sept. 23, 1881, 2; Brown, *Life and Public Service*, iii; the Reverend J. A. Cruzan, *Memorial Service at Fourth Street*, 7; the Reverend Luther Parad, *Chicago Tribune*, Sept. 26, 1881, 10; J. Z. Taylor's address in Kansas City, Sept. 16, 1881, in *World's Eulogies*, ed. McClure, 231.

79. Senator J. D. Maclaurin of South Carolina, in *Memorial Life*, ed. Townsend, 228; declaration by an Indian leader in *McKinley and Men of Our Times*, ed. Pell, Buel, and Boyd, 202; Halstead, *Life of McKinley*, 370.

80. *Chicago Tribune*, Sept. 14, 1901, 7.

81. The Reverend L. B. Bates, Boston, Sept. 15, 1901, in *Boston Evening Transcript*, Sept. 16, 1901, 2; Dr. Talmage's article in the *Christian Herald*, in Halstead *Life of McKinley*, 391; Elizabeth Stuart Phelps Ward, in *Memorial Life*, ed. Townsend, 407; Senator Hoar's tribute, Sept. 19, 1901, in *Boston Evening Transcript*, Sept. 20, 1901, 3; the Reverend F. D. Powers, in *Life of McKinley*, ed. Everett, 399. John Henry Bartlett, *An Address*, delivered at the McKinley birthday banquet held in Dayton, Ohio, on Jan. 17, 1928.

82. The Reverend Cumming's sermon in Chicago, *Chicago Tribune*, Sept. 26, 1881, 5; Senator Joseph B. Foraker, an address in Cincinnati, *Life of McKinley*, ed. McClure and Morris, 406; Charles M. Pepper, in Halstead, *Life of McKinley*, 386; Father Lavelle's speech in St. Patrick's Cathedral, New York, Sept. 17, 1901, in *Life of McKinley*, ed. Everett, 398; the Reverend W. H. Chapman, in ibid., 395–96, Bishop Andrews's funeral sermon, in ibid., 363; Pell, Buel, and Boyd, *McKinley and Men of Our Times*, 88; *Boston Evening Transcript*, Sept. 20, 1901, 3.

83. *Pamphlets on Biographies* 9: 1; *New York Times*, Sept. 26, 1881, 4; *New York*

Times, Sept. 20, 1901, 6; *San Francisco Chronicle* Sept. 16, 1901, 5; *Atlantic Monthly* 48 (1881): 708; *Chicago Tribune,* Sept. 16, 1901, 4.

84. The Reverend T. K. Noble, an address at the memorial of the Grand Army of the Republic, San Francisco, Sept. 25, 1881, in *World's Eulogies,* ed. McClure, 174; the Reverend F. E. Morse of New York, *New York Times,* Sept. 16, 1901, 5; the Reverend C. E. Manchester at the funeral of William McKinley, Canton, Ohio, in *Life of McKinley,* ed. Everett, the Reverend Moss Olivet, in Halstead, *Life of McKinley,* 289.

85. Highton, *Two Orations,* 17.

86. Gordon, *William McKinley,* 89–90.

87. Townsend, *Memorial Life,* 395–96.

88. Blaine, *Memorial Address,* 57.

89. McClure, *World's Eulogies,* 227.

90. Brown, *Life and Public Service,* viii

91. The Reverend F. Osbore, *Boston Evening Transcript,* Sept. 20, 1901, 6; Father Lavelle, an address in New York, Sept. 17, 1901, in *Life of McKinley,* ed. Everett, 398; Rabbi Grossman, an address in Temple Rodeph Shalom, New York, in Halstead, *Life of McKinley,* 288; the Reverend Charles Goodel, Methodist Episcopal Church, Brooklyn, in ibid.; the Reverend Dean R. Rabbitt, Church of Epiphany Brooklyn, in ibid.; the Reverend Hugh B. Ward, Roman Catholic Church, Brooklyn, in ibid.; the Reverend David D. Gregg, Presbyterian Church, Brooklyn, in ibid.

92. Everett, *Life of McKinley,* 397; *New York Times,* Sept. 16, 1901, 5; Grover Cleaveland's address at Princeton University, in *Life of McKinley,* ed. McClure and Morris, 411; *San Francisco Chronicle,* Sept. 16, 1901, 5.

93. *San Francisco Chronicle,* Sept. 16, 1901, 5.

94. James McGranhan, a memorial poem, *Chicago Tribune,* Sept. 26, 1881; Professor Swing's oration in Chicago Central Church, Sept. 25, 1881, in *New York Times,* Sept. 26, 1881, 6; William R. Balch, memoir, in *Garfield's Words,* ed. Balch 27; Henry Watterson, an address, in *World's Eulogies,* ed. McClure, 67; "Humanitas Regans," a poem by M. J. Savage, in Brown, *Life and Public Service,* 380; "James A. Garfield," a poem by Julia Ward Howe, in ibid., 383; Henry Wadsworth Longfellow, a poem, in ibid., 368–369; "Fatherless," a poem by Kate T. Woods, in ibid., 383; Charles Edward Loke, address at the funeral service in Milburn House in Buffalo, Sept. 15, 1901, in *Life of McKinley,* ed. Everett, 335; Bishop Andrews's funeral oration, in ibid., 365; Grover Cleaveland's address at Princeton University, in *Life of McKinley,* ed. McClure and Morris, 409; S. W. Small, a poem, in ibid., 420.

95. *New York Times,* Sept. 7, 1931, 16.

96. Brandegee, *Address* delivered before the McKinley Association of Connecticut at New Haven, Jan. 29, 1904; Vincent, *Story of Garfield;* Taft, *Address,* delivered at the banquet of the Tippecanoe Club, Cleveland Ohio, Jan. 29, 1912.

5. Progressive Reformers and Martyrdom: Mixed Attitudes

1. Wendell Phillips Stafford, associated justice of the Supreme Court of the District of Columbia, defined him as a radical Progressive. *Wendell Phillips,* 30.
2. As early as 1839, William L. Garrison wrote to Wendell Phillips:

   We feel that, in a worldly sense, few in the expanded ranks of American abolitionists have made larger sacrifice upon the altar of Humanity than yourself. . . . You turned your back upon the blandishment of a seductive world, repudiated all hope of political preferment and legal eminence . . . and became the associate of those, who for seeking the abolition of slavery by moral and religious instruments, are up to this hour subjected to popular odium, to violent treatment, to personal insult. (Quoted in Bartlett, *Wendell and Ann Phillips,* 24)

   Carlos Martyn, one of the first biographers of Wendell Phillips wrote that he repudiated not only his social status but his whole national heritage when he openly condemned the Constitution of the United States, calling it a covenant with death. "Henceforth he stood a man without country. He became a political Ishmael, his hand against everyman and everyman's hand against him. Whatever may be the thought of his wisdom, no one can deny his self sacrifice." Martyn, *Phillips,* 166; see also William Lloyd Garrison, Jr., in a memorial meeting in Massachusetts, before the Women's Suffrage Association, Feb. 28, 1884, in Austin, *Phillips,* 397; Beecher, *Phillips,* 417, 422, delivered in Plymouth Church, Brooklyn, Feb. 10, 1884; eulogy on Wendell Phillips by John Davis Long, Washington, D.C., Feb. 22, 1884, in *Orations,* ed. Hazeltine 24: 10218; Stafford, *Wendell Phillips,* 31; Higginson, *Wendell Phillips,* vii; Barrows, *Eulogy,* delivered at the memorial service to Wendell Phillips in Central Music Hall, Chicago, Feb. 17, 1884, 12–13.
3. Grimké, A., *Eulogy,* delivered in Tremont Temple, Boston, Apr. 9, 1884, 21.
4. *Exercises,* July 5, 1915, 14.
5. Phillips, *Speeches,* 279–84.
6. Stafford, *Wendell Phillips,* 57.
7. "The reformer is careless of numbers, disregards popularity, and deals only with ideas, conscience and common-sense," he declared in one of his many Boston addresses. "He feels . . . that as God waited long for an interpreter, so he can wait for his followers." Martyn, *Phillips,* 262.
8. In an address before the Grand Lodge of the Knights of Saint Crispin in Boston, Apr. 1872, he declared: "Let me tell you why I am interested in the Labor question. . . . I sympathize with sufferers there; I am ready to fight on their side." Phillips, *Speeches,* 172.
9. Early in 1839 he wrote in the *Liberator* that in the abolition movement "lives the religion of the present while the pulpit was busying itself with forms of sin." *Liberator,* June 21, 1839.
10. Martyn, *Phillips,* 177, 388–89, 527.

11. Wendell Phillips, "Christianity Is a Battle Not a Dream," in Phillips, *Speeches*, 279–84.

12. When radical Republicans failed in their effort to impeach President Johnson, Phillips noted: "Our whole success for thirty years past has been fed by such defeats as this. The annexation of Texas, the Compromise of 1850, Kansas trampled in blood, Bull Run, the second election of Lincoln, his murder, all these seeming defeats were victories in disguise." Quoted in Sears, *Phillips*, 279.

13. Russell, *Phillips*, 7–8, 183.

14. Ibid., 179.

15. Early in 1843 the New England poet James Russell Lowell dedicated a poem to Wendell Phillips in which among others, he wrote:

He saw God stands upon the Weaker side . . .
And humbly joineth him to weaker part
Fanatic named, a fool, yet well content
So he could be the nearer to God's heart
And feel its solemn pulses sending blood
Through the widespread veins of endless good.

See Stafford, *Wendell Phillips*, 43; see also Frederick Douglass's address in Washington, D.C., after the funeral, in Austin, *Phillips*, 420; Julia Ward Howe in a commemoration meeting at Faneuil Hall, Feb. 9, 1884, in Boston, ibid., 391; Martyn, *Phillips*, 41; Russell, *Phillips*, 8.

16. Beecher, *Phillips*, 417, 423.

17. Address by Theodore D. Weld in *Memorial Service*, Nov. 29, 1885, at the residence of William Sumner Crosby, 7–8, 13.

18. Ibid., 27.

19. Mrs. Mary E. Black in a poem to Wendell Phillips written at the request of the memorial committee of Boston, declared:

The broken fetter of the slave
The right of manhood to be free—
What nobler signs could make thy grave
A sacred shrine to Liberty.

Appeared in *Memorial of Wendell Phillips*, 27–28.

20. A letter from Phillips Brooks in *Memorial Service*, 39; Madison, *Critics*, 65; Curtis, *Phillips*, 16; *Memorial of Wendell Phillips*, 1.

21. Eulogy on Wendell Phillips by John Davis Long, Washington, D.C., Feb. 22, 1884, in *Orations*, ed. Hazeltine 24: 10216.

22. Stafford, *Wendell Phillips*, 7

23. Declaration of the Board of Aldermen in the City of Boston, *Memorial of Wendell Phillips*, 25; N. G. M. Chamberline in a commemoration meeting, Feb. 9, 1884, Boston, in Austin, *Phillips*, 390; Stafford, *Wendell Phillips*, 6, 9, 33–35; Madison, *Critics*, 69; Wentworth, *Phillips*, an address delivered in Faneuil Hall, Boston, Dec. 4, 1906, under the auspices of the Socialist Party Clubs of Massachusetts, 32.

24. Using Phillips's career as a universal lesson, Rev. Minot J. Savage, who delivered a prayer at the Boston memorial meeting to honor Wendell Phillips, declared:

> Let us not be content until humanity is redeemed, until the poor are lifted up, the ignorant enlightened, until every chain is broken and all ugliness is transformed into the divine beauty. And when we have accomplished this, the dream of all ages shall have been realized, the desire of all nations shall have come, the kingdom of God, which is the true kingdom of man, shall have descended from on high to abide with us here on earth. (*Memorial of Wendell Phillips*, 29)

25. Curtis, *Phillips*, 31, 36.
26. Austin, *Phillips*, 389; Martyn, *Phillips*, 111, 166; Stafford, *Wendell Phillips*, 9; Sears, *Phillips*, 305; Wentworth, *Phillips*, 4–5.
27. Frederick Douglass's address in Austin, *Phillips*, 416, 421.
28. *Memorial Service*, 25–26.
29. Woodberry, *Phillips*, 45–46.
30. Theodore D. Weld, in *Memorial Service*, 22–24; Higginson, *Wendell Phillips*, vii.
31. Archibald Grimké, a black leader, declared in a meeting in Tremont Temple in Boston on Apr. 11, 1884, that "Phillips' negro friends thoroughly appreciated his sacrifice for them," and Frederick Douglass echoed this deep appreciation in his tribute. Austin, *Phillips*, 399–421.
32. Ibid., 391–92.
33. *Memorial of Wendell Phillips*, 25–26.
34. Russell, *Phillips*, 8.
35. *Memorial of Wendell Phillips*, 11.
36. Mann, *Yankee Reformer*, 179.
37. McNeill, *Labor Movement*, 468–69.
38. Mann, *Yankee Reformer*, 183.
39. Quoted in ibid., 88.
40. Jones, *Kingdom*, 198.
41. Ibid., 214.
42. Mann, *Yankee Reformer*, 88.
43. Quoted in ibid., 89.
44. Ibid., 90.
45. Bliss, "Church," 13.
46. Mann, *Yankee Reformer*, 235.
47. Herron, *Christian State*, 26–27.
48. Quoted from Crunden, *Ministers of Reform*, 44.
49. Herron, *Between Caesar and Christ*, 39.
50. Ibid., 49.
51. Ibid., 50.
52. Ibid., 53.
53. Ibid., 57.
54. Ibid., 67–68.

55. Crunden, *Ministers of Reform*, 5, 39, 164.
56. Sinclair, *Autobiography*, 108.
57. Ibid., 238.
58. Mann, *Yankee Reformer*, 127–31.
59. Edwin D. Mead, "Tribute to Professor Parsons," *Arena* 40, no. 228 (Dec. 1908): 641.
60. See Benjamin O. Flower, *Civilization's Inferno* (Boston, 1893), 231, 233–34.
61. Benjamin O. Flower, "Professor Frank Parsons, Ph.D.: An Appreciation," *Arena* 40, no. 227 (Nov. 1908): 497, 500.
62. Benjamin O. Flower, "Then Dawned at Light in the East," *Arena*, 10, no. 57 (Aug. 1894): 342–52.
63. Benjamin O. Flower, "John Ruskin: A Type of Twentieth Century Method," *Arena* 12, no. 92 (July 1897): 70–72, 78.
64. Benjamin O. Flower, "Some Civilization's Silent Currents" *Arena* 6, no. 36 (Nov. 1892): 768.
65. M. D. W. Howe, *Holmes-Laski Letters*, 119, 227, 689, 772.
66. "Holmes to Laski," Dec. 15, 1917, in ibid., 119.
67. "Holmes to Laski," Aug. 7, 1925, in ibid., 772.
68. M. D. W. Howe, *Holmes-Pollock Letters*, 252–53.
69. George Santayana, "The Genteel Tradition in American Philosophy," in Santayana, *Winds of Doctrine*, 200.
70. Ibid., 210–11.
71. Josiah Royce, "The Problem of Job," in *American Thought*, ed. P. Miller, 21, 25.
72. Quoted in Clebsch, *American Religious Thought*, 156.
73. James, *The Will to Believe*, 31
74. On the ways in which Jane Addams became a national myth, see Lasch, *Social Thought*, Introduction.
75. After the founding of Hull House, Jane Addams gave a lecture in Plymouth, Massachusetts, in which she described it as "my subjective necessity for social settlement." She emphasized three main impulses that motivated her to devote her life to reform:

    1) The desire to make the entire social organism democratic and extend democracy beyond its political expression. . . . 2) The impulse . . . to bring social energy and accumulation of civilization to those portions of the race which have little. . . . 3) Renaissance of Christianity, a movement towards its early humanitarian aspects.

    Such statements demonstrated that Addams never totally abandoned the belief in the morality of the universe, but her acceptance of modern culture prevented her from appropriating the martyr tradition. Jane Addams, "The Subjective Necessity for Social Settlement," in *Social Thought*, ed. Lasch, 29.
76. Ibid., xxiv
77. Lynn, *Jane Addams*, 429.
78. Ibid., 430.
79. Addams, *Peace and Bread*, 132, 150.

80. Ibid., 150–51.
81. Randolph Bourne, "The Price of Radicalism," *New Republic* 4 (Mar. 11, 1916): 161.
82. Randolph Bourne, *Untimely Papers,* quoted in Moreau, *Bourne* 135.
83. Quoted from Sillen, "Randolph Bourne," 29.
84. Quoted in Moreau, *Bourne,* 155.
85. In this article Bourne expresses personal disappointment with the Progressive tradition as expressed by Wilson or Dewey. "One has a sense of having come to a sudden short stop at the end of an intellectual era. . . . To those of us who have taken Dewey's philosophy almost as our American religion, it never occurred that values could be subordinate to technique." Bourne, "The Twilight of Idols," in Bourne, *War and the Intellectuals,* 59–60.
86. Quoted in Moreau, *Bourne,* 166.
87. Ibid., 209.
88. Dos Passos, *1919,* 105–6.
89. Quoted in Moreau, *Bourne,* 204.
90. V. W. Brooks, *Randolph Bourne,* xiv, xxx.
91. Bourne, *War and the Intellectuals,* xiii–xiv.
92. Herron, *Germanism.*
93. Royce, "The Duties of Americans," *Address,* delivered at Tremont Temple, Boston, Jan. 30, 1916.
94. Lucian Lamer Knight, "Woodrow Wilson—Behold the Dreamer Cometh" (an address in Druid Hall Presbyterian Church, Atlanta, Georgia, Feb. 10, 1924) in *Woodrow Wilson,* ed. Knight, 15–17.
95. Ibid., 8–10, 30–31; Alderman, *Woodrow Wilson,* 33, delivered before the Congress of the United States, Dec. 25, 1924; McAllister, *Selected Poems,* 24, 58; Dr. Edward Parker Davis, class poet of the Princeton class of '79, "Poem," in *True Woodrow Wilson,* ed. Black, 250; Senator Tom Connally's centennial address, "Woodrow Wilson—A Remembrance," Feb. 21, 1956, Richmond, Virginia, in *Woodrow Wilson in Retrospect,* ed. Pinsley, 67; Reid, *Woodrow Wilson,* 239.
96. Quoted from Rowse, *Woodrow Wilson,* 283.
97. Knight, *Woodrow Wilson,* 12; McAllister, *Selected Poems,* 218; Dr. Francis P. Gaines, "Reflection of Woodrow Wilson" (delivered in Staunton, Virginia, Nov. 12, 1940), in *Woodrow Wilson in Retrospect,* ed. Pinsley, 10; D. H. Miller, *Woodrow Wilson,* 3 (memorial address delivered at the Madison Avenue Presbyterian Church, Feb. 10, 1924).
98. Alderman, *Woodrow Wilson,* 38.
99. Black, *True Woodrow Wilson,* 260.
100. Ibid., 307; White, *Woodrow Wilson,* 1; Alderman, *Woodrow Wilson,* 26; Reid, *Woodrow Wilson,* 232, 236–37; Payne, *Address,* 21 (Hall of the House of Delegates, Richmond, Virginia, Nov. 17, 1931); D. H. Miller, *Woodrow Wilson,* 4; S. M. Wilson, *Woodrow Wilson,* 17 (memorial address delivered at the New Lexington Opera House in Lexington, Kentucky, on Feb. 10, 1924).
101. Bliss Perry, "Woodrow Wilson—Commemorative Tribute," prepared for the

American Academy of Arts and Letters, *American Academy of Arts and Letters,* no. 50 (1925): 18–19.

102. Daniels, *The Wilson Era,* 636.

103. McAllister, *Selected Poems* 40, 44, 48–49, 51, 67, 69, 75, 79, 80, 87, 90–91, 94–96, 102–3.

104. Quoted from Daniels, *The Wilson Era,* 367–68.

105. Bender, *Woodrow Wilson,* 7; Raymond B. Fosdick, undersecretary general of the League of Nations, a tribute in the *New York Times,* Feb. 4, 1924; Senator Joseph F. Guffey, address on the eighty-fifth anniversary of President Wilson's birthday, Dec. 28, 1943, in *Woodrow Wilson,* ed. Harley, 120; Ray Standard Baker, address at Woodrow Wilson Memorial Dinner, Los Angeles, Dec. 28, 1943, in ibid., 144; Reid, *Woodrow Wilson,* 220; Josephus Daniels quoted from Wilson's last article in the *Atlantic Monthly* of 1923, to show how far was the president from self-interested politicians, Daniels, *The Life of Woodrow Wilson,* 353.

106. "He was a power and not a puppet with strings to be pulled by designing politicians." Knight, *Woodrow Wilson,* 18.

107. Alderman, *Woodrow Wilson,* 30.

108. Reid, *Woodrow Wilson,* 221–23.

109. Knight, *Woodrow Wilson,* 10.

110. On the various reactions of politicians who supported Wilson to his death see Brewster, *Passing of Woodrow Wilson.* The theme of Wilson the freedom fighter appeared in many poems dedicated to his memory, see McAllister, *Selected Poems* 56–57, 60.

111. Quoted from Brewster, *Passing of Woodrow Wilson.*

112. Quoted in ibid.

113. Cranston, *Story of Woodrow Wilson,* 456; Payne, *Address,* 10, 19.

114. Bailey, *Woodrow Wilson,* 100, 135; tribute of Governor Al Smith, Judge John McIntyre, and ex-Ambassador John W. Davis, all quoted in Brewster, *Passing of Woodrow Wilson;* Edith Cherrington, "Woodrow Wilson," a poem, in *Selected Poems,* ed. McAllister, 56; Knight, *Woodrow Wilson,* 26; Payne, *Address,* 19; S. M. Wilson, *Woodrow Wilson,* 14.

115. Josephus Daniels, *The Life of Woodrow Wilson,* 17.

116. Articles in the *World,* and the *San Francisco Chronicle,* and an address by Joseph P. Tumulty, in Brewster, *Passing of Woodrow Wilson;* undersecretary general of the League of Nations in an article in the *New York Times,* Feb. 4, 1924; in Harley, *Woodrow Wilson,* 141–42.

117. Daniels, *The Life of Woodrow Wilson,* 334.

118. Senator Joseph F. Guffey's address on the eighty-fifth anniversary of President Wilson's birthday, Dec. 28, 1941, in Harley, *Woodrow Wilson Still Lives,* 120. Sumner Wens, undersecretary to the State Department in 1941, in a memorial address on Armistice Memorial Day, ibid., 114.

119. Ibid., 9.

120. McAllister, *Selected Poems,* 48, 51, 90, 109.

121. Ibid., p. 98.

122. Joseph Tumulty's address in Brewster, *The Passing of Woodrow Wilson;* McAllister, *Selected Poems,* 27, 40, 49, 112; "Reflection on Woodrow Wilson," speech by Dr. Francis P. Gaines, president of Washington and Lee University, Lexington, Virginia, delivered on Nov. 12, 1940 in Staunton, Virginia, in *Woodrow Wilson in Retrospect,* ed. Pinsley, 10, Harley, *Woodrow Wilson,* 124.

123. Knight, *Woodrow Wilson,* 26.

124. "The Road Away from Revolution," the last article by Woodrow Wilson, appeared in the *Atlantic Monthly,* Aug. 1923, reprinted in Daniels, *Life of Woodrow Wilson,* 353.

125. Wilson's popular biographers quoted him on this subject. Thomas Bailey wrote that early in 1912 Wilson made the following prophetic statement: "I would rather lose in a cause that I know that some day will triumph, than triumph in a cause that I know some day will lose." Bailey, *Woodrow Wilson,* 123. Likewise, Josephus Daniels wrote that after his stroke Wilson consoled him: "Do not trouble about the things we fought for. They are sure to prevail. . . . It may come in a better way than we provided." Daniels, *The Wilson Era,* 12. See also Alderman, *Woodrow Wilson,* 31; Knight, *Woodrow Wilson,* 26; Bender, *Woodrow Wilson,* 15; McAllister, *Selected Poems,* 39, 44.

126. B. Perry, "Woodrow Wilson," *American* 19–20.

127. Bailey, *Woodrow Wilson,* 22, 100.

128. Alderman, *Woodrow Wilson,* 24.

129. Knight, *Woodrow Wilson,* 17; Connally, "Woodrow Wilson—A Remembrance," 67.

130. White, *Woodrow Wilson,* 471; Rowse, *Woodrow Wilson,* 12–13.

131. Bailey, *Woodrow Wilson,* 137–38.

132. Ibid., 368–69.

133. Crunden, *Ministers of Reform,* 273.

6. On Revolution's Altar

1. Levine, *Jane Addams,* xv.

2. William P. Black, in *The Knights of Labor,* Oct. 8, 1887, quoted from *Haymarket Martyrs,* ed. Foner, 16.

3. Eugene Victor Debs, "Looking Backward," *Appeal to Reason,* Nov. 23, 1907, reprinted in *Debs,* 284–86.

4. "An Address by August Spies," quoted from *Twenty-Fifth Anniversary,* 24.

5. Ibid., 36.

6. Ibid., 33.

7. See *Haymarket Martyrs,* 46.

8. Quoted from *Twenty-Fifth Anniversary,* 38.

9. "Captain Black's Eulogy at the Tomb," in *Albert Parsons,* 246–47.

10. Ibid., 200.

11. William P. Black, "Introduction to the Autobiographies of the Haymarket

Martyrs," originally published in *The Knights of Labor,* Oct. 8, 1887, quoted here from *Haymarket Martyrs,* ed. Foner, 18–19.

12. *Twenty-Fifth Anniversary,* 10.
13. For an interesting analysis of Emma Goldman's attitude toward suffering as compared with figures such as Christ, Socrates, and Gandhi who accepted the "theosophy of suffering," see Ganguli, *Emma Goldman,* 2–3.
14. Goldman, *Political Violence,* 29.
15. Quoted from Hippolyte Havel, "Emma Goldman," New York, Dec. 1910, in *Anarchism,* ed. Goldman, 40.
16. Goldman, *Anarchism,* 50, 62, 65.
17. "Emma Goldman and Alexander Berkman to Dear Friends," Dec. 19, 1919, Ellis Island, in *Nowhere at Home,* ed. Drinnon and Drinnon, 13.
18. Goldman, *Living My Life* 1: 56.
19. Ibid., 87–88.
20. Goldman, *Political Violence,* 2, 8, 29.
21. Goldman, *Anarchism,* 12–13.
22. Goldman, *Living My Life* 1: 221, 227.
23. Ibid., 307.
24. Ibid. 2: 508–9.
25. Reacting to the antianarchist hysteria after McKinley's assassination she tried to explain the relationship between radical martyrs and the people. "Sasha [Berkman] had done something for the people; and our brave Chicago martyrs, and the others in every land and time. But the people are asleep; they remain indifferent." Ibid. 1: 304.
26. Ibid., 304.
27. Emma Goldman to Emily Scott, June 26, 1928, St. Tropez, in *Nowhere at Home,* ed. Drinnon and Drinnon, 85.
28. Late into night we talked of our plans for further activities," wrote Goldman. "When separated, we had made a pact—to dedicate ourselves to the cause in some supreme deed, to die together if necessary, or to continue to live and work for the ideal for which one of us must give his life." Ibid., 62.
29. Ibid., 13.
30. Goldman, *Living My Life* 1: 61.
31. Ibid.
32. Quoted in Kornbluh, *Rebel Voices,* 1.
33. The case of Valentino Modestino, who was killed by the police in Paterson, New Jersey, demonstrated such an attitude. The members of the union commemorated the scene of violence with the "Pageant of the Paterson Strike," written by the radical author John Reed and performed by Paterson strikers themselves in Madison Square Garden on June 7, 1913. The *New York Tribune* noted that episode 3, which described the funeral of Modestino provided the audiences and sympathizers of the strikers with an emotional climate that reinforced their solidarity. "A coffin supposed to contain Modestino's body, was borne across the stage, followed by the strikers in funeral procession to

the heavy tones of the 'Dead March.' As they passed, the mourners dropped red carnations and ribbons upon the coffin, until it was buried 'beneath the crimson symbol of the worker's blood.' " Kornbluh, *Rebel Voices*, 213.

34. *Industrial Worker*, Nov. 3, 1917, 1; When the IWW published *The Everett Massacre* it emphasized the same element of anonymous martyrdom. "This book is dedicated to the loyal soldiers of the great class war who were murdered . . . in the struggle for free speech . . . FELIX BARAN, HUGO GERLOT, GUSTAV JOHNSON, JOHN LOONEY, ABRAHAM RABINOWITZ, and those unknown martyrs whose bodies were swept out to unmarked graves on Sunday, November 5, 1916." W. C. Smith, *Everett Massacre*, 4.

35. Eulogy to a free-speech martyr, delivered over the remains of Michael Hoey by Laure Payne Emerson, published in the *San Diego Labor Leader*, Apr. 5, 1912. Quoted from Foner, *Fellow Workers*, 143–44.

36. The poem "To Frank Little" by Viola Gilbert Snell appeared in *Solidarity* on Aug. 25, 1917, and the poem "When The Cock Crows" by Arturo Giovannitti appeared in *Solidarity* on Sept. 22, 1917. See Kornbluh, *Rebel Voices*, 306–9.

37. Chaplin, *Centralia Conspiracy*.

38. Dos Passos, *1919*, 456–61.

39. *Industrial Worker*, Oct. 23, 1920, 2.

40. For the spreading of the Joe Hill legend see G. M. Smith, *Joe Hill*.

41. Renshaw, *The Wobblies*, 190.

42. Ibid., 191.

43. *New Solidarity*, Nov. 28, 1918, 1.

44. Kornbluh, *Rebel Voices*, 127.

45. Ibid., 152.

46. Ibid., 146.

47. G. M. Smith, *Joe Hill*, 179–90.

48. Stegner, "I Dreamed I Saw Joe Hill," 187; see also G. M. Smith, *Joe Hill*, 193–96.

49. *International Socialist Review* 16, no. 6 (Dec. 1915): 331.

50. Quoted from Kornbluh *Rebel Voices*, 155.

51. *International Socialist Review* 16, no. 6 (Dec. 1915): 331.

52. *New Solidarity*, Nov. 28, 1918, 1.

53. Ibid., Nov. 23, 1918, 2.

54. A committed socialist such as Walter Hurt wrote, "History proved that despite the purpose for which they were designed, prisons have always been instruments of progress, unfailing agencies of human advancement. Capitalism thought it had destroyed Debs. It merely had made him. When it sentenced Debs to jail Capitalism signed its own death warrant." *Appeal to Reason*, Nov. 23, 1907, reprinted in *Debs*, 497–98.

55. John Spargo, "Eugene V. Debs, Incarnate Spirit of Revolt," in *Debs*, 507, 508.

56. Eugene V. Debs, "A Poem" (1926), in Salvatore, *Eugene V. Debs*, 303.

57. Eugene V. Debs, "John Brown: History's Greatest Hero," *Appeal to Reason*,

Nov. 23, 1907, reprinted in *Debs,* 272; Debs, "Looking Backward"; "Martyn Irons, Martyr," Dec. 9, 1900, in *Debs,* 275; "The Martyred Apostles of Labor," *New Time,* Feb. 1898, reprinted in ibid., 263–67.

58. Ibid., 323.
59. Eugene V. Debs, "Jesus the Supreme Leader," *Coming Nation,* Mar. 1, 1914, 2, quoted in Currie, *Eugene V. Debs,* 120.
60. Ginger, *Bending Cross,* 399.
61. Ibid., 391.
62. After his release Debs wrote *Wall and Bars,* a book on prisoners' lives, in which he stated, "In going to prison myself I came to know them well . . . and I came also to realize the moral obligation resting on me to espouse their cause and to wage their war against the vicious system." 248.
63. Debs to his brother Theodore, Nov. 27, 1919, in Salvatore, *Eugene V. Debs,* 316.
64. Quoted from Salvatore, *Eugene V. Debs,* 311.
65. Le Prade, *Debs and the Poets,* 3, 18, 20, 25, 31, 34, 38, 42, 43, 71.
66. *Debs Has Visitors,* play by Charles Erskine Scott Wood, in ibid., 88–93.
67. Karsner, *Debs,* 226; Owen Lovejoy, in Le Prade, *Debs and the Poets,* 144; Witter Bynner, in ibid., 52; Schnittkind, *Story of Eugene V. Debs,* 188.
68. "Calmly he walked into the living death that had been prepared for him— and his soul sang; for he had stood the test . . . kept his faith—and deemed his life a little thing to lay upon the altar of his dream." Le Prade, *Debs and the Poets,* 50–51.
69. Ibid., 51.
70. Ibid., 30.
71. Mabel Curry, Debs's close friend, in a letter to Debs from Apr. 11, 1921, in Salvatore, *Eugene V. Debs,* 313; Guy Bogart, a socialist poet from California and John Milton Scott, a minister close to socialism, regarded Debs as a martyr for the salvation of the workers of the world, and Witter Bynner, a poet from Berkeley confessed that he was moved by Debs's humane passion for the betterment of his species. See Le Prade, *Debs and the Poets,* 35, 38, 52.
72. Karsner, *Debs Goes to Prison,* 58.
73. Schnittkind, *Story of Eugene V. Debs,* 190.
74. *Debs,* 332–33.
75. Ginger, *Bending Cross,* 373.
76. Quoted from David Karsner, *Debs Goes to Prison,* 1.
77. Ginger, *Bending Cross,* 372.
78. The socialist and Progressive writer Upton Sinclair wrote that "the government regards him as a . . . felon. . . . But there are a great many people in the United States and other countries who . . . regard him as hero, a martyr, even a saint." Sinclair, Introduction to Le Prade, *Debs and the Poets,* 5. Such a theme appears also in other poems, ibid., 9, 28, 44.
79. For early analogies with Lincoln see John Swinton, "Lincoln 1860—Debs 1894," in *Debs,* 503; W. E. P. French, "A Love Shared by Lincoln and

Debs," in ibid., 513. For later analogies, see James Oppenheim's comment on Debs in Le Prade, *Debs and the Poets,* 17, 63–64; Henry Ridely's comparison to John Brown's idealism without his violence, in ibid., 49; and Percy McKaye's poem, "The Three Guardsmen of Atlanta," describing John Brown, Abraham Lincoln, and William Lloyd Garrison as guardsmen of Debs's prison, in ibid., 10.

80. Ibid., 70.
81. Le Prade, *Debs and the Poets,* 84.
82. Ibid., 84–87.
83. Ibid., 6; David Star Jordan, the president of Stanford University, poets Charles Sanburg and William Ellery Leonard, and Jewish leader Israel Zangwill, uttered similar opinions. Ibid., 28, 40, 48, 49.

7. Contemporary America: Decline and Resurrection of the Martyr

1. Nevins, *Lincoln and the Gettysburg Address,* 89.
2. For an interesting discussion of the cultural revolution of our time and its origins see May, *American Innocence.*
3. Bellah et al., *Habits of the Heart,* 232.
4. For interesting discussions on the impact of the Progressive movement and the meaning of its failure, see Richard Abrams, "The Failure of Progressivism" and Arthur Link, "What Happened to the Progressive Movement in the Twenties" in *Twentieth-Century America,* ed. Abrams and Levine, 207–24, 267–83; Daniel Rodgers, "In Search of Progresivism," *Reviews in American History,* Dec. 1982, 113–27; Kolko, *Triumph of Conservatism;* Weinstein, *Corporate Ideal;* Wiebe, *Search for Order;* Samuel Hays, "The Politics of Reform in Municipal Government in the Progressive Era," *Pacific Northwest Quarterly* 55 (Oct. 1964): 157–69.
5. Quoted from Orlansky, "Reactions," 263–64.
6. The attitude of a "true believer" (willing to sacrifice his life for the revolution) became central among left-wing intellectuals. Journals like the *New Masses,* the *Daily Worker,* and the *Partisan Review,* used a rhetoric of radical commitment, praised martyrs for the working class and called for further sacrifices to promote the revolution. The quest for martyrdom appeared in the well-known play *Waiting for Lefty,* by Clifford Odets. The crowd at the end participates in a ritual of commitment and sacrifice: it echoes and reiterates the player's vow to fight capitalism at any price till the final victory. This drama reached national prominence during the 1930s and brought its message far beyond the ranks of the committed radical. See Clifford Odets, *Waiting for Lefty,* in Odets, *Six Plays,* 1–33.
7. See Hofstadter, *Age of Reform,* 302–28.
8. Orlansky, "Reactions."
9. "When Kennedy Died," *Newsweek,* Sept. 14, 1964, 61–62; Sheatsley and Feldman, "Assassination of President Kennedy," 197, 206–7.

10. Toscano, *Since Dallas*, 14.
11. *Christian Century* 80 (1963): 1487.
12. *Saturday Evening Post*, Dec. 14, 1963, 19.
13. Ibid., 32a.
14. On the various analogies to Abraham Lincoln, see Toscano, *Since Dallas*, 1; *Ebony*, a black magazine, wrote that both Kennedy and Lincoln had died martyrs for the cause of freedom, but that Kennedy had surpassed Lincoln by working to achieve complete equality between the races. *Ebony* 19, no. 4 (Feb. 1964): 25, 27.
15. *Christian Century* 80 (1963): 1568.
16. Toscano, *Since Dallas*, 17.
17. *Christian Century* 81 (1964): 37.
18. Arthur M. Schlesinger, Jr., "A Eulogy," *Saturday Evening Post*, Dec. 14, 1963, 32–32a; Richard Gilman, "The Fact of Mortality," *Commonweal* 79, no. 12 (Dec. 13, 1963): 337–38; *Christian Century* 80 (1963): 1487.
19. Gilman, "Fact of Mortality," 338.
20. Toscano, *Since Dallas*, 40.
21. Quoted in Fairlie, *Kennedy Promise*, 353.
22. Fairlie, "Man for One Season," 28–29, 129–31.
23. *Time*, Feb. 1, 1971, 10.
24. Ibid.
25. Midge Decter, "Kennedyism," *Commentary* 49, no. 1 (Jan. 1970): 27.
26. Harris, *Anguish of Change*, 201; Toscano, *Since Dallas*, vii, ix, 16, 59, 62. In their report on various presidential performance studies, Robert K. Murray and Tim H. Blessing showed that in the polls of 1966, 1977, 1981, and 1982, experts on American presidents, while always ranking Lincoln as the "greatest" president, never viewed Kennedy as more than an "above average" president. He was never considered by experts in American history and politics as one of the ten best presidents in the United States. Murray and Blessing, "Presidential Performance," 541–42.
27. Martin, *Hero for Our Time*, 568, 574.
28. Fairlie, "Man for One Season," 131.
29. Wills, *Kennedy Imprisonment*, 300–301.
30. *Nation* 206 (Apr. 15, 1968): 490.
31. Quoted in Newsweek, Apr. 15, 1968, 38.
32. Oates, *Let the Trumpet Sound*, 28, 32.
33. Ibid., 78–79, 86.
34. Ibid., 110–11.
35. Ibid., 136, 140, 146.
36. Ibid., 190.
37. Ibid., 162.
38. Martin Luther King, Jr., *Letter from a Birmingham Jail*, in *Nonviolence in America*, ed. Lynd, 462.
39. Ibid., 477–78.
40. Ibid., 466.

41. Ibid., 479.
42. Ibid., 472.
43. Ibid., 479.
44. Responding to the demand to wait for the gradual enforcement of the deseg-
    regation laws, King wrote:

    But when you have seen vicious mobs lynch your mothers and fathers at will and drown
    your sisters and brothers at whim; when you have seen hate-filled policeman curse,
    kick, brutalize, and even kill your black brothers and sisters with impunity; when you
    see the vast majority of your twenty million Negro brothers smothering in an air-tight
    cage of poverty in the midst of an affluent society; . . . when you are harried by day and
    haunted by night by the fact that you are a Negro, living constantly at tip-toe stance,
    never quite knowing what to expect, when you are forever fighting a degenerating sense
    of "nobodiness"—then you will understand why we find it difficult to wait. (Ibid., 466–
    67)

45. "One day the South will know that when these disinherited children of God
    sat down at lunch counters they were in reality standing up for the Judeo-
    Christian heritage, and thus carrying our whole nation back to great wells of
    democracy which were dug deep by the founding fathers in the formulation
    of the Constitution and the Declaration of Independence." Ibid., 481.
46. Oates, Let the Trumpet Sound, 236, 269.
47. Ibid., 321.
48. King taped this speech and it was used at his own funeral two months later.
    Newsweek, Apr. 22, 1968, 26.
49. Smylie, "On Jesus," 85–86. For King's biblical interpretation of his struggle,
    see also Elder, "King and Civil Religion"; Smith and Zepp, Beloved Commu-
    nity, 12, 80–81, 119–31; Downing, Promised, Land, 221, 223.
50. King, Where Do We Go, 133.
51. Oates, Let the Trumpet Sound, 455.
52. Ibid., 341.
53. Ibid., 406.
54. Ibid., 413–14.
55. Martin Luther King, Jr., "A View From the Mountaintop," appeared in many
    books and journals. Quoted from Newsweek, Apr. 15, 1968, 34–38; Renewal
    9, no. 4 (Apr. 1969): 5; and Washington, Testament of Hope, 280–86.
56. Crisis 5, no. 4 (Apr. 1968): 115. In a poem dedicated to King's memory,
    Natalie S. Robins wrote in the Nation 210 (June 22, 1970): 765:

    The city streets a hundred years
    from now will wear his blood as
    sun.
    A free man has the choice to live or die
    . . . He chose to have no
    choice, knowing all along he chose
    his death.

57. Commonweal 88, no. 5 (Apr. 19, 1968): 126.
58. Ibid., 88, no. 11 (May 31, 1968): 315.

59. *Crisis* 5, no. 4 (Apr. 1968): 115.

60. It was surprising to find how many religious and educational periodicals devoted articles to Martin Luther King, Jr. Among the themes discussed in the educational journals were suggestions to compare King and Thomas Becket in English classes, the use of King's example as a moral approach to the study of U.S. history, and many children's poems in honor of King's birthday. For example, see *English Journal* 57 (Nov. 1968): 1147–48; *Social Education* 39 (Jan. 1975): 36–39; *Elementary English* 52 (Jan. 1975): 108; *Childhood Education* 46 (Apr. 1970): 374–75. The religious themes varied from the traditional analogy to Jesus, and discussion of the martyr as a suffering servant killed by the people and atoning in his death for their sins, to the impact of King's religious imagery on American politics. See for example, *Interpretation* 24 (1970): 74–92; *America* 118 (Apr. 1968): 532; *Criterion* 7 (Winter 1968): 3–4; *Christian Century* 85, no. 16 (Apr. 1968): 475–76; ibid., no. 18 (May 1968): 578; ibid. 90, no. 1 (Jan. 1973): 35–36.

61. Smylie, "On Jesus," 89.

62. Two years after King's assassination *Newsweek* noted with some surprise that King's name retained its huge symbolic strength even while his principles, his strategies, and many of his apparent accomplishments were sliding into deepening eclipse. *Newsweek,* Jan. 26, 1970, 26.

63. Peter Schrag, "The Uses of Martyrdom," *Saturday Review* 51 (Apr. 20, 1968): 28–29.

64. "He was seeking not consensus but the cleansing action of revolutionary change. America had made progress toward freedom, but measured against the goal the road ahead is still long and hard." *Nation* 206 (Apr. 15, 1968): 490.

65. Many variations of the American dream appeared also in addresses, rituals, and artefacts commemorating American martyred heroes outside the political sphere. Themes such as broken dreams were common in eulogies to James Dean, Judy Garland, Marilyn Monroe, Elvis Presley, and other "martyrs" from the realm of art and entertainment. Similarly, a call to carry on the unfulfilled technological dream characterized many tributes to the six astronauts killed in January 1986 in the explosion of the Challenger space shuttle.

66. Cormish R. Rogers, "MLK and the Bicentennial," *Christian Century* 92, no. 13 (Apr. 1975): 348.

67. *New York Times,* Jan. 20, 1986, pt. Y, p. 5.

68. "Saving Dissenter from His Legend," ibid., 12.

69. Ibid.

70. Ibid.

71. "He is . . . the richest symbol in the American experience," wrote Clinton Rossiter on Lincoln. "He is, as someone has remarked neither irreverently nor sacrilegiously, the martyred Christ of democracy's passion play." Rossiter, *American Presidency,* 108.

Select Bibliography

Primary Sources

Addams, Jane. *Peace and Bread in Time of War*. New York: King's Crown Press, 1945, first published 1922.

Alderman, Edwin Anderson. *Woodrow Wilson—Memorial Address*. Washington, D.C.: Government Printing Office, 1925.

Alger, Horatio. *From Canal Boy to President*. New York: John Anderson, 1881.

American Academy of Arts and Letters, no. 50 (1925).

Andrew, John. *Message to the Senate and House of Massachusetts*. Boston: Apr. 17, 1865.

Annin, Robert Edwards. *Woodrow Wilson—A Character Study*. New York: Dodd, Mead, 1924.

Annual Report of the American Anti-Slavery Society, by the Executive Committee, for the John Brown Year. New York: Negro University Press, 1969, first published 1861.

Arnold, Isaac N. *Abraham Lincoln*. Chicago: Fergus, 1881.

Austin, George Lowell. *The Life and Times of Wendell Phillips*. Boston: B. B. Russell, 1884.

Avey, Elijah. *The Capture and Execution of John Brown*. Chicago: Afro-American Press, 1969, first published 1906.

Bailey, Thomas. *Woodrow Wilson and the Great Betrayal*. New York: Macmillan, 1945.

Balch, William R., ed. *Garfield's Words*. Boston: Houghton Mifflin, 1881.

Barrett, W. Z. *Mourning for Lincoln*. Philadelphia: John C. Winston, 1909.

Barrows, John H. *Eulogy*. Chicago: Jamson and Printing, 1884.

Bartlett, Colb P. *The Martyr's Return*. Wantagh, N.Y.: Bartlett, 1915.

Barton, William E. *Abraham Lincoln and the American Ideal*. Casper, Wyo.: *Casper Daily Tribune*, Printed by the Commercial Printing Co., 1928.

————. "John Brown and Abraham Lincoln." *Lake Placid News*, May 18, 1928.

Barton, William E. *The Soul of Abraham Lincoln*. New York: George H. Doran, comp. 1920.

Beecher, Henry Ward. *Wendell Phillips: A Commemorative Discourse*. New York: Fords Howard and Hulbert, 1884.

Bender, Robert J. *Woodrow Wilson: Scattered Impressions of a Reporter*. New York: United Press Association, 1924.

Benet, Stephen Vincent. *John Brown's Body — A Poem*. New York: Heritage Press, 1927.

Black, Harold Garnet, *The True Woodrow Wilson — Crusader for Democracy*. New York: Fleming H. Revell, 1946.

Blaine, James G. *Memorial Address Before the Department of the Government of the United States*. Washington, D.C.: Government Press Office, 1882.

Bliss, W. D. P. "The Church of the Carpenter and Twenty Years After." *Social Preparation for the Kingdom of God* 11, no. 13 (Jan. 1922).

Bourne, Randolph. *War and the Intellectuals*. New York: Harper and Row, 1964.

Brakeman, N. L. *A Great Man Fallen: A Sermon*. Baton Rouge, La.: New Orleans Times Book and Job Office, 1865.

Brandegee, Frank B. *Address on the Life, Character, and Public Service of William McKinley*. Washington, D.C.: Judd and Detweiler Printers, 1904.

Brewer, David Josiah, ed. *The World's Best Orations*. 10 vols. St. Louis: E. P. Kaiser, 1899.

Brewster, Eugene, V., ed. *The Passing of Woodrow Wilson*. New York: Brewster Publication, 1924.

Brooks, Phillips. *Perfect Freedom — Addresses*. Boston, 1893.

Brooks, Van Wyck. *Randolph Bourne — History of a Literary Radical*. New York: B. W. Huebsch, 1920.

Brown, E. E. *Life and Public Service of President Garfield*. Boston: D. L. Guernsey Cornhill, 1881.

Brown, Robert E. *The Meaning of Abraham Lincoln*. Oakland: First Congregation Church, 1929.

Bryant, William Cullen, and Gay Sydney Howard. *A Popular History of the United States*. Vol. 4. New York: Charles Scribner's Sons, 1881.

Bulkley, Edwin A. *A Discourse Commemorative of the Death of Abraham Lincoln*. Plattsburgh, N.Y.: J. W. Tuttle Book and Job Printer, 1865.

Bundy, J. M. *The Life of James A. Garfield*. New York: Barnes, 1881.

Burgess, John W. *The Civil War and the Constitution*. Vol. 1. New York: Charles Scribner's Sons, 1901.

Chaplin, Ralph. *The Centralia Conspiracy*. Chicago: Central Defence Committee, [1920].

Conwell, Russell H. *The Life of James A. Garfield*. Portland, Maine: Stinson, 1881.

Cowgill, Frank Brooks. *Columbia Martyr*. N.P., 1941.

Cranston, Ruth. *The Story of Woodrow Wilson*. New York: Simon and Schuster, 1945.

Curtis, George William. *Wendell Phillips — A Eulogy*. New York: Harper and Brothers, 1884.

Daniels, Josephus, *The Life of Woodrow Wilson*. New York: Will H. Johnson, 1924.

————. *The Wilson Era—Years of War and After*. Chapel Hill: University of North Carolina Press, 1946.

Davis, Harold E., ed. *Garfield of Hiram*. Hiram, Ohio, 1931.

Debs, Eugene V. *Wall and Bars*. Chicago: Socialist Party Press, 1927.

Debs: His Life, Writings, and Speeches. Chicago: Charles H. Kerr, 1908.

Deihm, C. F., ed. *President James A. Garfield Memorial Journal*. New York: C. F. Deihm, 1882.

Dimmock, Thomas. *Lovejoy*. St. Louis, 1888.

Dos Passos, John. *1919*. New York: Harcourt Brace, 1932.

Draper, Andrew S. *What Makes Lincoln Great*. Cedar City, Iowa: Torch Press, 1940.

Drinnon, Richard, and Drinnon, Anna Maria, eds. *Nowhere at Home—Letters from Exile of Emma Goldman and Alexander Berkman*. New York: Shocken, 1975.

Drummond, S. A. *Abraham Lincoln: The Ideal American*. Sawtelle, Calif., 1927.

Du Bois, W. E. B. *John Brown*. Philadelphia: George G. Jacobe, 1909.

Eddy, Daniel C. *The Martyr President*. Boston: Graves and Young, 1865.

Egar, John H. *The Martyr President*. Leavenworth, Kans.: Bulletin Job Printing Establishment, 1865.

Everett, Marshall, ed. *The Complete Life of William McKinley*. Chicago: Chicago Historical Press, 1901.

Eversol, Henry Kelso. *Sir Knight William McKinley: An Address*. Cincinnati, 1943.

Exercises at the Dedication of the Statue of Wendell Phillips, July 5, 1915. City of Boston: Printing Department, 1916.

Foner, Phillip S., ed. *The Autobiographies of the Haymarket Martyrs*. New York: Humanities Press, 1969.

————, ed. *Fellow Workers and Friends—IWW Free Speech Fight as Told by Participants*. Westport, Conn.: Greenwood Press, 1981.

French, Charles Wallace. *Abraham Lincoln—The Liberator*. New York: Funk and Wagnalls, 1891.

Galbreath, C. B. "John Brown," *Ohio Archeological and Historical Quarterly* 30 (1921): 184–354.

Garrison, Wendell Phillips, and Francis Jackson Garrison. *The Words of Garrison*. Boston: Houghton Mifflin, 1905.

Goldman, Emma. *Living My Life*. 2 vols. New York: Dover, 1970, first published 1931.

————. *The Psychology of Political Violence*. New York: Mother Earth Publisher, 1911.

————, ed. *Anarchism and Other Essays*. New York: Dover, 1969, first published 1911.

Gordon, Charles Ulysses, ed. *William McKinley: Commemorative Tributes*. Chicago: Lourier, 1942.

Greeley Horace. *The American Conflict*. Hartford: O. D. Case, 1864.

Green, Beriah. *The Martyr*. Boston: American Anti-Slavery Society, 1838.

Grimké Archibald H. *A Eulogy on Wendell Phillips*. Boston: Rockwell and Churchill, 1884.

Grimké, Francis J. *The Works of Francis J. Grimké*. 2 Vols. Washington, D.C.: Associated Publishers, 1942.

Gurley, Phineas Densmore. *Faith in God: A Sermon at the Funeral of Abraham Lincoln*. Philadelphia: David Warde, 1940, first published 1865.

Halstead, Murat. *Illustrious Life of William McKinley*. Chicago, 1901

Harley, Eugene J., ed. *Woodrow Wilson Still Lives—His World Ideals Triumphant*. Los Angeles: Center for International Understanding, 1949.

Haskell, Thomas Nelson. *True Greatness and Goodness*. Denver, 1881.

Hassard, F. R. G. "Apology for John Brown." *Catholic World* 42 (1885–86): 515–27.

Hazeltine, Mayo W., ed. *Orations—From Homer to McKinley*. Vol. 24. New York: Collier and Son, 1902.

Herndon, William H. *Herndon's Lincoln—The True Story of a Great Life*. Springfield, Ill.: Herndon's Lincoln Publishing, 1921, first published 1889.

Herron, George D. *Between Caesar and Christ*. New York: Thomas Y. Crowell, 1899.

———. *Christian State*. Boston: Thomas Y. Corwell, 1895.

———. *Germanism and the American Crusade*. New York: M. Kennerley, 1918.

Hertz, Emanuel, ed. *Abraham Lincoln—A Tribute of the Synagogue*. New York: Bloch, 1927.

Higginson, Thomas Wentworth. *Wendell Phillips*. Boston: Lee and Shepard, [1884].

Highton, Henry E. *Two Orations*. San Francisco: Bacon, 1883.

Hill, John Wesley. *Abraham Lincoln: Man of God*. New York: G. P. Putnam's Sons, 1920.

Hoar, George F. *James A. Garfield*. Boston: Houghton Mifflin, 1882.

Holst, Herman Von. *John Brown*. Boston: Cupples and Hurd, 1888.

Horton, Rushmore G. *A Youth History of the United States*. New York: Von Evrie and Horton, 1868.

Howe, Julia Ward. *Reminiscences*. Boston: Houghton Mifflin, 1899.

Howe, Mark De Wolf, ed. *Holmes-Laski Letters*. Cambridge: Harvard University Press, 1953.

———, ed. *Holmes-Pollock Letters*. Cambridge: Harvard University Press, 1961.

———, ed. *The Memory of Lincoln—Selected Poems*. Boston: Small Maynard, 1899.

Howells, William Dean. "Old Brown." *Ohio Archeological and Historical Review* 30 (1921): 181.

Ingalls, J. J. "John Brown's Place in History." *North American Review* 138 (Feb. 1884): 138–50.

James, William. *The Will to Believe*. New York: Longmans, Green, 1923, first published 1896.

Johnson, Oliver. *William Lloyd Garrison and His Times*. Boston: Houghton Mifflin, 1881, first published 1879.

Jones, Jesse H. *The Kingdom of Heaven*. Boston: H. O. Houghton, 1871.

Karsner, David. *Debs: His Authorized Life and Letters*. New York: Boni and Liveright, 1919.

———. *Debs Goes to Prison*. New York: Irving Kaye Davis, 1919.

Keifer, Joseph Warren. *Oration.* Springfield, Ohio: Globe, 1887.

Kimball, George. "Origin of the John Brown Song." *New England Magazine* 20, no. 4 (Dec. 1889): 371–76.

King, Martin Luther, Jr. *Where Do We Go From Here?* New York: Harper & Row, 1967.

Knight, Lucian Lamer, ed. *Woodrow Wilson — The Dreamer and the Dream.* Atlanta, Ga.: Johnson Dallis, 1924.

Kornbluh, Joyce L., ed. *Rebel Voices: An IWW Anthology.* Ann Arbor: University of Michigan Press, 1964.

Legislative Honors to Abraham Lincoln from the State of New York. Albany: Weed Parsons, 1865.

Le-Prade, Ruth. *Debs and the Poets.* Pasadena, Calif.: Upton Sinclair, 1920.

Lewis, Lloyd. *Myths after Lincoln.* New York: Harcourt, Brace, 1929.

Lincoln and Herndon — Religion and Romance. N.p.: Holman Hamilton, 1959, first published 1879.

Lynn, James Weber. *Jane Addams — A Biography.* New York: D. Appleton Century, 1935.

McAllister, B. C., ed. *Selected Poems on Woodrow Wilson.* New York: Dean, 1926.

McCabe, James D. *Our Martyred President — The Life and Public Service of James A. Garfield.* Philadelphia: National, 1881.

McClellan, Katherine Elizabeth. *A Hero's Grave in the Adirondacks.* Saranac Lake, N.Y.: Published by the author, 1896.

McClure, Alexander D., and Charles Morris eds. *The Authentic Life of William McKinley,* Philadelphia: City Printing House 1901.

McClure, J. B., ed. *The World's Eulogies on President Garfield.* Chicago: Rhodes and McClure, 1881.

McNeill, George, ed. *The Labor Movement and the Problem of Today.* Boston: James Cooper, 1886.

Marineau, Harriet. *The Martyr Age of the United States.* Boston: Weeks Jordan, 1839.

Martyn Carlos. *Wendell Phillips: The Agitator.* New York: Funk and Wagnalls, 1890.

Martyr's Monument of Abraham Lincoln Exhibited by His Speeches. New York: American News, 1865.

Mayo, A. D., *The Martyr President,* Cincinnati, Ohio: Steam Press, 1866.

A Memorial of James A. Garfield from the City of Boston. Boston: City Council Print, 1881.

A Memorial of Wendell Phillips from the City of Boston. Boston: City Council Print, 1884.

Memorial Service to Wendell Phillips. Boston: James Cooper, 1886.

Mewell, Robert Henry. *The Martyr President.* New York: Carleton, 1865.

Miller, David Hunter. *Woodrow Wilson.* New York: Appeal Printing, 1924.

Miller, Perry, ed. *American Thought — Civil War to World War I.* New York: Holt, Rinehart and Winston, 1954.

Niccolls, Samuel J. *A Discourse on the Assassination of Abraham Lincoln*. St. Louis: Serman Spencer Printer, 1865.

Nicolay, John G. *Campaigns of the Civil War*. Vol. 1. New York: Charles Scribner's Sons, 1890.

Odets, Clifford. *Six Plays of Clifford Odets*. New York: Modern Library, 1939, first published 1933.

Olcott, Charles S. *The Life of William McKinley*. 2 vols. Boston: Houghton Mifflin, 1916.

Our Martyred President: Voices from the Pulpit of New York and Brooklyn. New York: Tibbals and Whiting, 1865.

Pamphlets on Biographies. Vols. 4, 9, 13.

Parsons, Lucy E., ed. *Life of Albert Parsons*. Chicago: Lucy E. Parsons, 1889.

Payne, John Barton. *An Address at the Unveiling of the Bust of Woodrow Wilson*. Richmond, 1931.

Pell, Edward L., James W. Buel, and James P. Boyd, eds. *McKinley and Men of Our Times: A Memorial Volume of American History*. Washington, D.C.: Historical Society of America, 1901.

Phillips, Wendell. "The Lesson of President Lincoln's Death." In *Universal Suffrage and Complete Equality*. Boston: Geo. C. Rand and Avery, 1865.

———. *Speeches, Lectures, and Letters*. Boston: Lee and Shepard, 1891.

Pinsley, Raymond F. ed. *Woodrow Wilson in Retrospect*. Verona, Va.: McClure Press, 1978.

Poetical Tributes to the Memory of Abraham Lincoln. Philadelphia: J. B. Lippincott, 1865.

Powler, Charles. *Patriotic Orations*. New York: Eaton and Mains, 1910.

Quarles, Benjamin, ed. *Blacks on John Brown*. Urbana: University of Illinois Press, 1972.

Rauschenbusch, Walter. *Christianizing and the Social Order*. New York: Macmillan, 1912.

Realf, Richard. *Poems*. New York: Funk and Wagnalls, 1898.

Reid, Edith G. *Woodrow Wilson—the Caricature, the Myth, and the Man*. London: Oxford University Press, 1934.

Rhodes, James Ford, *History of the United States*. Vols. 2, 5. New York: Harper and Brothers, 1920, first published 1893, 1904.

Rice, Allen Thorndike, ed. *Reminiscences of Abraham Lincoln by Distinguished Men of His Times*. New York: Harper and Brothers, 1909, first published 1865.

Root, David. *A Memorial of the Martyred Lovejoy*. Boston: Anti-Slavery Society [1837].

Rose, A. L., ed. *Woodrow Wilson and the American Liberalism*. New York: Macmillan, 1948.

Royce, Josiah. "The Duties of Americans in the President War." In *Address*, Boston, 1916.

Ruchames, Louis, ed. *John Brown—The Making of a Revolutionary*. New York: Grosset and Dunlap, 1969, first published 1959.

Russell, Charles Edward. *The Story of Wendell Phillips*. Chicago: Charles Herr, 1914.

Sanborn, Franklin B., ed. *The Life and Letters of John Brown*. Concord, Mass.: Sanborn, 1910, first published 1885.

Santayana, George. *Winds of Doctrine*. New York: Charles Scribner's Sons, 1926.

Schnittkind, Henry. *The Story of Eugene V. Debs*. Boston: National Committee, Independent Workingmen's Circle, 1919.

Sears, Lorenzo. *Wendell Phillips: Orator and Agitator*. New York: Page, 1909.

Sinclair, Upton. *Autobiography*. Pasadena, Calif.: Upton Sinclair, 1918.

Smith, Walker C. *The Everett Massacre*. Chicago: IWW Publishing Bureau, 1917.

Stafford, Wendell Phillips. *Wendell Phillips—A Centennial Oration*. New York: NAACP, 1911.

Stearns, Charles B. *The Fugitive Slave Law of the United States*. Boston, 1851.

Stone, Lucy. *Tributes to William Lloyd Garrison at the Funeral Service*. Boston: Houghton Osgood, 1879.

Stone, Thomas T. *The Martyr of Freedom*. Boston: Isaac Knapp, 1838.

Strong, J. D. *The Nation's Sorrow*. San Francisco, 1865.

Strong, Josiah. *The New Era; or, the Coming of The Kingdom*. New York: Baker and Taylor, 1893.

Sumner, Charles. *Eulogy on Abraham Lincoln*. Boston, 1865.

Taft, William H. *Address*. Washington, D.C., 1912.

Tanner, Henry. *The Martyrdom of Lovejoy*. Chicago: Fergus, 1881.

Thayer, William M. *From Log-Cabin to the White House*. London: Ward Lick, 1920.

Thompson, George. *Prison Life and Reflection*. Oberline, Ohio: J. M. Fitch, 1847.

Thompson, Maurice. *Lincoln's Grave*. Cambridge: Stone and Kimball, 1884.

Thoreau, Henry David. *The Writings of Henry David Thoreau*. Boston: Houghton Mifflin, 1894.

———. *Yankee in Canada*. Boston: Houghton Mifflin, 1888.

Townsend, G. W., ed. *Memorial Life of President McKinley*. Washington, D.C.: Government Publishing House, 1903.

Tributes to William L. Garrison at the Funeral Service. Boston: Houghton Osgood, 1879.

Twenty-Fifth Anniversary of November, Memorial Edition, November 11, 1882–1912. Chicago: Lucy E. Parsons, 1912.

United States Congress Memorial Address to President Lincoln. Washington, D.C.: Government Printing Office, 1866.

Villard, Fanny Garrison. *William Lloyd Garrison on Non-Resistance*. New York: Nation's Press, 1924.

Villard, Oswald Garrison. *John Brown—A Biography Fifty Years Later*. Boston: Houghton Mifflin, 1911.

Vincent, Edgar L. *The Story of Garfield*. Portland, Maine: L. H. Nelson, 1908.

Webb, Edwin B. *Memorial Sermons*. Boston: Randy and Avery Press, 1865.

Webster, Jackson Clay. *The Foe Unmasked—A Poem*. New York, 1865.

Wells, Wells. *Wilson—The Unknown*. New York: Charles Scribner's Sons, 1931.

Wentworth, Franklin H. *Wendell Phillips.* New York: Socialist Literature, 1909.

White, William Allen. *Woodrow Wilson: the Man, His Time, and His Task.* Boston: Houghton Mifflin, 1924.

Whitehead, John. *Memorial Sketch of the Life of Compatriot William McKinley.* New Haven: John Polhemus Printing, 1903.

Whitman, Walt. *Death of Abraham Lincoln.* Chicago: Black Cat Press, 1960.

Wilson, Hill Peebles. *John Brown—Soldier of Fortune.* Boston: Cornhill, 1918, first published 1913.

Wilson, Woodrow. *A History of the American People.* 5 vols. New York: Harper and Brothers, 1908.

Wine, Frederick Howard. *The Greatness of Abraham Lincoln.* Springfield, Ill., 1905.

Winkley, J. W. *John Brown: The Hero—Personal Reminiscences.* Boston: James H. West, 1905.

Woodberry, George Edward. *Wendell Phillips—The Faith of an American.* New York: Woodberry Society, 1912.

Secondary Sources

Aaron, Daniel. *The Unwritten War.* New York: Alfred A. Knopf, 1973.

Abrams, Richard M., and Lawrence W. Levine. *The Shaping of Twentieth-Century America.* Boston: Little, Brown, 1965.

Albanese, Catherine. "Requiem for Memorial Day: Dissent in the Redeemer Nation." *American Quarterly* 26 (Oct. 1974): 387–98.

Anderson, Dwight G. *Abraham Lincoln: The Quest for Immortality.* New York: Alfred A. Knopf, 1982.

Auden, W. H. *Collected Shorter Poems, 1927–1957.* New York: Random House, 1966.

Bartlett, Irving H. *Wendell and Ann Phillips.* New York: W. W. Norton, 1979.

Barton, William E. *Abraham Lincoln and Walt Whitman.* Indianapolis: Bobbs-Merrill, 1928.

Bellah, Robert N. *The Broken Covenant: Civil Religion in Time of Trial.* New York: Seabury Press, 1975.

Bellah, Robert N., et al., *Habits of the Heart.* Berkeley: University of California Press, 1985.

Bercovitch, Sacvan. *The American Jeremiad.* Madison: University of Wisconsin Press, 1978.

———. *The Puritan Origins of the American Self.* New Haven: Yale University Press, 1975.

Berlin, Isaiah. *Four Essays on Liberty.* London: Oxford University Press, 1969.

Bloch, Ruth. *Visionary Republic.* Cambridge: Cambridge University Press, 1985.

Bloomenfield, Maxwell H. *Alarms and Diversions: The American Mind Through American Magazines.* The Hague: Mouton, 1967.

Bowker, John. *Problems of Suffering in Religions of the World.* Cambridge: Cambridge University Press, 1970.

Boyer, Richard. *The Legend of John Brown.* New York: Alfred A. Knopf, 1973.

Brodie, Fawn M. "The Political Hero in America: His Fate and His Future." *Virginia Quarterly Review* 46 (Winter 1970): 46–60.

Burns, Edward M. *The American Idea of Mission.* Westport, Conn.: Greenwood Press, 1957.

Chapman, John Jay. *William Lloyd Garrison.* New York: Moffat, Yard, 1913.

Clebsch, William A. *American Religious Thought—A History.* Chicago: University of Chicago Press, 1973.

Crosby, Ernest. *Garrison—The Non-Resistant.* Chicago: Public Publishing, 1905.

Crunden, Robert M. *Ministers of Reform.* New York: Basic Books, 1982.

Currie, Harold W. *Eugene V. Debs.* Boston: G. K. Hall, 1976.

Davidson, James West, and Mark Hamilton Lytle, eds. *After the Fact.* Vol. I. New York: Alfred A. Knopf, 1982.

Diggins, John P. *The Lost Soul of American Politics.* Chicago: University of Chicago Press, 1984.

Dillon, Merton L. *Elijah P. Lovejoy: Abolitionist Editor.* Urbana: University of Illinois Press, 1964.

Dixon, John. "Poetry Honors Dr. Martin Luther King, Jr." *Elementary English* 52 (January 1975): 108.

Doenecke, Justus D. *The Presidencies of James A. Garfield and Chester A. Arthur.* Lawrence, Kans.: Regents' Press, 1981.

Donald, David. *Lincoln Reconsidered.* New York: Alfred A. Knopf, 1956.

Dougherty, Flavian, ed. *The Meaning of Human Suffering.* New York: Human Sciences Press, 1982.

Douglas, Ann. " 'Heaven Our Home' Consolation Literature in the Northern United States 1830–1880." *American Quarterly* 26, no. 5 (Dec. 1974): 496–516.

Downing, Frederick L. *To See the Promised Land,* Macon, Ga.: Mercer University Press, 1986.

Duberman, Martin, ed. *The Anti-Slavery Vanguard—New Essays on the Abolitionists.* Princeton: Princeton University Press, 1965.

Elder, John Dixon. "Martin Luther King, Jr., and the American Civil Religion." *Harvard Divinity School Bulletin* 1–3 (Spring 1968): 17–18.

Eliade, Mircea. *The Sacred and The Profane.* New York: Harcourt Brace Jovanovich, 1959, first published 1957.

Fairlie, Henry. "He Was a Man Only for One Season." *New York Times Magazine,* November 21, 1965, 28–29.

————. *The Kennedy Promise—The Politics of Expectation.* Garden City, N.Y.: Doubleday, 1973.

Foss, Martin. *Death Sacrifice and Tragedy.* Lincoln: University of Nebraska Press, 1966.

Ganguli, B. N. *Emma Goldman—Portrait of a Rebel Woman.* Bombay: Allied Publishers, 1979.

Ginger, Ray. *The Bending Cross—A Biography of Eugene V. Debs*. New York: Russell and Russell, 1969, first published 1949.

Girard, René. *Violence and the Sacred*. Baltimore: Johns Hopkins University Press, 1977, first published 1972.

Gold, Michael. *The Life of John Brown*. New York: Roving Eye Press, 1960.

Harris, Louis. *The Anguish of Change*. New York: W. W. Norton, 1973.

Hartnell, Rodney T., and Carol U. Libby. "Agreement with Views of Martin Luther King, Jr., Before and After the Assassination." *Pylon* 33, no. 1 (Spring 1972): 79–87.

Hartz, Louis. *The Liberal Tradition in America*. New York: Harcourt Brace Jovanovich, 1955.

Hay, Robert. "Providence and the American Past." *Indiana Magazine of History* 65, no. 2 (June 1969): 79–102.

Historical Society of Israel, ed. *Holy War and Martyrology*. Jerusalem: Academon, 1967.

Hoffer, Eric. *The True Believer*. New York: Harper and Brothers, 1951.

Hofstadter, Richard. *The Age of Reform*. New York: Vintage Books, 1955.

Holzer, Harold, Gabor S. Boritt, and Mark E. Neely, Jr. *The Lincoln Image: Abraham Lincoln and the Popular Print*. New York: Charles Scribner's Sons, 1984.

Horbury, William, and Brian McNeil, eds. *Suffering and Martyrdom in the New Testament*. Cambridge: Cambridge University Press, 1980.

Hume, John F. *The Abolitionists*. New York: G. P. Putnam's Sons, 1905.

Kolko, Gabriel. *The Triumph of Conservatism*. New York: Free Press, 1963.

Lasch, Christopher, ed. *The Social Thought of Jane Addams*. Indianapolis: Bobbs-Merrill, 1962.

Levine, Daniel. *Jane Addams and the Liberal Tradition*. Westport, Conn.: Greenwood Press, 1980, first published 1971.

Lewis, R. W. B. *The American Adam*. Chicago: University of Chicago Press, 1955.

Lynd, Staughton, ed. *Nonviolence in America*. Indianapolis: Bobbs-Merrill, 1965.

Madison, Charles A. "Anarchism in The United States." *Journal of History of Ideas* 6 (1945): 46–66.

———. *Critics and Crusaders*. New York: Henry Holt, 1947.

Mann, Arthur. *Yankee Reformer in an Urban Age*. Cambridge: Harvard University Press, 1954.

Marcus, Robert D. "James A. Garfield: Lifting the Mask" *Ohio History* 88 (1979): 78–83.

Martin, Ralph G. *A Hero for Our Time: An Intimate Study of the Kennedy Years*. Macmillan, 1983.

May, Henry. *The End of American Innocence*. New York: Alfred A. Knopf, 1959.

Merrill, Walter. *Against Wind and Tide*. Cambridge: Harvard University Press, 1963.

Monaghan, Jay. "An Analysis of Lincoln Funeral Sermons." *Indiana Magazine of History* 41, no. 1 (March 1965): 31–44.

Moorhead James. "Between Progress and Apocalypse: A Reassessment of Millennialism in American Religious Thought, 1800–1880." *Journal of American History* 71, no. 3 (Dec. 1984): 538–41.

Moreau, John. *Bourne: Legend and Reality*. Washington, D.C.: Public Affairs Press, 1966.

Murray, Robert K., and Tim H. Blessing. "The Presidential Performance Study: A Progress Report." *Journal of American History* 70, no. 3 (Dec. 1983): 535–55.

Nevins, Allen. *Lincoln and the Gettysburg Address*. Urbana: University of Illinois Press, 1964.

Niebuhr, Reinhold. *The Irony of American History*. New York: Charles Scribner's Sons, 1952.

Nimmo, Dan and James E. Combs. *Subliminal Politics—Myth and Mythmakers in America*. Englewood Cliffs, N.J.: Prentice-Hall, 1980.

Ninde, Edward S. *The Story of the American Hymns*. New York: Abigdon Press, 1921.

Oates, Stephen B. "John Brown and His Judges." *Civil War History* 17 (Mar. 1971): 5–24.

———. *Let the Trumpet Sound: The Life of Martin Luther King, Jr*. New York: New American Library, 1983, first published 1982.

———. *Our Fiery Trial: Abraham Lincoln, John Brown, and the Civil War Era*. Amherst: University of Massachusetts Press, 1979.

———. *To Purge This Country with Blood*. Cambridge: University of Massachusetts Press, 1984, first published 1970.

Orlansky, Harold. "Reactions to The Death of President Roosevelt." *Journal of Social Psychology* 26 (Nov. 1947): 235–65.

Perry, Louis. *Radical Abolitionism—Anarchy and Government of God in Anti-Slavery Thought*. Ithaca: Cornell University Press, 1973.

Quandt, Jean B. "Secularization of Postmillennialism." *American Quarterly* 25 (Oct. 1973): 390–409.

Quarles, Benjamin. *Allies for Freedom—Blacks and John Brown*. New York: Oxford University Press, 1974.

Renshaw, Patrick. *The Wobblies*. Garden City. N.Y.: Doubleday, 1967.

Rogin, Michael. "The King's Two Bodies." *Massachusetts Review* 20 (Autumn 1979): 553–73.

Rosenberg, Bruce. *Custer and the Epic of Defeat*. Philadelphia: Pennsylvania State University Press, 1974.

Rossiter, Clinton. *The American Presidency*. New York: Harcourt Brace and World, 1960, first published 1956.

Roth, Ruth, M. "Martyrdom." *English Journal* 62 (Nov. 1968): 1147–48.

Salvatore, Nick. *Eugene V. Debs—Citizen and Socialist*. Urbana: University of Illinois Press, 1982.

Sanford, Charles L. *The Quest for Paradise*. New York: AMS Press, 1979, first published 1961.

Schneider, Louis, and Sanford M. Dorbusch. *Popular Religion: Inspirational Books in America*. Chicago: University of Chicago Press, 1958.

Sheatsley, Paul B., and Jacob J. Feldman. "The Assassination of President Kennedy: A Preliminary Report on Public Reactions and Behavior." *Journal of Public Opinion* 28 (Summer 1964): 189–215.

Sillen, Samuel. "The Challenge of Randolph Bourne." *Masses and Mainstream*, 6 (Dec. 1953): 29.

Smith, Gibbs M. *Joe Hill*. Salt Lake City: University of Utah Press, 1969.

Smith, Kenneth L., and Ira G. Zepp, Jr. *Search for the Beloved Community*. Valley Forge, Pa.: Judson Press, 1974.

Smith, Thomas Ventor. *Lincoln: Living Legend*. Chicago: University of Chicago Press, 1940.

Smylie, James H. "On Jesus, Pharaohs, and the Chosen People." *Interpretation* 24 (1970): 74–92.

Sorin, Gerald. *Abolitionism*. New York: Praeger Publishers, 1972.

Stavis, Barrie. *The Man Who Never Died*. New York: Heaven Press, 1951.

Stegner, Wallace. "I Dreamed I Saw Joe Hill Last Night." *Pacific Spectator* I (Spring 1947): 184–87.

Stewart, Charles J. "Lincoln's Assassination and the Protestant Clergy of the North." *Journal of the Illinois State History* 54, no. 3 (Autumn 1961): 268–93.

Stewart, James Brewer. *Holy Warriors*. New York: Hill and Wang, 1976.

Stone, Michael K. "Heaven's Rescued Land: American Hymns and American Destiny." *Journal of Popular Culture* 10, no. 1 (1976): 133–40.

Strout, Cushing. *The New Heaven and New Earth—Political Religion in America*. New York: Harper and Row, 1974.

Stulter, Boyd B. "Abraham Lincoln and John Brown." *Civil War History* 8 (Sept. 1962): 290–99.

Swift, Lindsey. *William Lloyd Garrison*. Philadelphia: George W. Jacobes, 1911.

Toscano, Vincent L., *Since Dallas: Images of John F. Kennedy in Popular and Scholarly Literature, 1963–1973*. San Francisco: Robert D. Reed, and Adam S. Eternovich, 1978.

Turner, Thomas Reed. *Beware the People Weeping*. Baton Rouge, La.: Louisiana State University Press, 1982.

Tuveson, Ernest Lee. *Redeemer Nation*. Chicago: University of Chicago Press, 1968.

Warren, Robert Penn. *John Brown—The Making of a Martyr*. New York: Payson and Clarke, 1929.

Washington, James M., ed. *A Testament of Hope—The Essential Writings of Martin Luther King Jr*. New York: Harper and Row, 1986.

Weaver, Phillips. "Moral Education and the Study of United States History." *Social Education* 39 (Jan. 1975): 36–39.

Weinstein, James. *The Corporate Ideal in the Liberal State, 1900–1918*. Boston: Beacon Press, 1968.

Wiebe, Robert. *The Search for Order, 1877–1920*. New York: Hill and Wang, 1967.

Wills, Garry. *The Kennedy Imprisonment*. Boston: Little, Brown, 1984.

Wilson, Jackson R. *In Quest of Community*. New York: John Wiley and Sons, 1968.

Wolf, Hazel Catherine. *On Freedom's Altar*. Madison: University of Wisconsin Press, 1952.

Wolf, William J. *The Almost Chosen People—A Study of the Religion of Abraham Lincoln*. Garden City, N.Y.: Doubleday, 1959.

Index